A Political History of the
Texas Republic
1836–1845

STANLEY SIEGEL

A Political History of the
Texas Republic
1836–1845

AUSTIN · UNIVERSITY OF TEXAS PRESS · *1956*

Library of Congress Catalog Card No. 56-7478

© 1956 by the University of Texas Press
Manufactured in the United States of America

For Norma

Foreword

THE GREAT MOVEMENT westward which characterized American history from the turn of the nine-
teenth century until the disappearance of the frontier incidentally embraced the migration to Texas. The pioneering services of Moses and
Stephen F. Austin led to the development of this particular wilderness,
and the colonizing efforts of the *empresarios* which followed made
Texas a flourishing colony under Mexican rule. This happy state of affairs underwent a gradual transition between 1829 and 1836, for the
American colonists could not live at peace with their Mexican officials.
Differences of temperament and character were accentuated by the
desires of the Americans to perpetuate slavery in Texas and to be free of
the practice of the Roman Catholic faith. Squabbles over taxation and
disputes concerning the lack of judicial safeguards led to the calling of
a series of conventions which culminated in the Texas declaration of in-

dependence, March, 1836. Though badly defeated at Goliad and at the Alamo, the decisive victory at San Jacinto assured the independence of Texas.

The annexation of Texas by the United States brought to a close the Republic of Texas' nine-year period of independent existence. During this short era the nation enjoyed all the attributes of sovereignty. A legitimate government, an army in the field, the beginnings of a navy, and the operation of a diplomatic system on a major scale were all features of the Republic's power and affluence. Though hampered by the bad times, which also struck with such devastation in the United States, and by the reliance upon paper-money issues which characterized the administrations of Sam Houston and Mirabeau B. Lamar, Texas was able to weather the storm and to maintain its independence until the date of annexation.

This work is concerned with the political history of the Republic. It is true that political divisions existed prior to the Revolution, and in this period political differences were based upon distinct principles. The faction led by William H. Wharton in the early stages of the trouble with Mexico was eager for a complete break; the faction led by Austin counseled a moderate program and did not agree on the wisdom of independence until late in 1835. However, the political divisions on the basis of principles did not continue in the period of the Republic. Politics were almost wholly of a personal nature between 1836 and 1845. The personality of Sam Houston dominated Texas in that era and made possible the two Houston administrations as well as the election of Anson Jones, who was Houston's chosen candidate. Also, it can be said that the election of Lamar was nothing more than a reversion from the first Houston term in office. There were no political parties in Texas comparable to the Whigs or Democrats in the United States. There were political techniques, appropriate to a developing, more sophisticated nation, but politics in the Republic were primarily of a personal nature.

In conclusion, the individual citizen of the Republic was much like his counterpart in the United States. His principles were in the Jacksonian mold, and his devotion to agrarian pursuits resulted in a distrust of any type of corporate monopoly. Texas was akin to any other Southern state in the ante bellum period, with cotton the chief source of wealth and with slavery a recognized institution. The development of the Republic continued along these lines, so that the state of Texas naturally became a part of the Confederacy at the time of the Civil War. Also, social historians have asserted that the germination of the distinct Texas character and tradition had its origin in the period of the Republic.

Acknowledgments

I WOULD LIKE TO EXPRESS my gratitude to the following librarians and archivists who made the writing of this book a much easier task. The staffs of the Anderson Library of the University of Houston, the Rosenberg Library at Galveston, and the San Jacinto Museum of History were most courteous in their service and interest. Miss Llerena Friend, librarian of the Eugene C. Barker Texas History Center of the University of Texas Library; Mrs. Bertha Brandt, assistant archivist of the Archives Division of the Texas State Library; Mr. Richard Ducote of the Houston Public Library; and Mrs. Lorraine Gresham of the Fondren Library at Rice Institute, have also been helpful in making research materials available.

My greatest debt is to Dr. William H. Masterson of Rice Institute. He suggested the topic, directed the study in its original form as a doctoral thesis in history at the Rice Institute, and reread portions of the manuscript. Dr. Masterson has continued to give graciously of his time and advice, and my thanks are due to him and to my parents.

STANLEY SIEGEL

Houston, Texas
March, 1956

Contents

Illustrations

Between pages 118 and 119

Stephen F. Austin's empresario notice, 1829
Santa Anna captures the Alamo, March 6, 1836
Broadside issued by Houston as commander-in-chief of the Texas Army
Call for Texas Army volunteers
Santa Anna surrenders to Houston after the Battle of San Jacinto
Leading political figures of the Republic
  Stephen F. Austin
  William H. Wharton
  James Pinckney Henderson
  James Hamilton

A Political History of the
Texas Republic
1836–1845

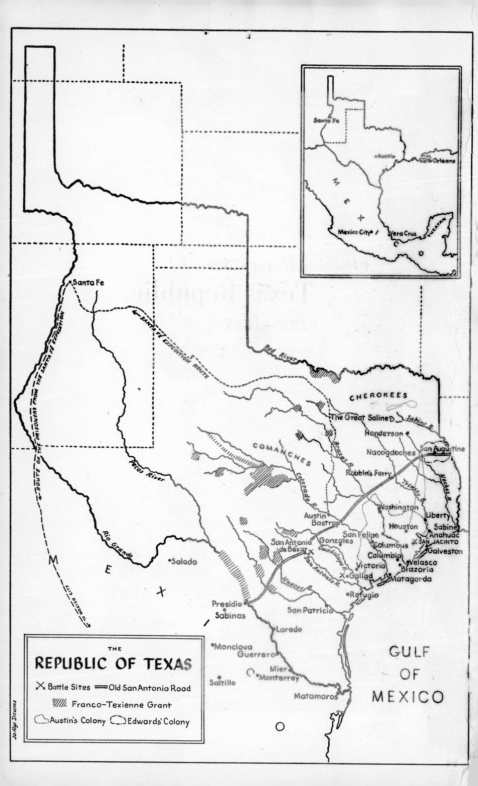

Revolution and Independence

FOR MORE THAN FIFTY YEARS, that is, from the very period of their political infancy, the prevailing thought in the United States of America has been the acquisition of the greater part of the territory that formerly belonged to Spain, particularly that part which to-day belongs to the Mexican nation. Democrats and Federalists, all their political parties, whatever their old or new designations, have been in perfect accord upon one point, their desire to extend the limits of the republic to the north, to the south, and to the west, using for the purpose all the means at their command, guided by cunning, deceit, and bad faith. It has been neither an Alexander nor a Napoleon, desirous of conquest in order to extend his dominions or add to his glory, who has inspired the proud Anglo-Saxon race in its desire, its frenzy to usurp and gain control of that which rightfully belongs to its neighbors; rather it has been the nation itself which, possessed of that roving spirit that moved the barbarous hordes of a former age in a far remote north, has swept away whatever has stood in the way of its aggrandizement.[1]

WELL MIGHT THE MEXICAN SECRETARY OF WAR, José María Tornel y Mendívil, thus reflect bitterly in the spring of 1836 upon the rapid sequence of events which had followed the migration of American colonists into Mexican territory. These events had largely come without warning and therefore were harder to bear. Official Mexico had congratulated itself upon the amicable relations that existed between the central government and the colonists, and, conversely, no one was more conscious of his duties and responsibilities as a loyal Mexican citizen than Stephen F. Austin.[2] The immigration agents, or *empresarios*, as a class adopted the course set by Austin and pursued a moderate policy throughout all the internal troubles which beset Texas and which finally culminated in revolution. Such men as Frost Thorn, David G. Burnet, Sterling C. Robertson, and others, while they ultimately took part in the struggle against Mexico, were originally anything but firebrand revolutionaries.

It is also evident that the members of the various colonies under Mexican rule were generally happy with their lot. Generous bounties of land, complete freedom from taxation, and the practical enjoyment of religious toleration despite the official attitude combined to give Texas the aura of a paradise. The ravages of sickness, the constant fear of Indian attack, the loneliness of frontier life, and the general privations incidental to the establishment of new settlements in the wilderness were experiences in which they all had shared, yet spirits were always revived by the natural beauty and fertility of the land.[3] The original settlers, because of their common pioneering experience and jealousy of new arrivals, constituted a class by themselves and came to be known as the "Old Three Hun-

[1] José María Tornel y Mendívil, *Relations between Texas, the United States of America, and Mexico,* quoted in Carlos E. Castañeda, *The Mexican Side of the Texan Revolution,* 287. Tornel's pamphlet was published in 1837 and contained a scathing denunciation of the favorable sentiment in the United States for the Texans.

[2] Eugene C. Barker, *The Life of Stephen F. Austin, Founder of Texas, 1793–1836: A Chapter in the Westward Movement of the Anglo-American People,* 69.

[3] Noah Smithwick, *The Evolution of a State: or Recollections of Old Texas Days,* 9–10.

4

dred."[4] This was significant politically because the original colonists maintained their loyalty to Austin throughout his career in Texas. Though at no time did they take the lead in the political sniping that preceded the war, the early settlers were conspicuous by their bravery at the siege of Béxar, the slaughter at the Alamo, and the victory at San Jacinto.

Migration to Texas can be traced to a few basic reasons, the most important of which was the land hunger current in the United States in the early 1820's. This desire for land was stimulated by the panic of 1819 and by the need to abolish the issuing of national land grants on credit because of the general hard times. As a result of the panic many wildcat state banks failed, wiping out many people's savings, and paper money was further restricted because of the reorganization of the United States Bank by Langdon Cheves.[5] On the other hand, land could be had virtually for the asking in Mexico. In 1825 the *Missouri Advocate,* published at St. Louis, reflected the dissatisfaction with the federal land system and the advantages to be gained by migration to Texas by observing: "The difference is too great not to produce its effect between a republic which gives first rate land gratis, and a republic which will not sell inferior land for what it is worth."[6] Land fever and the resulting passion for land speculation were uppermost in the minds of many who came to Texas in this period.[7]

The prevailing hard times in the United States also contributed colonists who left their native states to escape creditors. Various laws of imprisonment for debt were still effective in many of the states, and a hasty removal to Texas provided a solution for numbers of harassed debtors. In many Southern states the expression "Gone to Texas" (or simply G.T.T.) written on the doors of recently abandoned homes gave information that the occupants had departed one step ahead of the local sheriff.[8] This is not to imply

[4] William Fairfax Gray, *From Virginia to Texas, 1835: Diary of Col. Wm. F. Gray Giving Details of His Journey to Texas and Return in 1835-36 and Second Journey to Texas in 1837,* 81.

[5] Eugene C. Barker, "Notes on the Colonization of Texas," *Mississippi Valley Historical Review,* X (1923), 152.

[6] *Missouri Advocate,* August 27, 1825, quoted in *ibid.,* 143.

[7] Elgin Williams, *The Animating Pursuits of Speculation: Land Traffic in the Annexation of Texas,* 21.

[8] William R. Hogan, *The Texas Republic: A Social and Economic History,* 5.

that all who came to Texas in this period were fugitives from justice; the majority of those who migrated had previously been poor but solvent farmers, residing primarily in the Southern states. However, enough undesirables did come to Texas to give some credence to the characterization of the new area as the "Botany Bay" of the United States.[9]

Correspondence to Stephen F. Austin, as a representative *empresario*, gives a good indication of the reasons impelling migration to Texas. Samuel Ayres, representing the Texas Emigrating Society of Lexington, Kentucky, wrote to Austin: "This society is Composed of Farmers, and Mechanics and Manufacturers, with a few Merchants and Professional Characters. Some of them are wealthy, others have been wealthy, but have fallen Victims to the Changes and difficulties of the time, through the unguarded Policy of our Country, and some are young beginners."[10] From Mississippi, James A. E. Phelps wrote to Austin in this vein: "The emigrating or Texas *fever* prevails to an extent that your *wishes* would no more than anticipate—It has pervaded all classes of the citizens of this state and the adjoining; from the men with capital, to the man that wishes to acquire a living."[11]

These and many other accounts are confirmation that the desire for land and the wish to start life in a new country, free from debt and removed from painful surroundings, were the primary reasons for the lure of Texas.

The Mexican federal constitution of 1824 represented the fruits of independence. Both American and Spanish influences were important in the drafting of this document: The framers felt that the principles of republicanism and free immigration, both of which had proved so beneficial to the growth of the United States, would also aid in the political development of Mexico.[12] In addition, they retained such features of the Spanish constitution of 1812 as the responsibility of individual cabinet members to Congress, a pro-

[9] Thomas A. Bailey, *A Diplomatic History of the American People*, 249.

[10] Samuel Ayres and others to Austin, June 6, 1822, Eugene C. Barker (ed.), *The Papers of Stephen F. Austin*, I, 522.

[11] James A. E. Phelps to Austin, January 16, 1825, in *ibid.*, II, 1020.

[12] James Q. Dealey, "The Spanish Sources of the Mexican Constitution of 1824," *Quarterly of the Texas State Historical Association*, III (1900), 162. This periodical became known as the *Southwestern Historical Quarterly* with the publication of Volume XVII in 1913.

vision respecting freedom of the press, and Sunday elections. The national colonization law governing all foreign settlements in Texas, except Austin's first colony, was enacted by the Mexican Congress on August 18, 1824. In December, 1820, Moses Austin, Stephen's father, had asked the Spanish government's permission to settle three hundred families in Texas. With the aid of Baron de Bastrop, an influential citizen whom Austin had previously known in the United States, the petition was granted on January 17, 1821. Moses Austin soon died, but his grant was transferred to Stephen. Mexico was so torn by revolution and internal disorder between 1821 and 1824 that the Austin grant was unique. The *empresarios* who followed the Austins enjoyed their own rights under the law of 1824.[13]

The national colonization statute fixed certain general regulations for the administration of the public lands and also transferred to the respective states the right of developing the local details of the colonization program. The most important restrictions imposed upon the states by the federal act were: (1) that foreigners should not be settled within twenty leagues of the national boundary nor within ten leagues of the coast without the concurrent approval of both the state and federal executives; (2) that no individual should be allowed to hold title in his own person to more than 49,000 acres of land; (3) that Congress should retain authority at its discretion to stop emigration from any particular nation.[14]

In accordance with the terms of the federal act, the legislature sitting for Coahuila and Texas passed a state law dated March 24, 1825. Heads of families who met the requirements of the statute could obtain 4,428 acres of land for the very low fee of $30, payable to the state in installments of four, five, and six years. Clerical expenses, stamped paper for the title, surveyor's charges, and other fees, however, increased the total cost of such a grant to about $200. In order to stimulate the settlement of the vacant lands, the law further provided for the employment of *empresarios*. These men could obtain exclusive contracts for a term of six years to settle a stipulated number of families in designated areas. Within six weeks or so after the passage of the state law the governor let con-

[13] Dudley G. Wooten, *A Complete History of Texas*, 131.
[14] Eugene C. Barker, *Mexico and Texas, 1821–1835*, 12.

tracts to a number of *empresarios* for the settlement of some 2,400 families in Texas. By 1830 there were contracts for nearly 7,000 families, and almost the entire area of eastern Texas was covered by grants to the colonizers.[15]

Although Texas was a land of opportunity for many Americans in financial straits, there were two factors which partially tended to operate against migration. The questioned right to bring slaves into Texas and the uncertainty of religious toleration are of major significance in understanding the reluctance of many families to move to Texas. Correspondence to Austin here again proves a good index to the sentiments of the times. A prospective emigrant wrote from Alabama: "The most Interesting subjects to the people here appear to be that of Slavery and Religion the latter being a constitutional matter I have no expectation of as early a change But would like to know what is the present state or prospect relative to the admission of slavery."[16] Another wished to know the probable attitude of the Mexican government on the matter of religious toleration:[17]

I wish to know what the feelings of the Govt are at this time upon the subject of religion. Will it wink at liberty of conscience and permit good and worthy inhabitants to peaceably assemble and worship their God in the way most agreeable to their feelings without evincing any disposition to make proselytes or to interfere with the prevailing religion of the country. This is a subject of vast importance to the people of these U States and has a most powerful effect in preventing respectable families from removing from this to your country.

Concerning the slavery question, a Mississippi planter commented: "Nothing appears at present, to prevent a portion of our wealthy planters from emigrating immediately to the province of Texas but the uncertainty now prevailing with regard to the subject of slavery. . . . If this be a fact it will check the tide of emigrating spirits at once; and indeed it has had its influence already."[18] Finally, from New Orleans one Nathaniel Cox wrote to Austin that he had assured a prospective settler that slaves could be taken into

[15] *Ibid.*, 13.
[16] Richard R. Royal to Austin, August 23, 1825, *Austin Papers*, II, 1183.
[17] Charles Douglas to Austin, February 15, 1825, *ibid.*, 1046–47.
[18] James A. E. Phelps to Austin, January 16, 1825, *ibid.*, 1020.

Texas. Cox then noted: "I hope he will find no difficulty with his, as it would ruin an helpless family should he lose them."[19] These and many other inquiries of the same tenor addressed to the *empresarios* reveal the importance of slavery and religious toleration to those planning to go to Texas.

It was certain that as American immigrants poured into Texas latent racial and cultural distinctions would come to the surface and cause trouble between the Mexicans and the newcomers. Apart from personal qualities of difference, the American colonists were imbued with a heritage of political freedom which stood in strong contrast to the record of servitude that the Mexicans had known under Spanish rule. The American political experience had involved participation in government and the frequent and orderly change of government officials; the Mexican experience, in the short span of independence, had resulted in complete turmoil, with one revolution rapidly following another. Racial and cultural differences are significant in explaining the events that followed. They bred in the early settlers a contempt for their Mexican neighbors which hastened the ultimate conflict.[20]

Legal rights and procedures in Texas were far different from those the American colonists were accustomed to. In November, 1826, Austin wrote to Baron de Bastrop, the representative from Texas in the Mexican federal legislature: "One of the most important subjects to the people of the State of Coahuila and Texas is a speedy organization of the Judiciary on a system which promises permanency, more uniformity in the interpretation of laws, and convenience to the people."[21] The constitution of 1824 merely provided for the framework of a judicial system and stipulated that the details should be filled in by law. This was done by an act of June 21, 1827, yet no basic improvements were effected in the judicial system in Texas.[22] In his letter to De Bastrop, Austin suggested that the alcalde, the local judicial officer, be given adequate and clearly defined powers in order to avoid the time and expense of

[19] Nathaniel Cox to Austin, April 21, 1825, *ibid.*, 1079.

[20] Mattie Austin Hatcher (ed.), *Letters of an Early American Traveller: Mary Austin Holley, Her Life and Her Works, 1784–1846*, 157. Paul Horgan, *Great River: The Rio Grande in North American History*, II, 479.

[21] Austin to Baron de Bastrop, November ?, 1826, *Austin Papers*, II, 1486.

[22] Barker, *Mexico and Texas*, 94.

appeals to higher courts. The act of 1827 provided that the alcalde's verdict was final in civil suits involving up to $300 but that cases involving larger amounts were subject to appeal to one of the three members of the Supreme Court, which sat at Saltillo. In like manner, the alcalde's jurisdiction was supreme in criminal cases in which the penalty did not exceed a fine of $100 or imprisonment for more than one month. Verdicts of corporal punishment, however, had to be referred to the Supreme Court whether or not the defendant appealed, and such sentences as death, deportation, or ten years at hard labor had to be successively confirmed by two chambers of the Supreme Court.[23] Since neither this law nor the constitution of 1824 made any provision for trial by jury, the colonists were without the enjoyment of this basic right.[24]

Difficulties over land matters also plagued the settlers in their relations with the Mexican government. Titles to land were not certain, and, if the local *empresario* could not provide relief, petitions to the central government were of no avail.[25] The short-lived revolt led by Haden Edwards in 1826-27 was indicative of the underlying causes of resentment. On April 18, 1825, permission was granted to Edwards to settle nearly eight hundred families in eastern Texas in an area which included the important town of Nacogdoches. The site of the grant was particularly unfortunate because the district had previously been occupied by the Spaniards and Spanish land titles still retained their legality. As a further complication, this area, the "neutral ground" lying on the border between Texas and Louisiana, had long served as the meeting place for renegades of every description as well as for scattered bands of Cherokee Indians. Trouble actually began when Edwards contested the validity of the Spanish land titles, many of which undoubtedly were forged. The attempted mediation of Austin and Baron de Bastrop failed, and Edwards soon proclaimed himself ruler of the "Republic of Fredonia." Alliances were signed with some of the Indian tribes, and the revolt also received support from desperadoes on

[23] *Ibid.*, 95.
[24] Austin to "Gentlemen of the Convention," April 1, 1833, *Austin Papers,* II, 938. This circular presents the judicial reforms which Austin desired.
[25] Austin to B. W. Edwards, September 15, 1825, *Austin Papers,* II, 1202–1203.

both sides of the border. The outbreak was quickly put down by the Mexican authorities, but as a result the federal government was apprehensive of further immigration from the United States.[26] Thus the questions of slavery and religious toleration, the fundamental racial and cultural distinctions between the colonists and the Mexicans, and the difficulties over land ownership and speculation all played their part in precipitating the Revolution.

In the summer of 1828, General Manuel Mier y Terán was sent to Texas to observe conditions following the suppression of the Fredonian rebellion. Vicente Guerrero had succeeded Gomez Pedraza as Mexico's president, and it had been decided that action would be taken against further disturbances in Texas. In September, 1829, Mier became commanding general of the Eastern Interior Provinces and therefore responsible for the defense of Texas. Primarily because of his recommendations, the law of April 6, 1830, was enacted by the Mexican government, an act of exceeding importance to the political relationship between the federal government and the colonists in Texas.[27] The provisions of the law were well defined: (1) a loan to be financed by the existing duties on cotton and woolen imports was authorized to meet the cost of transporting Mexican colonists to Texas; (2) the coasting trade was opened to foreign vessels for a period of four years; (3) authority was vested in the federal commissioner to supervise the execution of the contracts and to see that they did not violate the provisions of the general colonization law; (4) the general passport law of March 12, 1828, was changed to read that foreigners entering by the northern frontier must show passports issued by the Mexican representatives at their place of residence; (5) existing slavery within Texas was recognized but further introduction of slaves into the area was forbidden.[28] General Mier then took up residence in Texas to administer the terms of the decree.

In many respects the law of 1830 represented a turning point for the Texans. For the first time a statute had been passed which attempted to stimulate Mexican settlement as a buffer against the

---

[26] Wooten, A Complete History of Texas, 146–47.
[27] Ohland Morton, Terán and Texas: A Chapter in Texas-Mexican Relations, 112.
[28] Ibid., 116.

Americans. The unrestricted right of slave ownership within Texas was destroyed by the article on slavery,[29] and the monopoly that the colonists had enjoyed in the coasting trade was also abolished. The clause concerning immigration was a practical recognition by the Mexican government of the differences in temperament that existed between the native Mexicans residing in Texas and their American neighbors.[30] More important, the act seemed to undermine Austin's faith in the intentions of the central government. From this point until his decision to back the movement for war in 1835, his loyalty to Mexico suffered. At the same time, discerning colonists began to realize that Texas would never have peace under the Mexican flag. The concept became widespread that the continual revolutions in Mexico would result only in a steady flow of new rulers and different acts, all bearing upon Texas.[31]

In accordance with the terms of the new law, General Mier proceeded to establish military garrisons throughout Texas. One of these, the post at Anahuac on Galveston Bay, was commanded by Colonel John Bradburn, an American from Kentucky. Perhaps the Texans felt particularly angered by the sight of one of their fellow countrymen in the role of a Mexican official, for trouble soon occurred. William Barret Travis, acting as attorney for a Louisiana slaveholder, attempted to recover two runaways, and for this Bradburn forced his arrest.

Patrick C. Jack, who had incurred Bradburn's displeasure by playing a series of practical jokes, was then held on a trumped-up charge. Both Travis and Jack were very popular in east Texas and a force soon started to their rescue. The insurgents sent to Brazoria for two cannon, and a skirmish took place there between the Texans and the Mexican troops stationed in the area. After the Mexicans had been forced to withdraw, the settlers drew up the "Turtle Bayou Resolutions," by which they pledged their support to the cause of Santa Anna in his supposed revolt against the principles of Centralism. This took place in June, 1832, and on August 22 the

[29] Eugene C. Barker, "The Influence of Slavery in the Colonization of Texas," *Southwestern Historical Quarterly*, XXVIII (1924), 32. Also see Lester G. Bugbee, "Slavery in Early Texas," *Political Science Quarterly*, XIII (1898), 398.

[30] Alleine Howren, "Causes and Origin of the Decree of April 6, 1830," *Quarterly of the Texas State Historical Association*, XVI (1913), 395.

[31] Barker, *Mexico and Texas*, 144.

alcaldes of San Felipe issued a call for a general convention to meet on October 1. This was the first in a series of conventions that preceded the final declaration of independence.[32]

Fifty-eight delegates assembled at San Felipe in October and elected Austin president, over the candidacy of William H. Wharton. Patrick C. Jack, representing the district of Liberty, was present, as was Philip A. Sublett, for the district of Ayish Bayou. However, except for these two men and Wharton, the convention was controlled by the moderate elements.[33] Committees were appointed to prepare memorials to the national and state governments on the following matters: (1) to secure repeal of the parts of the decree of April 6, 1830, which dealt with emigration from the United States; (2) to petition for a uniform tariff exemption; (3) to petition for a separation from Coahuila and the establishment of state government in Texas. The vote on the demand for statehood stood 36 to 12 in favor of the measure, and it resolved the first test of strength between the temporizing forces led by Austin and the insurgents represented by Wharton. It is still too early to refer to the Wharton and Austin factions as "War" and "Peace" parties, for differences at this point were more on the basis of personalities than on political principles, but it can be said that alignments were forming.[34]

The period from October, 1832, to April, 1833, was one of relative tranquillity in Texas. Reflecting this sentiment, Jonas Harrison a prominent settler of the Teneha District, wrote to Austin: "The idea of a separate, distinct, and independent government I do not believe exists in the mind of any man of common sense in the district. Nor do they want to belong to the United States of the North, there are some fiew exceptions to this last opinion, but not many, scarsely one to ten."[35] A week later Harrison returned from a trip to the Ayish Bayou District and reported that the inhabitants there "deprecate the idea of being *independent of the Mexican Republic.* Their sole wish is to be dependent on it, and to afford it all the sup-

[32] *Ibid.*, 118–19.
[33] E. K. Lindley (comp.), *Biographical Directory of the Texan Conventions and Congresses, 1832–1845,* 17.
[34] Walter P. Webb, "William Harris Wharton," in Dumas Malone (ed.), *Dictionary of American Biography,* XX, 35.
[35] Jonas Harrison to Austin, November 30, 1832, *Austin Papers,* II, 895.

port and protection in their power—to protect all its rights and interests, and in return to participate of all its benefits and advantages, and particularly of its liberal policy in relation to its lands."[36] However, in contrast to these feelings of loyalty, as discerning a political observer as Sam Houston informed the President of the United States that "Texas will by her members in convention by the 1st April, declare all that country as Texas proper, and form a State Constitution."[37] Differences of opinion were current, but the interim prior to the convention of 1833 allowed for the further molding of public sentiment.

In January, 1833, the Central Committee, a standing committee of citizens elected at the convention in October, issued a call for another convention to meet on the first of April. Austin was in Béxar (San Antonio) at the time but hurried back to attend the deliberations, which were again held at San Felipe. The roll call of delegates assembled at the tiny village gives a good indication of the political scene at this point. William H. Wharton was elected president, defeating Austin for the office, and other prominent members of the radical faction, such as Patrick C. Jack, Philip A. Sublett, Robert McAlpin Williamson, and Sam Houston, were much in evidence.[38] The delegates first drew up a provisional constitution and petitioned the Mexican federal Congress for approval of the document. The petitions against the anti-immigration clause of the 1830 act and for general tariff exemption were repeated. Sam Houston was named chairman of the committee that drew up the provisional Constitution, and David G. Burnet received the appointment as chairman of the group that prepared the memorial arguing for approval of the Constitution and consequent organization of state government. Austin, Dr. James B. Miller, and Erasmo Seguin, a native Mexican friendly to the Texas cause, were elected to make the journey to Mexico City to place these proposals before the national Congress. Since Miller and Seguin were not delegates

[36] Harrison to Austin, December 8, 1832, *ibid.*, 900.
[37] Sam Houston to Andrew Jackson, February 13, 1833, Amelia W. Williams and Eugene C. Barker (eds.), *The Writings of Sam Houston, 1813–1863*, I, 275.
[38] Duncan W. Robinson, *Judge Robert McAlpin Williamson; Texas' Three-Legged Willie*, 82. Williamson lost a leg before coming to Texas and then employed a wooden leg, thus the colorful sobriquet.

to the convention and had no taste for the trip, Austin was left to travel alone.[39]

Just prior to his departure for the Mexican capital, Austin forcefully indicated his own attitude toward the existing situation in a letter to a favorite cousin:[40]

Should this application be refused it will be the greatest error ever committed by the Mexican Government. Texas is now in the budding, and impulsive vigor of youth, and a wise direction of its energies will make it one of the most efficient, faithful, and devoted States of the Union. But, under dissapointment it will be an unmanageable and wayward child. For young as it is in some respects, it is far advanced in energy of character, and an unbending determination of purpose. In short, *Texas is determined to have a state Government.*

The Texas commissioner was in a difficult position as he set out on his journey, for many of the settlers doubted his enthusiasm for the mission and others were personally jealous of his position. Writing to Anthony Butler, the American minister at Mexico City, John P. Coles, a member of Austin's colony, noted that "Co. Austin's sincerity in this matter is much doubted by many people in Texas I hope however that Austin will not forget himself and his Friends   He is closely watched and his future prospects depend greatly upon his Conduct in this matter."[41] Austin's awareness of these suspicions can be seen in a letter he directed to his brother-in-law, James Perry:[42]

There is, I am told, some uneasiness that I shall not insist on the approbation of the constitution as formed by the late convention—I shall try and get the law of 6 April 1830 repealed and *a declaration that the people of Texas may legally convene in convention to make a constitution*—This much I expect to effect and no more. . . . No one need have any fears that I will compromise Texas improperly—The interest of Texas is my interest. . . . Unfortunately we have some *personal parties* amongst us—but this is an evil that will correct itself in time.

Austin left Texas in late April and arrived in Mexico City in the

[39] Barker, *Life of Austin,* 361–62.
[40] Austin to Mary Austin Holley, April 20, 1833, *Austin Papers,* II, 955–56.
[41] John P. Coles to Anthony Butler, July 15, 1833, *ibid.,* 988.
[42] Austin to James F. Perry, April 22, 1833, *ibid.,* 960.

middle of July. On August 1 he filed his petition in support of statehood for Texas with Carlos García, minister of foreign relations, and then occupied himself by visiting the sessions of the national legislature. In Texas the people continued to watch his course of action with great interest, the suspicion of his sincerity lingering still.

In Mexico City the messenger from Texas chafed under the usual parliamentary delay. Congress showed no disposition to deal with the memorials from Texas and, to add to his woes, an epidemic of cholera broke out in the city, forcing a legislative recess until the end of September. In August Austin wrote to his cousin, John Austin: "I think the decision of Congress will be in favor of a State, but I fear they will send it to the other States for their approbation, this will cause some delay, tho my friends here think it will be dispatched by the first of January."[43] Congress resumed its sessions but again showed no desire to debate the Texas matter. This disappointment, coupled with the fact that he himself was in poor health after an attack of cholera, led Austin to pour out his disillusionment and chagrin in a letter to J. Miguel Falcón, the Mexican *ayuntamiento* at San Antonio. Writing this letter was an unfortunate act, for it was ultimately responsible for Austin's arrest and detention in the capital. In his communication to Falcón, Austin took note of the existing situation and then observed:[44]

In this state of affairs, I recommend that the ayuntamientos of Texas place themselves in communication with each other without a moment's delay for the purpose of organizing a local government for Texas as a state of the Mexican federation according to the law of May 7, 1824, so as to have everything in readiness to effect the organization in union and harmony as soon as it is known that congress has refused its approval. This step is indispensable as a preparatory measure for there is no doubt but that the fate of Texas depends upon itself and not upon this government.

In time, a copy of this letter reached the Minister of Foreign Relations, García, and Austin was arrested at Saltillo on January 3,

[43] Austin to John Austin, August 6, 1833, *ibid.*, 997.
[44] Austin to Ayuntamiento of San Antonio, October 2, 1833, quoted in Barker, *Life of Austin,* 373–74.

1834. He was taken to Mexico City and on February 13 was placed in solitary confinement in the old Inquisition prison.

The affairs of Texas improved early in 1834 because of internal Mexican politics. Santa Anna, whose fame rested on his military exploits, placed Gómez Farías in the presidential chair, though for all practical purposes ruling Mexico himself. Santa Anna had become a self-styled "true liberal," and to give stature to this conception Farías secured the passage of legislation pointing toward the abolition of clerical taxes and the equal distribution of land taxation in Mexico. Santa Anna also posed as a reformer who would aid the disgruntled provinces in their disputes with the central government.[45] The repeal of the anti-immigration clause of 1830 was announced simultaneously with Austin's arrest, and there was also a promise of tariff exemption at a later date. During the following spring the national legislature granted Texas many basic and long-desired reforms.

Local autonomy was strengthened in Texas by creating four new municipalities at Bastrop, San Patricio, Matagorda, and San Augustine and by creating the political departments of Brazos and Nacogdoches. Texas was given an additional representative in the state legislature, so that three members represented the province while nine spoke for Coahuila. The federal Congress also passed a law permitting the use of English in legal documents and, as a rider to an insignificant land law, passed the declaration that no person should be molested for religious opinions provided he did not disturb public order. The legislators also passed a judiciary act which gave appellate circuit courts to Texas and granted the right of trial by jury.[46] Thus, by the reforms of 1834, the standing complaints against religious conformity, a faulty judicial system, and the restrictions against immigration from the United States were lifted, and the colonists looked upon Santa Anna as a liberator. But time would come, much in the fashion of the American Revolution, when Santa Anna would be referred to as a "petty tyrant."

With Austin in prison, party alignments became more discern-

---

[45] Willfrid Hardy Callcott, *Santa Anna; the Story of an Enigma Who Once Was Mexico*, 108–109.
[46] Barker, *Mexico and Texas*, 130.

ible in Texas. Growing restive under his restraint, the prisoner unburdened his feelings to his brother-in-law, James Perry:[47]

It is very likely that I may be hammered and pummeled about for a year before I get home again, but I think that good will come of it for Texas. The April law is repealed and before I quit the matter I hope to see some other remedies. I did not like the manner this question was started I wanted Bexar to take the lead—but so it is—you must all now harmonize more with Bexar and Goliad and have union—and no more *party spirit.* I suppose that some of my enemies in the colony will rejoice at what they think or *hope* will be my ruin—no good man will envy them their joy, nor participate in it.

Austin was determined to take his imprisonment philosophically, but as the months passed and there was no attempt by the political departments in Texas to petition for his release, he grew increasingly bitter. Writing to Oliver Jones, he stated his belief that "a mild and respectful representation of facts from the Ayuntamientos of Texas" would secure his freedom. Rumor led him to believe that his personal enemies were plotting against him in Texas, but he did not believe that his friends would also desert him: "a few may do so, but not the mass—not the farmers—the honest and sound part of the community."[48]

In this surmise Austin was probably correct, but it is true that a concerted opposition to him did exist in the faction led by William H. Wharton. Political differences were accentuated by strongly conflicting personalities. In his excellent study of the life of Stephen F. Austin, Eugene C. Barker draws this contrast:[49]

The two differed fundamentally in temperament. Wharton was masterful, quick to anger, uncontrolled, somewhat domineering, one imagines that he made no allowance for the blundering interference of Mexican authority, and was ready at all times to try to right a real or fancied grievance by the most direct means, regardless of the consequences of failure either to himself or to others. Austin was almost the opposite in every respect.

In the fall of 1833 John Wharton, William's brother, established

[47] Austin to James F. Perry, January 14, 1834, *Austin Papers,* II, 1033.
[48] Austin to Oliver Jones, May 30, 1834, *ibid.,* 1058.
[49] Barker, *Life of Austin,* 386.

a newspaper, *The Advocate of the People's Rights,* published at Brazoria. The paper appeared irregularly from November, 1833, to February, 1834, and its columns were dedicated to an attack on the "watchful waiting" policy adopted by Austin.[50]

While Austin was in prison, events transpired at Monclova, a political department within the state of Coahuila and Texas, that had a direct bearing on the approaching revolution. The state legislature, meeting at Monclova, passed laws of March and April, 1834, which gave to the governor the sole right of disposing of lands in four-hundred-league units to individuals in Texas,[51] and a similar law was enacted on April 19, 1835. Under the terms of these enactments, the public lands in Texas were made the subject of particularly notorious speculation. These laws were quickly vetoed by the federal Congress, but again the internal distresses of the nation had a distinct reaction in Texas. The legislation had resulted from the renewal of a quarrel between the districts of Saltillo and Monclova over the location of the capital of the state of Coahuila and Texas. The government at Monclova, hostile to Santa Anna, had sanctioned the speculations in an attempt to provide funds to defend the established state government against possible attack. Shortly thereafter, General Martín Perfecto de Cós, Commandant General of the Eastern Interior Provinces and brother-in-law of Santa Anna, declared the laws of 1834 and 1835 unconstitutional and proceeded to arrest the governor of Monclova, the legislature having adjourned just prior to his raid.[52] The immediate reaction in Texas was one of complete disgust at the shameful speculations sanctioned by the Monclova legislature.[53] Also, the belief was becoming widespread that Texas should free itself of the continual internal warfare besetting the Mexican government.

Politically, the Monclova incident proved damaging to the Austin group. Chief among those present at the sessions of the state legislature had been Samuel Williams, private secretary to Austin

[50] Eugene C. Barker, "Notes on Early Texas Newspapers, 1819–1836," *Southwestern Historical Quarterly,* XXI (1917), 139.

[51] Eugene C. Barker, "Land Speculation as a Cause of the Texas Revolution," *Quarterly of the Texas State Historical Association,* X (1906), 81.

[52] Barker, *Mexico and Texas,* 135–36.

[53] Barker, "Land Speculation as a Cause of the Texas Revolution," *Quarterly of the Texas State Historical Association,* X, 89.

and business agent for his colony. It was Williams who had introduced the law authorizing the sale of land up to four hundred leagues, and he ultimately received a handsome share of the profits. Other men associated in the speculations were Ben Milam, James Bowie, General John T. Mason, representative of a New York land company, and others, but no prominent men of the Wharton faction were implicated.[54] Williams' conduct in the matter was of major importance in the political alignments prior to the revolution, since it was well understood that he had always acted with Austin's sanction and that the two men were personally very friendly. Austin's awareness of the damage done by Williams' participation in the Monclova affair can be seen by a subsequent letter to Williams. The two had become estranged, and when Williams pleaded for a reconciliation Austin wrote repudiating[55]

those cursed Monclova speculations and Contracts by which you have involved yourself and friends and country in evils which you certainly never even drempt of and know nothing of now. . . . You spared no kind of pains to precipitate the country into war immediately, an event which you must have known would have perpetuated my imprisonment indefinitely—you also must have known that all the odium of those things, would be cast on me by the envious and slanderous owing to our long friendship and relations.

The lasting result of the speculations was that those who had been at Monclova wished to make their transactions good by a declaration of independence from Mexico. Thus the Wharton group, while not tainted with the shame of the speculations, at the same time secured the support of a small but vocal group desiring revolution.[56]

Events moved rapidly to a climax in the troubled province of Texas. Armed with petitions from many of the political departments in Texas, Peter W. Grayson and Spencer H. Jack, both competent attorneys, arrived in Mexico City from Texas. By virtue of their diligent efforts Austin was soon released on bond and in time given his complete freedom under a general amnesty statute. At

[54] Williams, *The Animating Pursuits of Speculation*, 46–48.
[55] Austin to Samuel Williams, October 12, 1836, *Austin Papers*, III, 435–36.
[56] Robinson, *Judge Robert McAlpin Williamson*, 108.

last, after two years of imprisonment, Austin was allowed to return to Texas in July, 1835.

In Texas, however, the colonists were alarmed by the display of Santa Anna's true tendencies. In January, 1835, the Mexican Congress, in accordance with the dictator's wishes, deposed President Farías. On March 31 the legislators passed a law reducing the militia to one man for every five hundred inhabitants, thereby ending effective opposition from the individual states of the union. On May 2 Congress passed the extraordinary declaration that it possessed in itself the sovereign power to set aside the constitution of 1824 for the good of the nation.[57] General Cós was continued in his position as Commandant General of the Eastern Interior Provinces and Colonel Domingo de Ugartechea was created commandant in Texas. Finally, the tariff exemptions that had been granted in 1832 for a period of two years expired, and the customhouses, along with the accompanying soldiery, were revived. The colonists were now forced to pay a duty on most imports, and a profitable smuggling trade to the interior, which should have paid duty at Matamoros, was effectively choked off.[58]

In January, 1835, Captain Antonio Tenorio with a detachment of soldiers and a customs collector arrived at Anahuac to reopen the customhouse. A deputy collector was stationed at Brazoria and trouble soon developed. Andrew Briscoe, a local merchant, refused to obey the tariff laws because he felt that they were not being enforced on a uniform basis throughout Texas. He showed his contempt for the Mexican soldiery in a series of practical jokes, one of which led to his arrest and that of a friend. News of the arrest reached San Felipe, and on June 22 a meeting was held there to discuss the matter. Meanwhile, General Cós assured Tenorio that Ugartechea was on his way to aid the garrison at Anahuac. The colonists decided to act first. Captain William Barret Travis delivered an impassioned speech at San Felipe, enlisted volunteers, and

[57] Wooten, A Complete History of Texas, 182.
[58] Carlos E. Castañeda (trans.), "Statistical Report on Texas, 1835," Southwestern Historical Quarterly, XXVIII (1925), 186. In January, 1834, Colonel Juan Almonte, a high-ranking army officer, was sent to Texas on a general tour of inspection. In his report, which was published at Mexico City in 1835, much attention was devoted to the smuggling activities of the Texans.

forced Tenorio to surrender.[59] Upon his return to San Felipe, Travis found that his course of action was condemned by many and that the moderate group still retained the upper hand. A letter from Travis to James Bowie, also a member of the group desiring immediate independence, gives a good indication of the political conditions of the time. Writing from San Felipe, Travis commented that[60]

the people are much divided here. The *peace-party*, as they style themselves, I believe are the strongest, and make much the most noise. Unless we could be united, had we not better be quiet, and settle down for a while? There is now no doubt but that a central government will be established. What will Texas do in that case? ... I do not know the minds of the people upon the subject; but if they had a bold and determined leader, I am inclined to think they would kick against it.

The situation in San Felipe was common to the greater part of Texas. Meetings were held throughout the province attacking the action taken by Travis and asserting the loyalty of the individual communities. In many cases the proceedings of these meetings were broadcast in the hope that the Mexican government would recognize the feelings of the majority of the settlers.

Against this uncertain background Santa Anna overplayed his hand by ordering the arrest of Travis, Williamson, Samuel Williams, and others who had been conspicuous in the recent disturbances. General Cós refused to receive a peace mission until the men were delivered up to him; at the same time, he announced his intention to assume command in person at San Antonio. On August 20 at Columbia a committee of fifteen issued a call for another convention. The plan called for five elected delegates from each precinct within the political departments of Texas to meet at San Felipe on October 15. The impetus for this new convention came from the Wharton party and it marks the high point of their influence prior to the Revolution.[61]

The town of San Felipe itself, however, was controlled by the moderates and passed resolutions against the convention. More-

[59] Wooten, *A Complete History of Texas*, 183.

[60] Travis to Bowie, July 30, 1835, quoted in Henderson Yoakum, *History of Texas, from Its First Settlement in 1685 to Its Annexation to the United States in 1846*, I, 343.

[61] Eugene C. Barker, "Public Opinion in Texas Preceding the Revolution," *American Historical Association Annual Report, 1913*, I, 227.

over, as the capital of the department of the Brazos, and associated with the policy that Austin had always advocated, its attitude toward the wisdom of another convention was of major importance. Uncertainty prevailed in Texas, but deliberations were put aside with the return of Austin, who landed at Velasco on September 1. A public dinner in his honor was given at Brazoria, and he endorsed the convention without reservation, implying that in his mind war was inevitable. His complete approval of the plan set in motion by the Wharton party acted to unite the colonists on the necessity of preparing for war.

On September 21 Austin announced that General Cós had landed at Copano with a large force and that a group of Texans were gathering at San Antonio to prevent a meeting of Cós and Colonel Ugartechea, the commander at San Antonio. Ugartechea remembered that the colonists at Gonzales, a settlement east of San Antonio, possessed a brass six-pounder that had been given to them by the Mexican authorities as protection against Indians. Though the cannon was known to be unmounted, Ugartechea sent a small detachment to Gonzales to take it away.[62] A skirmish resulted, and on October 2 the Texans successfully attacked the Mexican position, forcing the soldiers to retreat toward San Antonio. The Texans had won the first engagement of the war, making necessary the formation of an army even before the meeting of the convention. Austin took the lead in preparing for war by creating a Central Committee. At his suggestion each municipality appointed one member to sit on a general council, and the sessions of the regular convention were then postponed until November. The general council, in the interim, elected Richard R. Royal of Matagorda as its president and designated Austin commander of the Texas Army.[63]

The new military leader decided to advance against San Antonio, but the council, wrestling with numerous difficulties, was full of dissension. Some of the delegates preferred to join the army, and those who met at San Felipe threatened to adjourn because of the absent members. Royal, who was having a difficult time, wrote to Austin that the delegates were like "volunteers in Camp (Very

[62] Wooten, A Complete History of Texas, 186.
[63] Ibid., 187.

Restless) and much is said about going home. . . . Our Proceedings have not had general Circulation all these circumstances render it necessary If not Indispensable to so arrange that the members Return to Hold the Convention as Speedily as Possible."[64] If this report failed to cheer Austin, it was all of a piece with his general situation. In the interests of unity, William Wharton had consented to accept the office of judge advocate general in the Texas Army, but then in a moment of anger had resigned. Bowie and Travis disagreed with their commander on the strategy for the siege of San Antonio, while Sam Houston, disgruntled at not receiving command of the army, sulked at San Felipe.[65]

The convention, called the "General Consultation," finally met at San Felipe on November 3 and drew up a declaration defending its actions against the Mexican government. The issue of complete independence was debated, and the Wharton faction mustered the support of Alexander Horton and Sam Houston, both representing the district of San Augustine, Wyly Martin, from San Felipe, and Judge Robert McAlpin Williamson, from the district of Mina.[66] Don Carlos Barrett, also from Mina, argued the necessity of conciliating the Mexican Federalists, who were Santa Anna's enemies, and stressed that an absolute declaration of independence would serve only to unite all factions in Mexico against the Texans.[67] The selection of Branch T. Archer as president of the consultation was a victory for the moderates, and the conventional wording of the declaration of causes as well as of a resolution endorsing the constitution of 1824 indicate the mild temper of the convention.[68] A provisional government was created, consisting of a governor, lieutenant governor, and a general legislative council who were to be elected by the delegates at the convention. On November 12 the group elected Austin, Archer, and William H. Wharton as commissioners to the United States to enlist financial aid and general sympathy for the cause of Texas. The organization of a regular

[64] Royal to Austin, October 16, 1835, *Austin Papers*, III, 187–88.
[65] Marquis James, *The Raven: A Biography of Sam Houston*, 214.
[66] Robinson, *Judge Robert McAlpin Williamson*, 113.
[67] William C. Binkley, *The Texas Revolution*, 40–41.
[68] Eugene C. Barker, "The Texas Declaration of Causes for Taking up Arms against Mexico," *Quarterly of the Texas State Historical Association*, XV (1912), 174–75.

army was provided for, and Sam Houston was appointed its commander. Then, just before its adjournment, the consultation agreed to meet again on March 1, 1836.

The Wharton party, though it failed to secure a declaration of independence, did gain two notable victories in the appointment of Sam Houston to command the army and in the election of Henry Smith as governor. Smith, representing the district of Columbia at the convention, had come to Texas in 1827. He had taught school for a living and had held a few minor political offices. He was not a major figure in the Wharton camp, but he had been identified with that faction since the convention of 1832. Smith was selected because, unlike Williamson or John Wharton, he was acceptable to the temporizing elements at the convention. According to Richard R. Stenberg, a scholar of this period of Texas history, the Wharton people were assiduous in contending that Austin could not be spared from the army and that the position of governor entailed less responsibility. From here it was an easy step to claim that Austin's services would be of greater value as a commissioner to the United States and to champion Sam Houston as commander of the army in the field.[69] Houston's previous military exploits were known, and it was felt that his friendship with President Jackson would be of aid to the Texans. Whether Houston conspired in Austin's defeat is not known; it is certain that he held a small opinion of the latter's military abilities and that he had violently disagreed with Austin's plan to storm Béxar. This test of party strength at the consultation was unique: the delegates voted for measures rather than men, a state of affairs not often duplicated during the period of the Republic.[70] In a short while, Austin, Archer, and Wharton set out for the United States, and the provisional government was left with the problem of waging war.

A bitter fight soon broke out between Governor Smith and his council. Lieutenant-Governor James Robinson sided with the council, and the quarrel became so intense that Texas was without a governing body worthy of the name. It was apparent that Smith

[69] Richard R. Stenberg, "Some Letters of the Texas Revolution," *Southwestern Political and Social Science Quarterly,* XXI (1941), 306–307. The material used here originally appeared in the unpublished reflections of Guy M. Bryan, a nephew of Austin's.

[70] Andrew J. Houston, *Texas Independence,* 67–68.

had a domineering nature. Colonel William Fairfax Gray, a native of Virginia traveling in Texas, was introduced to Governor Smith in February, 1836, and recorded the experience in his diary: "My impression of Governor Smith is, that he is a strongly prejudiced *party man*. Too illiterate, too little informed, and not of the right calibre for the station he has been placed in. Organs of self esteem and combativeness large; perceptive faculty good; intellectual, small; little reflection or imagination; no reverence."[71]

Military questions were at the bottom of the difficulties between Smith and his council. It will be remembered that the "declaration of causes" had affirmed an attachment to the principles of the Mexican Federalists; in time one of the leading opponents of Santa Anna, General José Antonio Mexía, offered his services to the Texans. The dilemma that confronted Smith was at once obvious because as a supporter of the Wharton party he was wedded to the idea of independence and thus could not reconcile himself to an association with the Federalists. Mexía won the endorsement of Austin prior to the commissioner's departure, and a resolution was adopted by the council stipulating that supplies should be provided for the Mexican military leader and the force he was to raise. Smith denounced the council's action in a strong veto message, but the resolution was then passed over his veto. Mexía, fully aware that he would never have the undivided backing of the provisional government, abandoned the expedition and returned to exile in the United States.[72]

Meanwhile, Béxar had fallen to the Texans. In the interim between Austin's resignation as commander of the army and Houston's appointment, Edward Burleson had served as commanding officer. A variety of plans were suggested to him for the capture of San Antonio, and, as is characteristic of volunteer armies, the soldiers remained disgruntled and restless. Finally, the old frontiersman Ben Milam took matters into his own hands. His challenge: "Who will follow old Ben Milam?" proved hard to resist, and some three hundred soldiers attacked the Mexican position. The battle raged for four days, and on December 9 the Mexican troops under

[71] Gray, *Diary*, 111.
[72] Ralph W. Steen, "Analysis of the Work of the General Council of Texas, 1835-1836," *Southwestern Historical Quarterly*, XLI (1938), 342.

General Cós were forced to surrender.[73] The battle was a complete success for the Texans, though, ironically, the one man lost was Milam. The Mexicans suffered heavy loss of life, and the defeat at San Antonio, coupled with the fact that the Texans had occupied Goliad and Gonzales, forced Cós to abandon Texas completely. The next Mexican army to appear in Texas would be led by Santa Anna.

The victory at San Antonio is also important in understanding the main point of contention between the governor and the council. In a message delivered on December 19, Smith called attention to the expense of maintaining an idle army and, though he did not expressly say so, implied that a Texas expedition directed against Matamoros would effectively secure independence. Interestingly enough, a military committee appointed by the council also recommended that the army be kept busy by an attack against the Mexican city. The committee noted that the army could not afford to remain idle because the impression would be created in the United States that no further volunteers were needed, and also because the enemy would be allowed time in which to fortify the Rio Grande frontier at Laredo and Matamoros.[74]

Although the Matamoros project was popular with all concerned, the Governor and council could not agree on leadership. General Houston, as the top-ranking military officer, was the logical man for the position, but he was opposed to the idea, probably because he thought the council would not effectively back him up. The Commander, who suffered in his relations with the council because of his political affiliations with Smith, had written to the Governor that the chairman of the military committee "has interposed every possible obstacle to the organization of the army; and, so far as I am identified with it, to delay the placing of Texas in a proper state of defense."[75] Houston instructed Bowie to undertake the expedition, but he also refused; the council then appointed Francis W. Johnson, who started for the Mexican frontier but later turned back. The command was next offered to James W. Fannin,

[73] Samuel A. Maverick, *Notes on the Storming of Bexar, in the Close of 1835*, p. 24.

[74] Eugene C. Barker, "The Texas Revolutionary Army," *Quarterly of the Texas State Historical Association*, IX (1906), 254.

[75] Houston to Henry Smith, December 17, 1835, *Houston Writings*, I, 321.

but he could not raise the necessary number of volunteers. At this point Houston and Johnson changed their minds once again and secured the sanction of both the Governor and the council to undertake the march. However, neither of the would-be commanders could enlist enough men to commence operations. Houston, in complete disgust, had Smith appoint him commissioner to the Cherokees to negotiate a treaty of alliance; Johnson marched on to San Patricio and encamped there with about a hundred men; and Fannin went into quarters at Goliad. The issue of a Mexican expedition was to plague further efforts of the Texans in their bid for independence.

On January 6 Smith received a letter from Houston that proved to be the proverbial last straw. Enclosed in the communication was a report from Lieutenant Colonel James C. Neill at Béxar. Neill complained that Francis W. Johnson had rifled all the provisions and clothing at Béxar before proceeding on to San Patricio and that as a result the men at San Antonio were suffering from want of supplies. Houston implored Smith to "send supplies to the wounded, the sick, the naked, and the hungry, for God's sake!"[76] Smith, regarding Johnson's act as a direct challenge to his authority, and suspecting that the council was in agreement with what had transpired, called a secret meeting of that body. He then read them a blistering lecture, accusing the members of the council of playing politics and of impeding the war effort. The council in turn created a committee to consider the governor's message and to draft a general course of action. The committee report stated that the members of the council were sovereign and that Smith had violated the national constitution of 1824 and was thus deposed. The Lieutenant-Governor, James Robinson, was made acting governor; and the commander in the field, the agents in the United States, and all other officials in Texas were made responsible to him.[77] Smith wrote to Robinson in a fury, accusing him of being a "stranger in the country" and observing that the council "did not make, nor can

[76] Houston to Smith, January 6, 1836, ibid., 333.
[77] W. Roy Smith, "The Quarrel between Governor Smith and the Provisional Government of the Republic," Quarterly of the Texas State Historical Association, V (1902), 325.

28

they break me; nor can you, with all the plastic power of your council chamber, upon what you may vainly conceive to be my ruin."[78] The dispute ran its bitter course. Smith refused to give up the archives of his office, and the council continued to meet at irregular intervals.

The citizens of Texas reflected the dissensions of their leaders. From his camp-site at Burnham's on the Colorado River, Travis wrote feelingly to Smith: "The people are cold & indifferent—They are worn down & exhausted with the war, & in consequence of dissentions between contending & rival chieftains, they have lost all confidence in their own Govt. & officers."[79] The important fact was that the people were moving toward a united desire for independence, and, in deposing Smith because of his alleged abuse of the constitution of 1824, the council displayed a woeful ignorance of the prevailing sentiment. As early as January 6, Lieutenant Colonel Neill, writing from his command at Béxar, said:[80]

I will say all to you that I Know about the feelings of the Citizens of this place on the subject of Independence—they Know not whose hands they may fall into, but if we had a force here that they Knew could sustain them I believe they would be ¾ths Americans and go for Independence and claim all to the Rio del Norte as they Know we want it and will have it.

Smith himself, soon after his removal from office, felt that "an unequevocal Declaration of Independence will save the country & that is all that can."[81] Many Texans reasoned that the war had already begun and that in reality the matter of independence was only splitting hairs. Ira Lewis, an early settler who had been a delegate at the consultation of 1835, must have reflected the majority opinion in Texas when he commented: "The consequences to Texas, will differ but little, whether we fight for Independence, or State rights, for in either case we must fight and whip Mexico."[82]

[78] Smith to Robinson, January 18, 1836, quoted in John Henry Brown, *Life and Times of Henry Smith, the First American Governor of Texas,* 247.
[79] Travis to Smith, January 28, 1836, in William C. Binkley (ed.), *Official Correspondence of the Texan Revolution, 1835–1836,* I, 352.
[80] J. C. Neill to Governor and Council, January 6, 1836, *ibid.,* 274.
[81] Henry Smith to L. W. Groce, January 18, 1836, *ibid.,* 305.
[82] Ira R. Lewis to Duncan S. Walker, January 26, 1836, Ira R. Lewis Papers.

Such was the rising sentiment, in fact, that when the question of independence was debated in March, 1836, the outcome was almost certain.

In the interim between the collapse of the provisional government and the meeting of the delegates in March, military affairs occupied the attention of the Texans. On February 1 Santa Anna set out for Texas at the head of 6,000 men. Upon reaching the Rio Grande, he dispatched General José Urrea to Matamoros for the purpose of engaging the force under Johnson and his principal aides, Dr. James Grant and Robert C. Morris, at San Patricio.

When Santa Anna reached San Antonio on February 23, the garrison of 150 men took refuge in the Mission of San Antonio de Valero (the Alamo). The Mexican commander caused a flag of truce to be flown and then demanded the surrender of the Texas position; Travis, in command of the defenders, answered with a cannon shot. It is said that the notes of the *degüello*, the medieval announcement that no quarter would be shown, were then blown, and the siege of the Alamo began. The bravery of Travis, Bowie, Crockett, and others is too familiar to require narration; it is enough to say that after a heroic defense the Alamo fell on March 6, four days after the Texans had declared their independence.

Meanwhile, Fannin had remained at Goliad. When news of Urrea's decisive victory at San Patricio on March 2 reached Fannin, he sent out companies under Captain Amon B. King and Major William A. Ward to engage Urrea in skirmish actions. Then, on March 11, Houston reached Gonzales and ordered Fannin to retire to Victoria on the Guadalupe River; but the impetuous commander disobeyed, preferring to await the return of King and Ward.[83] Fannin finally commenced his retreat on March 19 and was quickly attacked by Urrea. Upon the promise of amnesty and treatment in accordance with their status as prisoners of war, Fannin reluctantly surrendered his troops. The men were marched back to Goliad, where they were joined by a contingent of American volunteers who had been captured at Copano. Santa Anna then sent orders that the prisoners were to be put to death. On Palm Sunday, March 27, the Texans and the recent arrivals from the United States were massacred. Thus, Santa Anna was victorious, envisioning a quick

[83] Wooten, *A Complete History of Texas*, 218–19.

and complete conquest of Texas. To the Texans the military situation appeared extremely bleak.

For an understanding of political developments it is necessary to return to the convention of March, 1836, called at Washington-on-the-Brazos to declare Texas independent from Mexico and a nation in its own right. From New Orleans, Stephen F. Austin wrote to Sam Houston in January, 1836, that "a question of vital importance is yet to be decided in Texas, which is a declaration of independence." Austin then observed that though he had had reservations about independence when he left Texas he now wished to see the colonists "free from the trammels of religious intolerance and other anti-republican restrictions, and independent at once."[84] This letter put Austin's seal of approval on the approaching convention. It was common knowledge that the Wharton party was eager for an outright declaration of independence; thus the election of delegates to the convention turned on the candidates' positions toward the existing situation. The discerning among the electorate must have realized that unless the Texans tried to gain independence and create a new government which could bestow benefits in land, the high ratio of volunteers from the United States would be greatly curtailed.[85] Letters from Austin, Archer, and Wharton in the United States stressed the importance of independence as a talking point which they might use in negotiations with undecided capitalists.[86]

In the eyes of a traveler of that day, Washington-on-the-Brazos was a dismal place indeed:[87]

It is laid out in the woods; about a dozen wretched cabins or shanties constitute the city; not one decent house in it, and only one well defined street, which consists of an opening out of the woods. The stumps still

[84] Austin to Houston, January 7, 1836, *Austin Papers*, III, 298–99.

[85] Joseph E. Field, *Three Years in Texas*, 27–28.

[86] From Memphis, Wharton wrote to Smith in this manner: "I find the feelings in the country universal in our favor, *provided we war for independence*, or wish to attach ourselves to the United States of the North. But if our war is to be the Constitution of 1824, and is to terminate in anything short of a total dissolution of all connection with Mexico, we may expect no sympathy or assistance from this quarter." Wharton to Smith, January 27, 1836, quoted in Brown, *Life and Times of Henry Smith*, 289. Also see Austin, Archer, and Wharton to Smith, January 10, 1836, in George P. Garrison (ed.), *Diplomatic Correspondence of the Republic of Texas*, American Historical Association Annual Report, 1907, I, 57.

[87] Gray, *Diary*, 108.

31

standing. A rare place to hold a national convention in. They will have to leave promptly to avoid starvation.

The delegates assembled and elected Richard Ellis, representing the district of Red River, to be the presiding officer of the convention. On March 2 the declaration of independence was drawn up and unanimously signed by the members present; those delegates who arrived late signed it as they came in. The delegates took no official notice of the dispute between Smith and the council but merely demanded the transfer of the archives to the convention as the official government. On March 4 General Houston was confirmed as commander of all the military forces, and all able-bodied persons between the ages of seventeen and fifty were declared liable for military duty. An appeal to the United States for men, money, and supplies was announced, and liberal land bounties were offered to those who would volunteer their services in the cause of Texas independence.[88]

Though there was complete agreement on independence, there were areas of contention among the delegates. The wisdom of pledging the lands of Texas as security for any loan floated in the United States by the commissioners was debated, as was the extra-liberal land policy, which would benefit the volunteers instead of the old settlers. Gray noted that "the land question also requires much *log rolling* to make it suit the existing interests or selfish views of members."[89] After lengthy argument a law was passed which authorized the commissioners to contract a loan of one million dollars in the United States; this was followed by a statute which stipulated that the sale of public lands in Texas should cease until the end of the war. The convention then labored all day and night of March 16, drafting a new constitution for the state. The Constitution provided that the new government should have a president, a vice-president, and a Congress of two houses. An ad interim government was also created to serve in the existing emergency.[90] A judicial system based on the Constitution of the United States was established, and the new nation was divided into local areas for governmental purposes.

[88] Laws of the Republic of Texas, I, 20–21.
[89] Gray, *Diary*, 127.
[90] Yoakum, *History of Texas*, II, 72.

The main question of political importance at the convention centered around the election of officers to the ad interim government. Since all the delegates were united on the choice of independence, attention was directed to personalities rather than to issues. Among the comparative newcomers from the United States were men with previous legislative experience from which to choose, and it can certainly be said that this was the most talented assembly in Texas prior to the formation of the Republic. Such men as Robert Potter and Samuel Carson, both of whom had served in the North Carolina Legislature, and Thomas Rusk, a protégé of Calhoun's prior to his migration to Texas, gave a definite luster to this convention.[91] In addition there were such men as David Burnet, Sam Houston, and the Mexican liberal Lorenzo de Zavala. These men, and others like them, had been in attendance at the previous deliberations and already were a trifle contemptuous of the recent arrivals from the United States.

As early as March 8, Gray had confided to his diary that "the evil spirit of electioneering is among them for the *high offices* in prospect,"[92] but actually the Presidency of the ad interim government went by default. William H. Wharton, the leader of the independence party before the convention, was the logical choice for the position, but in a letter written from Nashville to Henry Smith he had made known his wishes: "In the new Organization I will have nothing to do with the Executive post. I prefer the post I am now in to any other if they choose to keep me in it."[93] It was also felt that Austin wished to remain in the United States, and the Monclova speculations still rankled in the minds of many to further disqualify him. The convention had also forestalled the chance of Houston's election by confirming his military rank as head of the Texas armies. Thus, with the three most prominent candidates disposed of, the convention elected David Burnet president of the ad interim government. Lorenzo de Zavala was made vice-president, and Samuel Carson was chosen to fill the office of secretary of state. The cabinet was completed with the selections of Bailey Hardeman as secretary of the treasury, Thomas Rusk as secretary of war,

[91] Sam H. Dixon and Louis W. Kemp, *The Heroes of San Jacinto*, 57.
[92] Gray, *Diary*, 127.
[93] Wharton to Smith, February 7, 1836, *Diplomatic Correspondence*, II, 66.

Robert Potter as secretary of the navy, and David Thomas as attorney general. The officers of the new government were sworn in at four o'clock on the morning of March 17, and the convention adjourned the following day. Provision was made for ratification of the Constitution by the people on September 1, and on the same day the first permanent officers of the new nation would be elected.[94]

The news of the fall of the Alamo had reached the convention during its sessions, and upon adjournment many of the delegates joined the general populace in the retreat toward Louisiana. This episode has come down in Texas history as the "Runaway Scrape," and it marked the lowest point of Texas' fortunes before the redemption of San Jacinto. Rain poured steadily for some two weeks as the settlers fled before the oncoming Mexican army, and those immigrants who reached Texas at this time prepared to turn back. Gray, who upon leaving the convention was caught up in the panic, has left this graphic description:[95]

Passed a number of people on the road flying from the invasion, and seeking a place of safety east of the Trinity. At the ferry were large crowds, all seeking a passage across for the same purpose, with their wives, children, negroes, horses, carts, wagons and droves of cattle. These they were trying to force to swim across the river.

Meanwhile, Houston had left for the west, where he gathered together the remnants of the Texas Army. As far as his intentions can be learned, he intended to make the Colorado River his line of defense and to wait there for reinforcements and news from Fannin. The tidings of Goliad reached him on March 25, and hoping to avert an engagement with General Ramírez y Sesma, who was advancing to Bastrop on the Colorado, he decided to retreat to the Brazos. The Texas commander was severely criticized at a later date for the failure to attack General Ramírez y Sesma; but Fannin's defeat at Goliad ultimately allowed General Urrea to join forces with Ramírez y Sesma, and a pitched battle under those circumstances would have been disastrous for the Texans.[96]

[94] Ordinances and Decrees of the Consultation and the Convention Which Assembled at Washington, March 1, 1836, 23–24.

[95] Gray, *Diary*, 152.

[96] Wooten, *A Complete History of Texas*, 226.

Continuing his retreat along the Brazos, Houston hoped to risk everything on a single decisive blow and thus waited for the most favorable moment to attack. His motives were suspect, and he was openly taunted with charges of cowardice by a few of his senior officers. It was known that General Edmund Pendleton Gaines was encamped at the Louisiana border, ostensibly to guard against Indian depredations. There were many who believed that Houston, in accordance with an understanding with Jackson, would continue his retreat into the territory of the United States and thus lure the Mexicans into a clash with American troops.[97] The cabinet officers of the ad interim government, themselves engaged in the wholesale retreat, added to Houston's woes by frequent visits to the army and by repeated admonitions to stop and fight. Houston expressed his anguish in a letter to the Attorney General, David Thomas, explaining that when he promised to keep the enemy from crossing the Brazos "I did not intend to convey the idea that either the army or myself possessed powers of ubiquity; but that they should not pass through my encampment." Houston then expressed his hope that "the president would understand, on *whom* to rely, and on *whom* for a while the burden must rest."[98] The Mexican forces, now united under Santa Anna, stepped up the tempo of their march and reached Harrisburg on April 15. The following day a Mexican scouting party just failed to capture Burnet and members of his cabinet at New Washington on Galveston Bay. Finally, Houston brought the retreat to a halt at Buffalo Bayou, where the Texans encamped in a dense wood on the east bank.

Houston's scouts soon brought word that Santa Anna and his army were at New Washington and that the terrain favored a Texas attack. Evidence indicates that a majority of the officers and men would not this time be denied a fight and that Houston also considered the situation advantageous. The Texas Army now numbered only about eleven hundred men, but it was felt that the element of surprise after so prolonged a retreat would more than counteract the Mexican superiority in number. As luck would have it, however, many of the soldiers now fell ill with measles and mumps, greatly reducing Houston's fighting force. Thus, when the Texans

[97] James W. Silver, *Edmund Pendleton Gaines, Frontier General*, 202-03.
[98] Houston to David Thomas, April 13, 1836, *Houston Writings*, I, 411.

crossed the bayou continuing their retreat, they numbered about eight hundred men; the other three hundred included the sick and those who were looking after them, and the members of the detachment left to guard the baggage.[99]

The army continued its march and turned toward Lynchburg Ferry. Houston placed his men in the timber skirting the bayou, and at this point the Mexican army appeared, retired to the timber (immediately behind the site of the present San Jacinto monument), and went into battle position. Actually, the positions of the two armies had cut off any mode of retreat for either. The Texans had the rain-swollen bayou to their right; the Mexicans had a swamp at their rear and to their right; and neither army could cross the prairie to the south without dangerously exposing itself to the fire of the other.[100] It was contended at a later date, when San Jacinto had become a political issue, that General Houston ordered a pontoon bridge built to move the army across Buffalo Bayou.[101] This order, if it was given, was never obeyed, though the soldiers did consent to destroy the bridge across Vince's Bayou, thereby cutting off a way of retreat for the Mexicans. As the Mexicans were enjoying their siesta in midafternoon of April 21, the Texans attacked and the rout was soon complete. Before sundown six hundred Mexicans lay dead and more than two hundred were wounded. On the Texas side nine men were killed and some thirty wounded. Among the wounded was General Houston who had been shot in the ankle—perhaps by one of his own men.[102]

The Texans spent the following day rounding up prisoners, and among the lot was Santa Anna, who had disguised himself as a common soldier, but had been inadvertently recognized by one of his own men. Houston made himself even more unpopular with certain elements of the army by refusing to allow the execution of the Mexican dictator, and the treatment of Santa Anna became a thorny problem for the ad interim government. General Houston filed a report of the battle with Burnet and soon afterwards bade farewell to the army. Upon the orders of his physicians the vic-

[99] Andrew F. Muir, "The Mystery of San Jacinto," Southwest Review, XXXVI (1951), 81.
[100] Ibid., 82.
[101] R. M. Coleman, Houston Displayed: or Who Won the Battle of San Jacinto, 3.
[102] Muir, "The Mystery of San Jacinto," Southwest Review, XXXVI, 83.

torious leader then left for New Orleans to have his wound treated. To a large segment of the army Houston was an incompetent leader who had been forced to fight and even then had been particularly lucky in catching the enemy napping. Yet with one blow he had put an end to Mexican pretensions in Texas. Though the armies of Texas lost every battle in the campaigns of 1836 save San Jacinto, Houston had not been personally associated with any of the defeats. On the contrary, the defeat at San Patricio and Fannin's surrender at Goliad could be directly traced to a refusal to obey his orders. With Austin and Wharton in the United States, the popular hero with the returning settlers was Sam Houston.

Old Sam Takes the Helm

S AM HOUSTON HAS BEEN generally proclaimed
the hero of San Jacinto. No fiction of the nov-
elist is farther from the truth. Houston was the only man on the battlefield that deserved censure. Was absolutely compelled into the fight. . . .
Houston only lacked the genius to become another Alcibiades. Had all
the vices without the virtues of the Athenian. Just before and immediately after the Battle of San Jacinto he was universally detested. The
army regarded him as a military fop, and the citizens were disgusted at
his miserable imbecility. But when wounded he visited New Orleans
and was treated there as a Hero and accounts of his reception were circulated throughout Texas and a complete reaction set in, and Sam Houston . . . never worthy to be called a brave man or a wise man became the
hero of San Jacinto and the Second President of the Republic.[1]

[1] Burnet to Mary Austin Holley, April 25, 1844, in *Calendar of H. R. Wagner*

THE REPUBLIC OF TEXAS in 1836 presented a vastly different sight from Texas prior to the Revolution. The increased immigration resulting from the struggle for independence led to a decided growth in the population of the young nation. When Houston came to the Presidency for the first time there were an estimated 30,000 Americans and 22,000 Mexicans, Indians, and Negroes residing in the Republic. The American settlers were located primarily at Houston, Galveston, and Nacogdoches. The city of Austin was unheard of as yet, and San Antonio was predominantly a Mexican center of some 2,000 people. There were also important Mexican settlements at Nacogdoches, La Bahía, and Victoria.[2]

The major Indian tribes in the Republic were the Cherokees, Comanches, and Wacos; the first two tribes posed a problem of frontier defense, but the Wacos were generally peaceable. The Lipan Apaches, Chickasaws, Delawares, and Caddoes also roamed the Texas plains but were never a significant force either for good or evil during the period of the Republic. The great majority of Negroes were slaves who had been brought by their masters from the Southern states. There were a small number of free Negroes in the Republic, but the usual restrictions were in operation against them.[3]

In the period just after the Revolution, immigration to Texas steadily increased. At this time the Republic was peopled by a great migration from the Mississippi Valley area south of the Ohio River. Organized companies from New York and Ohio had been enlisted in the Texas Army, and had come from almost every state in the Union.[4] The majority of the American settlers were people of the nonslaveholding, small-farmer class. Though regular church attendance was not a distinguishing feature of many of the settlers, the teachings of the Baptist and other Protestant faiths were held in great reverence. The society of the early Republic was predomi-

---

Manuscripts at Yale University, quoted in Richard R. Stenberg, "The Texas Schemes of Jackson and Houston," *Southwestern Political and Social Science Quarterly,* XV (1934), 250.

[2] Yoakum, *History of Texas,* II, 197–198.

[3] Harold Schoen, "The Free Negro in the Republic of Texas," *Southwestern Historical Quarterly,* XLI (1937), 83; Andrew F. Muir, "The Free Negro in Harris County, Texas," *Southwestern Historical Quarterly,* XLIV (1943), 224–25.

[4] Eugene C. Barker, "The United States and Mexico, 1835–1837," *Mississippi Valley Historical Review,* I (1914), 7–8.

nantly Jacksonian in philosophy.[5] Politics was permeated by a general opposition to corporate financial interests, to established banks, and to monopolies of any type and can better be understood as deriving from this Jacksonian background.

The government of this new nation was faced with two major problems: the ultimate disposal of Santa Anna and the question of recognition of Texas independence by the United States. As a condition to sparing his life at San Jacinto, Santa Anna had been compelled to order a general Mexican retreat. This was done, and the outlines of a temporary peace treaty were then drawn. Houston, General Rusk, in his official capacity as secretary of war, and Santa Anna agreed that in the final treaty to be ratified by both governments the independence of Texas would be *sine qua non*.[6] Upon Houston's departure for New Orleans for medical treatment, General Rusk was given the active field command. To replace Rusk in the cabinet, Mirabeau B. Lamar, who had distinguished himself by his bravery in leading a cavalry charge at San Jacinto, became secretary of war in the ad interim government.

After much thought, President Burnet decided to spare Santa Anna and to wring some concessions from the Mexican government in exchange for the safety of the dictator. Naturally this policy was opposed by the army, which looked upon Santa Anna as personally responsible for the Alamo and Goliad; but Burnet was resolved to carry his plan through in the face of popular opposition. Burnet's own words, "Santa Anna *dead* is no more than Tom, Dick, or Harry *dead*, but living he may avail Texas much,"[7] fully explain his attitude on the matter. In time the question of Santa Anna's disposal became a stalking horse for aspiring politicians, and a cabinet controversy resulted. It was known that the Secretary of the Navy, Robert Potter, was opposed to Burnet's plan, and Secretary of War Lamar disagreed so thoroughly that he felt compelled to issue a pamphlet explaining his position. In Lamar's opinion, Santa Anna's pledges of the use of his influence to secure Mexican recognition of Texas independence were "lighter than moonshine's watery

[5] Chauncey S. Boucher, "In Re That Aggressive Slaveocracy," *Mississippi Valley Historical Review*, VIII (1921), 15.

[6] Henry S. Foote, *Texas and the Texans*, II, 316–17.

[7] Burnet to Andrew Briscoe, May 21, 1836, Andrew Briscoe Papers.

beam." The Secretary of War felt that the defeat at San Jacinto would put an end to whatever power the Mexican leader enjoyed before the campaign. Finally, because of the butcheries at the Alamo and Goliad, Lamar regarded the tyrant as outside the pale of civilized warfare and thus subject to death regardless of his status as a prisoner of war.[8]

Disregarding the revolt within his own cabinet, Burnet on May 14 signed the two treaties of Velasco with Santa Anna. By the terms of the treaty which was published, Santa Anna pledged himself never again to take up arms against Texas and to use his influence to bring about a speedy end to the war. It was agreed that all hostilities should cease immediately and that the Mexican troops would continue to evacuate Texas. It was also stipulated that all property should be respected, that captured property should be restored, and that all prisoners held by the Mexicans should be exchanged on an equal basis for Mexican soldiers captured by the Texans. The second treaty signed at Velasco was secret in nature. It provided that upon his return to Mexico Santa Anna was to exert all his influence to obtain a recognition of Texas independence and the establishment of the boundary at the Rio Grande.[9]

In accordance with the terms of the treaties, Santa Anna was to be provided with passage back to Mexico. On June 1, he was placed aboard the Texas schooner-of-war *Invincible*, but his departure was delayed until final instructions were prepared for the commissioners who were to accompany him. At this point General Thomas J. Green arrived at Velasco with a number of volunteers from North Carolina and prevented the sailing of the *Invincible*. Santa Anna was taken off the ship over the protests of Burnet and his cabinet and placed under guard.[10] Green had just arrived in Texas, and his conduct did nothing to improve relations between the old settlers and the newcomers. The incident only further illustrated the weakness of the ad interim government.

In addition, the presence of Green and others like him did not ease Rusk's burden as commander in the field, for volunteer dele-

---

[8] Mirabeau B. Lamar, *Lamar's Prosecution of Santa Anna*, ed. Sinclair Moreland, 4.

[9] Wooten, *A Complete History of Texas*, 235.

[10] William C. Binkley, "The Activities of the Texan Revolutionary Army after San Jacinto," *Journal of Southern History*, VI (1940), 338.

gations led by such men as Memucan Hunt and Felix Huston, from Mississippi, and James Pinckney Henderson, from South Carolina, continued to arrive, displaying a decided unwillingness to obey orders. It was obvious that both the regular army and the volunteers strongly condemned the Burnet policy toward Santa Anna, and in an evident attempt to conciliate the army Rusk was deposed and Lamar appointed in his stead. This move completely backfired when Green, Felix Huston, and others, playing on the prevailing sentiment against the ad interim government, persuaded the army to refuse to accept Lamar. Deeply chagrined, and blaming Rusk for what happened, Lamar informed Burnet that "the whole has been produced by his desire of promotion. . . . I had an open rupture with Genl. Rusk."[11] There was some truth to Lamar's blaming Rusk, for Rusk had made no attempt to quiet the troublesome elements in the army and was only too willing to assume command again when the malcontents refused to accept Lamar.[12] The entire affair had ultimate political importance because it led to a breach between Rusk and Lamar and also strengthened the political association of Burnet and Lamar, an alliance which held firm through most of the Republic period.

The ad interim government's failure in domestic affairs was not redeemed by any significant accomplishments in relations with the United States. It will be remembered that the consultation of 1835 had sent Archer, Austin, and Wharton to the United States, where they had been at the time of San Jacinto. Prior to the decisive battle the commissioners were mainly concerned with private and official aid to the volunteer armies; after the battle they were concerned with official recognition of independence. The three men did noble work in securing three loans, which totaled nearly $75,000, as well as private donations of a smaller amount. They were successful in recruiting volunteers for Texas and in whipping up general enthusiasm which manifested itself in petitions and memorials to the United States government requesting the recognition of independ-

---

[11] Lamar to Burnet, July 17, 1836, Charles A. Gulick, Jr., and others (eds.), *The Papers of Mirabeau Buonaparte Lamar*, I, 417–18.

[12] Binkley, "The Activities of the Texan Revolutionary Army after San Jacinto," *Journal of Southern History*, VI, 340.

ence.[13] In the matter of official recognition, however, the commissioners were less successful. Wharton did secure an interview with Jackson and recorded the experience in a letter to Austin:[14]

> By special invitation I took a family dinner with the President on the day before yesterday and with the Vice President on yesterday. I was 4 or 5 hours alone with the President and the sole subject of conversation was *Texas*. He asked Where are your letters from your Government? Where Houston's official account of the Victory? Where your Presidents proclamation calling upon the inhabitants to return to their homes and attend to their crops? Where an official annunciation of the fact that the inhabitants are at their homes and in possession of the Most of Texas? Where the publication opening your ports and fixing your Tariff and Tonnage? Sir says he your President should send an express once a week to New Orleans to his agent and have published by authority the true situation of your country and every thing that goes to shew you are a *de facto government*.

Actually the Burnet government had failed to do any of the things suggested by Jackson. Houston had delayed in forwarding an official account of the victory at San Jacinto, and communication between Burnet and the Texas commissioners in the United States was extremely poor. The administration, hoping to expedite recognition, only made the situation worse by sending George Hamilton and Robert Childress as agents to the United States soon after San Jacinto. Thus two sets of commissioners moved about from Washington to New York, not communicating with each other and generally hurting the common cause.[15]

On May 26, only two months after the appointment of Childress and Hamilton, the government recalled all previous commissioners and sent Peter W. Grayson and James Collinsworth to Washington.

[13] Ethel Zively Rather, "Recognition of the Republic of Texas by the United States," *Quarterly of the Texas State Historical Association*, XIII (1910), 190–91.

[14] William H. Wharton to Austin, June 2, 1836, *Austin Papers*, III, 363–64.

[15] Rather, "Recognition of the Republic of Texas by the United States," *Quarterly of the Texas State Historical Association*, XIII, 196. Hamilton was sent to the United States in the hope that he might later secure a loan. Childress was selected because he had been chairman of the committee that had drafted the declaration of independence (and therefore had first-hand knowledge of that event) and because he had enjoyed a personal acquaintance with President Jackson.

Both men were originally from Tennessee, and it was hoped that their previous personal association with Jackson would prove valuable. The new agents were instructed to solicit the intervention of the United States to stop the war upon the basis of a recognition of Texas independence by Mexico, the acknowledgment of the independence of Texas by the United States, and the annexation of Texas by the United States.[16] Just before his departure, Collinsworth wrote to Rusk: "The objects of my mission I hope will prove successful & that is a consummation most devoutly to be wished for. We are in a deplorable condition Pecuniary morally & intellectually. Yet I hope all will be well."[17] However, Collinsworth's optimistic outlook soon underwent trial, for upon his arrival in Washington Congress had already adjourned and Jackson was on the point of leaving for "The Hermitage." In an informal interview the President gave the two commissioners to understand that a secret agent had been sent to Texas and that nothing could be done until his return.

Thus from November, 1835, until the inauguration of Sam Houston as first president of the Republic, three sets of agents represented the embryo nation at Washington. The total result of their efforts came when Henry Clay introduced a Senate resolution calling for recognition. The resolution provided that recognition would result when Texas had established a civil government and when the new state enjoyed all the attributes of sovereignty. Yet for all practical purposes the resolution left the matter untouched, and to improve the situation the Senate quickly passed another resolution, requesting the President to communicate to the Senate any pertinent information concerning Texas. By this provision, Jackson was enabled to appoint a secret agent to observe political conditions in Texas. Jackson's choice, Henry R. Morfit, was made kown to the Senate, and the appointment was confirmed by resolution. The House then gave its sanction to the plan by a resolution adopted July 4, the day that Congress adjourned.[18]

When Congress adjourned for the summer, it had already de-

---

[16] *Ibid.*, 201.

[17] Collinsworth to Rusk, May 31, 1836, Thomas Jefferson Rusk Papers.

[18] Rather, "Recognition of the Republic of Texas by the United States," *Quarterly of the Texas State Historical Association*, XIII, 220.

clared itself in favor of recognition whenever circumstances might justify it. Feeling that little could be accomplished in Washington with both Jackson and the members of Congress absent, Collinsworth determined to set out for Nashville and meet Jackson there. Grayson remained in Washington for some two months and then departed for Louisville. The agents felt confident of ultimate recognition because of Jackson's known penchant for Texas, but they did not reckon with his scrupulous desire to maintain the neutrality of the United States, or his wish not to embarrass his successor in office.[19] Grayson displayed a lack of political astuteness when he wrote to William H. Jack, then the secretary of state in the ad interim government: "As I have said before, there is in my mind no doubt that the present Administration, *can carry the measure of* Annexation. Genl. Jackson feels the utmost solicitude for it and we know how much that will count."[20] But Jackson would not trammel his hand-picked successor, Martin Van Buren, and refused to be rushed into precipitate action.

Meanwhile, political attention in the Republic was being focused on the first presidential election. The opportunity to choose governmental officials represented the hard-earned fruits of independence from Mexico, and the citizens of the Republic took an active interest in the developing campaign. The Constitution drawn up at Washington-on-the-Brazos in March, 1836, had stipulated that the first election should be held in September of the same year. It was this contest that engrossed the populace.

At the time of the March convention the Austin and Wharton factions were still the only "parties" in Texas, and they were not political parties as the term is understood today. Neither had an organization worthy of the name, nor was there a basic division of principles, for all were united on the necessity for independence. It had long been known in Texas that Wharton and Austin were personally at odds as a result of differences dating back to the convention of 1833, and the consultation, by sending both men to the United States, hoped to give the appearance of a united front in

[19] Eugene C. Barker, "President Jackson and the Texas Revolution," *American Historical Review*, XII (1907), 809.

[20] Peter W. Grayson to William H. Jack, August 11, 1836, *Diplomatic Correspondence*, II, 122.

Texas. However, upon his departure for the United States, Austin had felt a complete enmity for Wharton. Writing to Richard R. Royal, Austin complained: "I am associated in a mission to the United States with a man that I cannot act with—a man whose conduct proves he is destitute of political honesty, and whose attention is much more devoted to injure me than to serve the country. I mean Wharton."[21] Nevertheless, as the two men worked together in a common cause and came to respect each other's talents, a gradual reconciliation was effected. On January 21, 1836, Austin wrote to a friend: "There has been the most perfect harmony in the commission—we all agree as to the main principles, and especially as to independence. . . . John Wharton assures me that on his part, there will be no more restlessness and his brother says the same."[22] The long trip to Washington and the constant communication with each other continued to play on Austin's sentiments. A letter to James Perry reveals the complete change in his feelings:[23]

The most perfect harmony exists between all the commissioners—Archer is truly a noble fellow. I have never known him intimately before, and I am very much attached to him—Wharton and myself are on the best of terms and I have no doubt will always continue to be in the future—it is not my fault that we ever were otherwise—heretofore we have not known each other personally as we might and ought to have.

As events transpired, this change of heart on the part of both Austin and Wharton had far-reaching consequences for Texas politics.

The appointment of Grayson and Collinsworth had forced the return of the commissioners from the United States. Austin left Washington ahead of Archer and Wharton on May 24 and reached Texas in the latter part of June. He busied himself in making reports to Burnet suggesting that Santa Anna be sent to Washington to impress upon Jackson the urgent need for mediation. At the same time, Austin never lost sight of the approaching presidential election. A short while after his return he received a letter from Wharton, who wrote:[24]

[21] Austin to Richard R. Royal, December 25, 1835, *Austin Papers,* III, 293.
[22] Austin to Thomas F. McKinney, January 21, 1836, *ibid.,* 309.
[23] Austin to James F. Perry, March 4, 1836, *ibid.,* 318.
[24] Wharton to Austin, May 28, 1836, *ibid.,* 360.

It is understood at Nashville that Genl Houston is opposed to the annexation of Texas to the United States. If this be so it is truly and deeply to be deplored. Like all triumphant conquerors he will be omnipotent for a time at least. I plainly see before me the turmoil and confusion and injustice and the demagogueism which must ensue in *Texas* after the war is over before we can establish an orderly and harmonious independent government.

This letter did not amount to a personal disavowal of Houston, for in conclusion, and referring to Houston, Wharton noted that "we have always been and are the best of friends."[25] However, Wharton may have preferred Austin as a candidate, or he may have honestly believed that Houston did not intend to run.

It was well known that Wharton did not care to make the race; therefore, Austin could assume that if he himself agreed to be a candidate he would have the backing of his former associate. All doubts were set aside when Archer and Wharton returned to Texas. The three former commissioners met at Velasco on July 20 to prepare a joint report of their mission to the United States. The work completed, the talk soon turned to politics. Wharton and Archer, as well as Bailey Hardeman, S. Rhoads Fisher, and other prominent citizens of Texas, impressed upon Austin the necessity for his candidacy. Convinced of the wisdom of allowing his name to be used, Austin accepted the honor.[26] In a communication to General Rusk, Austin explained his decision: "I have consented to this for only one reason, which is that I believe I can be of material service in procuring the annexation of Texas to the U.S. should the people here wish it, as I have no doubt they do."[27]

On July 23 Burnet issued the national election proclamation. The electorate in Texas would choose national and county officials, ratify the Constitution, and decide on the wisdom of annexation to the United States. The election was then fixed for the first Monday in September. Soon after the proclamation appeared, the name of Henry Smith was put forward as a candidate. It would seem that the friends of the former Governor submitted his name in an attempt to vindicate his actions under the provisional government.

[25] *Ibid.*, 361.
[26] Memorandum by Austin, July 20, 1836, *ibid.*, 399.
[27] Austin to Rusk, August 9, 1836, *ibid.*, 412.

Branch T. Archer also permitted his name to be used as a candidate, but he was never a significant force in the election. There was an attempt to place Rusk's name in nomination, but he would not allow it.[28] The political situation in July, therefore, found Austin as the only major candidate. The obvious choice, Sam Houston, expressed a disposition not to run.

The tempo of the approaching election stepped up quickly in the month of August. Burnet, writing to Collinsworth and Grayson in the United States, reported: "The electioneering campaign has opened with Some activity and will probably be conducted with a good deal of Spirit. Austin is out for the Presidency. Archer is talked of by a few. No other candidate has yet passed the curtain."[29] But there was even more significant information relayed by General Rusk from the army: "We have had our difficulties in the Army. Many political Jugglers have tried their Hands here. . . . Smith and Austin are the only Candidates out as yet for President. Smith outruns Austin here."[30] In writing of "political jugglers" Rusk made reference to the troublesome element in the army led by Thomas J. Green and Felix Huston. Both men were once again dangling the Matamoros prize before the rank and file of the army. Rusk's letter to Houston informing him of the existing state of affairs in the army may have influenced Houston's decision to become a candidate. However, the Hero of San Jacinto continued to hold off, and well into the middle of August the contest centered about Austin and Henry Smith.

There was not much that could be said concerning Smith's record in Texas politics other than his dispute with the council. This breach had proved disastrous to Texas in the campaigns of 1836, and Smith was blamed by many for the defeats prior to San Jacinto. Coupled with this, it was well known that he had been the choice of the Wharton group in 1835 and that they had now disavowed him in favor of Austin. The case of Austin was a different matter. The issue of the Monclova speculations was brought forward once again, and Austin was also charged with undue regard for Santa

[28] John D. McLeod to Rusk, July 20, 1836, Rusk Papers.
[29] Burnet to Collinsworth and Grayson, August 10, 1836, *Diplomatic Correspondence*, II, 119.
[30] Rusk to Houston, August 15, 1836, Rusk Papers.

Anna's salvation. The nominee took notice of the existing situation in a letter to Rusk:[31]

> . . . there no doubt are many erronious reports in circulation—I have heard two—One that I am interested in the land speculations of Williams and others when they were at Monclova—This is utterly false—I have never been, am not, and never will be interested in those speculations. . . .
>
> The other report is that I have been the means of saving General Santa Anna. That man was saved by Gen. Sam Houston, as you know better than I do. . . . He was also saved by the Cabinet of Texas subsequently, and treaties made with him. I disapprove of all these measures —The first I think was almost ruinous to Texas for it saved the balance of the Mexican Army, and the other I think was wrong in principle, and more so in the *mode* or *manner* of using Santa Anna.

The explanation concerning Santa Anna proved satisfactory to a large number of voters, but the Monclova incident could not be downed.

Since the victory at San Jacinto, the most popular figure in Texas had been Sam Houston. This colorful personality, whose career dominates Texas history through the Civil War, had lived a full life prior to the Texas Revolution. Born in Virginia in 1793, Houston grew to manhood in the frontier state of Tennessee. As a young man he lived for four years with the Cherokee Indians, who adopted him and named him "the Raven." Tiring of Indian life, he joined the military and served with honor under Jackson in the Creek War.[32] As a protégé of Jackson he entered Tennessee politics and was sent to the national House of Representatives in 1823 and again in 1825. In 1827, with the full support of Jackson, he was elected governor of Tennessee by a majority of over 12,000 votes. In 1829 Houston was married to Eliza H. Allen, a daughter of John Allen, a prominent citizen of Gallatin, Tennessee, but a few months later a separation took place. This melancholy event proved to be the turning point of Houston's life. He immediately resigned as governor, and left by steamer for Little Rock, Arkansas.

In time Houston again took up residence with the Cherokees and

---

[31] Austin to Rusk, August 9, 1836, *Austin Papers*, III, 412–13.
[32] Alexander Hynds, "General Sam Houston," *Century Magazine*, XXVIII (1884), 494.

lived with them for about three years. It is a commentary upon his habits at this time that the Indians renamed him "Big Drunk." The reasons for the separation from his wife have never been definitely established. The majority of Houston's biographers accept the story of Houston's discovery that his wife did not truly love him, that her father had forced her into the union, and that her affections had been pledged to another.[33] Giving up his exile among the Indians, Houston appeared in Texas in 1832 as a secret agent of Jackson's empowered to interview a delegation of Comanches in the hope of inducing them to stop their raids on other Indian tribes across the American border. In 1833 he turned up as a member of the convention at San Felipe and decided to remain in Texas. At the convention of 1835 he was elected major general of the regular Texas Army, and San Jacinto ultimately endeared him to the general populace.[34]

Such a compelling figure was of particular importance in Texas, for the political emphasis was on personalities rather than principles. Looking back on the political scene in 1836, a member of the Texas Legislature wrote in 1843: "We here in Texas had nothing to do with parties in the United States. We were Sam Houston or anti-Sam Houston; Eastern Texas was largely for and Western Texas against him."[35] Though the Houston and anti-Houston division became even more pronounced after the General's first term in office, many who voted in 1836 supported Houston because of his military prowess or else voted against him because of the tales that were being circulated concerning his alleged cowardice in the field. Houston's private life prior to his decision to remain in Texas was also a matter of record. In addition to his known intemperance, Houston's friendly association with the Indians was also a topic of public discussion.

The impressions that Houston registered upon some of his contemporaries remain very interesting. Francis R. Lubbock, a Hous-

[33] James, *The Raven*, 139; Henry Bruce, *Life of General Houston, 1793–1863*, 48. See J. Frank Dobie, *The Flavor of Texas*, 1, for a unique guess why Houston and his wife were separated.

[34] Dixon and Kemp, *The Heroes of San Jacinto*, 38.

[35] Lucy A. Erath, "Memoirs of George Bernard Erath," *Southwestern Historical Quarterly*, XXVII (1923), 140.

ton man and later governor of Texas in his own right, observed:[36]

No person ever met Sam Houston in the early days of the Republic without being impressed with his greatness. He was then about forty-two years of age, just the prime of life. Standing largely over six feet in height, with a massive, well formed hand, a most remarkable foot, measuring more around the instep than in length, a large head, a piercing gray eye, a mouth and nose indicating character of fine proportions, and as straight as a majestic Indian. He was a most perfect specimen of physical manhood.

Another citizen of the Republic, Dr. John Washington Lockhart, observed:[37]

After serving in the civil war and seeing many of the leading military men on both sides, he was, in my judgment, vastly the superior of them all. General R. E. Lee came nearer him in soldierly bearing than any man I ever saw. He was a natural born ruler, both in the field and forum.

The first public nomination of Houston came at a meeting of the voters in San Augustine County, held in the Mansion House in the town of San Augustine on August 15. By the motion of Colonel Philip A. Sublett, a former member of the Wharton party who did not support Austin, it was unanimously resolved that Houston be nominated for the Presidency, and General Thomas J. Rusk for the Vice-Presidency. The chairman was instructed to send copies of the resolutions to Nacogdoches, Sabine, Shelby, Jasper, and Liberty. Similar meetings were held throughout eastern Texas, and on August 20, at the meeting of the citizens of Columbia, Houston was again nominated. The resolution drafted at Columbia pointed to the General's record as commander of the Texas armies, to the esteem with which he was regarded by Jackson and the cabinet at Washington and the advantage this would be to Texas in the negotiations for annexation, and also to Houston's previous executive experience as governor of Tennessee. Thomas F. McKinney, the business partner and personal friend of Samuel Williams, was

[36] Francis R. Lubbock, *Six Decades in Texas; or, Memoirs of Francis Richard Lubbock, Governor of Texas in War Time, 1861–63: A Personal Experience in Business, War, and Politics*, ed. C. W. Raines, 73.

[37] Jonnie Lockhart Wallis and Laurance L. Hill, *Sixty Years on the Brazos: The Life and Letters of Dr. John Washington Lockhart, 1824–1900*, 99.

the guiding force responsible for the Columbia meeting.[38] Houston's acceptance came but eleven days prior to the date of the election. In a letter addressed to a "gentleman in the army" he noted: "You will learn that I have yielded to the wishes of my friends in allowing my name to be run for President. The crisis requires it or I would not have yielded. Duty, I hope will not always require this sacrifice of repose and quiet."[39] The election slate was now complete.

Why Houston finally consented to run has never been fully explained. It is established that he had written to Rusk about the matter and that Rusk had assured him of his support.[40] At a later date, after the passions of the election had subsided, Houston wrote to Guy M. Bryan that he had allowed his name to be used only because of the irreconcilable differences between the Wharton and Austin parties, but in referring to Smith as the standard-bearer of the Wharton group Houston was mistaken.[41] He must have known that Wharton was championing Austin and that Smith was a candidate on his own. Indeed, Smith, whose strength lay with the army, withdrew from the race upon the announcement of Houston's candidacy, for it was evident that the majority of the army would now go for the General. A letter from Henry Austin to his sister throws some light on the situation and does lend credence to Houston's acknowledged purpose of running: "The government was formed on the spirit of compromise to save the country and those who voted for Houston say they did it for fear Henry Smith would beat Stephen and all be lost, while Houston with the votes of the army would be a sure candidate."[42] Archer allowed his name to remain in nomination, but he was at no time seriously considered the possible victor.

It was the practice at this time for political aspirants to place their name in nomination by advertisement in the local newspaper. A correspondent would then write the paper asking the candidate

---

[38] Houston *Telegraph and Texas Register*, August 23, 1836.

[39] Houston to "a gentleman in the army," n.d., *ibid.*, August 30, 1836.

[40] Rusk to Houston, August 9, 1836, quoted in James, *The Raven*, 265–66.

[41] Houston to Guy M. Bryan, November 15, 1852, *Houston Writings*, V, 367–68.

[42] Henry Austin to Mary Austin Holley, December 9, 1836, quoted in Nina Covington, "The Presidential Campaigns of the Republic of Texas of 1836 and 1838" (M.A. thesis, University of Texas, 1929), 40.

to state his convictions on certain basic matters. William H. Jack and Moseley Baker, both of whom were running for Congress, received two of these communications, which contain representative examples of the political issues involved in the campaign of 1836. The ultimate disposition of Santa Anna and the establishment of a land system were perhaps of the greatest importance.[43] Many were concerned that justice be granted to the volunteers in the disposition of land grants, but that favoritism not be shown them at the expense of the old settlers. There seemed to be unanimous agreement on the proposal to seek annexation of the new Republic to the United States and to give the first elected Congress the powers to amend the Constitution.[44] Finally, there were some who felt that the election of Houston would guarantee internal stability and thus favorable consideration on the part of the United States. At the same time, however, a letter addressed to Austin stating that his election would "hasten the proclamation of the President, acknowledging your Independence" was broadcast and received fairly wide circulation.[45]

The campaign was carried on in spirited fashion, though there were none of the organization facilities familiar to political campaigns today. Charges were hurled against Austin that he had fled Texas in its moment of greatest danger and that he had done nothing in the United States but "eat fine dinners and drink wine."[46] Such accusations were much less damaging than the old bogey of the Monclova speculations, and his indirect connection with these frauds hurt Austin in the extreme. Gail Borden, an old friend and political ally, sadly informed Austin that "from the sign of the times you can not be elected, unless you or some friend comes out in a circular to the people. The lamented land speculation is operating against you. . . . Some of your *old* devoted friends say, they cannot support you unless they are convinced that you had no hand in the big land purchase."[47] Though Austin wrote to Borden in answer to these charges, the general impression remained that Williams had acted at Monclova with Austin's approval. The persistence of this

[43] Houston *Telegraph and Texas Register*, August 9, 1836.
[44] Covington, "Presidential Campaigns of the Republic of Texas," 25–26.
[45] Joseph Ramage to Austin, July 27, 1836, *Austin Papers*, III, 405.
[46] Barker, *Life of Austin*, 511.
[47] Gail Borden to Austin, August 15, 1836, *Austin Papers*, III, 417.

idea was the chief cause of Austin's defeat. Austin himself must have felt that his chances were very slim, for on September 2 he wrote to James Perry: "Houston will, I am told, get all the east, and Red river now—Many of the old settlers who are too blind to see or understand their interest will go for him, and the army I believe will go for him, at least a majority of them."[48] Actually, the final result was never much in doubt, and in the official election returns Houston polled 5,119 votes to 743 for Smith and 587 for Austin.[49] Smith had formally withdrawn, yet he finished ahead of Austin. Archer received only a few scattered votes.

David Burnet, outgoing president of the ad interim government, explained the election results in concise fashion in a letter to Memucan Hunt: "Genl. Houston is beyond all question the President elect, he has beat my worthy friend, Austin, the pioneer of pioneers in Texas, as much as the splendor of military fame (no matter how acquired) excels the mild luster of meditative and intellectual worth."[50] Allowing for Burnet's known hatred of Houston, the military record of the General and his effective expulsion of the enemy from Texas were the chief factors in his favor. In addition, the recent arrivals in Texas, who represented an overwhelming majority at the polls, had no association with Austin and thus felt no gratitude for his pioneering efforts. Many of the voters also felt that Sam Houston, as President of the Republic, would continue to prosecute the war and secure an honorable peace on the basis of recognition by Mexico. The impression that Austin would adopt a temporizing policy if elected, and thus duplicate the failures of the ad interim government, also contributed to the downfall of the old *empresario*. Because Houston's frontier and Indian policies were not evident before the election, the eastern-western split which would later characterize the politics of the Republic was not an important factor at this point. In 1836 General Houston came as close to being a national hero in Texas as it was ever his lot to be.

James Morgan, an early settler in Texas, carried on a fairly regular correspondence with Samuel Swartwout, prince of thieves in

[48] Austin to James F. Perry, September 2, 1836, *ibid.*, 428.
[49] Election Returns, Journal of the Senate, First Congress of the Republic, First Session (1836), 10.
[50] Burnet to Memucan Hunt, September 16, 1836, Executive Department Journals, Ad Interim Government.

the Jackson era. In his own graphic fashion Morgan described the recent political race:[51]

The first general election of Texas is now all over and a majority of the candidates have the sad news by now. Austin knew long ago that he would be turned down by the people he had tried so hard to serve. Republics are proverbialy ungrateful and we feel certain that Austin anticipated just about the kind of political deal that was handed to him. The Result of the election was as follows: Sam Houston, who had been in Texas about three years, received 5119 votes; Henry Smith, who had made such a tragic and dismal failure of his position as provisional governor, and in a sense, had the blood of both Fannin and Travis on his hands polled a total of 743 votes, while Stephen F. Austin, who was even now dying for the Texas he loved so well and had served so long and made every sacrifice for, mustered the grand total of only 587 votes, and they were mostly the support of his Original 300 who remained loyal to him to the end.

The successful candidate for the vice-presidency was Mirabeau B. Lamar. The former Georgian had won his position virtually unopposed; the only other official nominee for the office, Alexander Horton, ran well behind the victor. Lamar's election in the face of the army's refusal to accept him as their leader after San Jacinto is explained by the facts that Thomas J. Green was busy running for Congress and that Felix Huston had been placated with a command in the army. It will be remembered that these two had led the malcontents against Lamar, and their decision not to actively oppose his candidacy was chiefly responsible for Lamar's election.

In the choice of his cabinet Houston displayed a decided wish to unite all former factions. He gave the portfolio of state to Austin, and that of the treasury to Henry Smith.[52] As his secretary of war the President chose General Thomas J. Rusk, thus keeping that popular personage within the cabinet and in support of Houston's policies. James Pinckney Henderson was appointed attorney general, and S. Rhoads Fisher, a defender of Austin at election time, was named to serve as secretary of the navy. To complete the ad-

[51] James Morgan to Samuel Swartwout, September 5, 1836, James Morgan Papers.

[52] Ernest W. Winkler (ed.), *Secret Journals of the Senate, Republic of Texas, 1836–1845*, 15.

ministration, Robert Barr was given the office of postmaster general.[53] Congress then elected James Collinsworth, former commissioner to the United States, as chief justice of the Supreme Court. Shelby Corzine, Benjamin C. Franklin, Robert McAlpin Williamson, and James W. Robinson were elected judges of the four judicial districts of the Republic, and also served in a dual capacity as associate justices of the Supreme Court. In time, district attorneys and county judges were also elected by Congress to complete the judicial branch of the Texas government.[54] The Legislature organized with Ira Ingram, representing Matagorda, as Speaker of the House, and Vice-President Lamar presiding over the Senate. In the House, Branch T. Archer, Thomas J. Green, John Wharton, and Moseley Baker were avowedly anti-Houston; in the Senate, opposition centered around Alexander Somervell and Stephen H. Everitt.[55]

In his inaugural address the "Hero of San Jacinto" outlined some of the basic problems facing his administration. He first referred to the problem of frontier defense and the wisdom of treating with the various Indian tribes on a fair and equitable basis. Houston maintained that the army should be kept in a state of preparedness and that the war against Mexico should be energetically waged until an honorable peace could be realized. The deplorable financial condition of the country was admitted, and a plea was made to Congress for judicious legislation as a remedy. The President expressed his pleasure that the people had shown their overwhelming desire for annexation and stated his belief that the United States would act quickly upon the matter. In conclusion, reference was made to Santa Anna, still in the custody of the Texans, and the ultimate advantages that might accrue from his release.[56]

Texas, in the winter of 1836, presented a depressing situation. The national treasury was empty, the land devastated, and the frontier harassed by Indians. A bedraggled army on the lookout for excitement constituted a danger to law and order, and there was a very clear possibility that the Mexican armies might at any time

[53] Joseph G. de Roulhac Hamilton, "James Pinckney Henderson," in Malone (ed.), *Dictionary of American Biography*, VIII, 526-27.
[54] Hogan, *The Texas Republic*, 253.
[55] Wooten, *A Complete History of Texas*, 246.
[56] *Houston Writings*, I, 449–52.

march against Texas. Times were hard, prices high, and the future anything but auspicious. A resident expressed his sentiments:[57]

The country has been completely ravaged by the armies. Houses have been robbed of their contents, provisions taken from them, the beeves have been driven out of the country, and the game frightened off. We have suffered during the summer exceedingly; some of us have tried to raise a late crop of corn by planting in June, but this experiment has not succeeded well. What we are to do I know not, but I trust some way will be provided for us.

Another Texan, in a letter to a relative in the North, gave his account of the troublesome times:[58]

Provision is very scarce and hard to be got. Flour is now selling at Lynch's at $18 pr BBl, and I am told it is 20 on the Brazos. Sugar 20 cts per lb. and no money to be had   Corn very scarce $1.50 pr Bushel on the Brazos   there is none to be had in our neighborhood. . . . I am told that there is 25000 Mexicans on their march and will be here early in the Spring. . . . I am fearful unless peace is made shortly or a sufficient force comes from the U.S. that we shall not be able to contend with so large a force.

Against this setting, Congress began its deliberations at Columbia and first attempted to locate a permanent seat of government. The ad interim government had concluded its functions at Velasco. Columbia served as a temporary location for the convening of the Legislature, but it was felt that a permanent capital should be established. House and Senate committees were appointed to draft recommendations, but the committees failed to agree, the House favoring Nacogdoches and the Senate the site at San Jacinto.[59] On November 14 an act was passed to temporarily locate the seat of government, and competition was then intensified between the contesting towns. In the Senate, petitions proposed the location of the capital at Matagorda, Fort Bend, Washington, Columbia, and

[57] William B. Dewees, *Letters From an Early Settler of Texas*, 208.
[58] A. M. Clopper to Nicholas Clopper, December 18, 1836, in "The Clopper Correspondence, 1834–1838," *Quarterly of the Texas State Historical Association*, XIII (1909), 137–38.
[59] Ernest W. Winkler, "The Seat of Government in Texas," *Quarterly of the Texas State Historical Association*, X (1906), 160–61.

Houston.[60] Since an agreement could not be reached, it was determined to locate the seat of government by joint vote of both houses of Congress. At this point the claims of the embryo city of Houston were put forth by John K. Allen, a member of the House, and his brother, Augustus C. Allen. The Allen brothers had conceived the idea of founding a town to take the place of the devastated Harrisburg and had purchased a tract of land on Buffalo Bayou five miles north of the former site of Harrisburg. When Congress assembled, the Allen brothers were able to offer sufficient inducements in the way of government buildings, private lodgings for congressmen, and a city "handsome and beautifully elevated, salubrious and well watered, and now in the very heart or center of population."[61] All of these benefits proved too hard to resist, and the legislators decided upon Houston as the seat of government. An act was passed on December 15, 1836, which provided that the capital should be located at Houston until the end of the legislative session of 1840.

Meanwhile, the question of the disposition of Santa Anna continued to vex the Texas government. The army had kept the illustrious Mexican prisoner at "Orozimbo," the plantation home of James A. E. Phelps. Before his inauguration, Houston paid the captive a visit and listened to Santa Anna's request that he be allowed to go to Washington to plead the Texas cause. As early as July 4, Santa Anna had written to Jackson asking him to use his influence to ensure that the provisions of the general agreement, signed just after the Battle of San Jacinto, be carried out in good faith by the Texas government.[62] Jackson replied some two months later that the Mexican minister in Washington had informed him that the government had officially repudiated Santa Anna and that consequently the United States could not deal with him. However, Jackson stated that his government would offer its good offices to the *de facto* Mexican government in an attempt to terminate the war.[63] On the same

[60] Journal of the Senate, First Congress, First Session, 62.

[61] Houston *Telegraph and Texas Register*, November 19, 1836, in Adele B. Looscan, *Harris County, 1822–1845*, 54.

[62] Santa Anna to Jackson, July 4, 1836. John Spencer Bassett (ed.), *Correspondence of Andrew Jackson*, V, 411.

[63] Jackson to Santa Anna, September 4, 1836, *ibid.*, 425–26.

day that he wrote to Santa Anna, Jackson unburdened himself to Houston on the matter:[64]

I have seen a report that Genl St. anna was to be brought before a military court, to be tried and shot. Nothing *now* could tarnish the character of Texas more than such an act at this late period. It was good policy as well as humanity that spared him—it has given you possession of Goliad and the alamo without blood, or loss of the strength of your army —his person is still of much consequence to you,. . . . He is the pride of the Mexican soldiers and the favorite of the Priesthood and whilst he is in your power the priests will not furnish the supplies necessary for another campaign, nor will the regular soldier voluntarily march when their reentering Texas may endanger or cost their favorite Genl. his life, therefore preserve his life and the character you have won.

Houston and his Secretary of State, Austin, well knew that no disposition of Santa Anna could be made without the sanction of Congress. As one of his first acts of office, Houston requested permission to send Santa Anna to Washington as a free man to treat with Jackson. Instead of granting this request, Congress enacted a resolution directing that Santa Anna be kept in Texas until the consent of the Senate could be secured for his removal.[65] The President immediately vetoed this resolution, and a general debate followed. In the Senate, Stephen H. Everitt, a leading opponent of the administration, argued a usurpation of the powers of the upper house, as well as the deplorable fact that the health of the prisoner might improve as a consequence of the trip to Washington.[66] Most of the opposition to Houston's plan came from the belief that the Mexican government would not respect any agreements made by the repudiated dictator. This sentiment was shared by many and was expressed in direct fashion by the most important newspaper of the period, the Houston *Telegraph and Texas Register:*[67]

Although Texas has not played the part of the robber with Santa Anna, yet the influence of what he and his government would call undue fear

[64] Jackson to Houston, September 4, 1836, *ibid.*, 425.
[65] Winkler (ed.), *Secret Journals of the Senate*, 21.
[66] Reverend Chester Newell, *History of the Revolution in Texas, Particularly of the War of 1835 & '36; together with the Latest Geographical, Topographical, and Statistical Accounts of the Country*, 125–26.
[67] Houston *Telegraph and Texas Register*, November 16, 1836.

was no less; and if his friends have not actually designated us by the honorable cognomen of bandits, they at least, have allowed us to rejoice in the titles of rebels, and would assuredly in their congress cause him, in the event of his release, to abjure any promises he might be induced to make, under present circumstances.

Congress continued in a rebellious mood. A resolution was secured, however, which made the President solely responsible for whatever treatment might be accorded Santa Anna. Houston quickly released the prisoner and also freed Colonel Juan Almonte, who had been captured at San Jacinto, to serve as Santa Anna's personal aide. Three Texans, Barnard E. Bee, George Hockley, and William H. Patton, were commissioned by the President to accompany the captive on the trip to Washington. On November 25 the party sailed for New Orleans, and they arrived in Washington on January 17, 1837.[68]

The hope of obtaining quick and favorable action on the annexation petition motivated Houston and Austin to favor Santa Anna's release. In writing to Henry Meigs, a friend of Texas and brother-in-law of John Forsyth, Jackson's secretary of state, Austin stated the case for Texas:[69]

Probably Mexico will not refuse to treat with the U.S. for a quit claim, or a final adjustment of limits, and thus give to Texas what she wants, without compromising her pride or prejudices by treating direct with Texas—or the same results may be attained by means of the mediation of the U.S. which Santa Anna has solicited from Genl. Jackson—Could not Santa Anna be used in this matter? and if he can, why not use him?

In much the same manner, Austin wrote to Senator Thomas H. Benton that "Santa Anna professes to be in favor of the independence of Texas, or its annexation to the U.S. etc. You are all wise and experienced politicians in Washington, and can judge better than

[68] The journey to Washington was made under very poor conditions in the winter season. Santa Anna, understandably enough, feared for his life and kept to his stateroom during the greater part of the trip. Upon reaching Washington, however, the prisoner was regarded as a social catch, and his attendance was requested at many dinner parties. It is said that Santa Anna borrowed a thousand dollars from Colonel Bee which he never returned. Callcott, *Santa Anna,* 148–49.
[69] Austin to Henry Meigs, November 7, 1836, *Austin Papers,* III, 449.

we can whether any important objects of general good to Mexico, the U.S. and Texas will result from his visit to your city."[70] After Santa Anna's departure, Houston named William H. Wharton minister to the United States, and the Senate unanimously confirmed the appointment.[71] Wharton had defended the President in his efforts to release Santa Anna, and Houston was not attempting to rid himself of a political foe by making this selection. Wharton was empowered to enter into negotiations for annexation, for it was felt that his previous experience in Washington and prior association with Jackson would be of value. This done, Houston wrote to Jackson informing him of Wharton's selection and confessing his own eagerness for annexation: "My great desire is that our country Texas shall be annexed to the United States and on a footing of Justice and reciprocity to the parties."[72] Wharton set out for Washington, arrived there before Santa Anna, and began working for recognition and eventual annexation.

In Texas, problems of finance were uppermost. The Republic was faced with a debt of about $1,250,000 expended in the recent war, and with no apparent means to satisfy it. The financial crisis was made even more difficult by the prevailing hard times in the United States. The Panic of 1837, and the resulting differences over monetary policy that occurred between Jackson and Nicholas Biddle, made the prospect of securing loans in the United States exceedingly dim. With only minimum chances for direct loans the government had the alternative of selling Texas lands in the United States. But again the times were unfavorable. The legislators were then compelled to find other means to raise money. A tariff, some types of direct taxes, and the disastrous expedient of paper-money issues were the answers ultimately devised.[73]

The land problem was inextricably related to the need for financial aid. The Republic of Texas embraced an area of some 237,906,-080 acres. When independence was declared, all of this vast area was unappropriated public domain except 26,280,080 acres which

[70] Austin to Thomas H. Benton, November 25, 1836, *ibid.*, 461.
[71] Winkler (ed.), *Secret Journals of the Senate*, 24.
[72] Houston to Jackson, November 20, 1836, *Houston Writings*, I, 488.
[73] Edmund T. Miller, *A Financial History of Texas*, 31–32. Also see Llerena Friend, *Sam Houston: The Great Designer*, 80.

had previously been granted to individuals by Spain and Mexico.[74] The provisional government and the ad interim government had granted extensive bounties in land to volunteers, and it was necessary that these lands be located, surveyed, and patented to the true owners. The Constitution of the Republic stipulated that all valid claims should be recognized and that a general land office should be established. Also, in accordance with the Constitution, all heads of families living in Texas at the time of the declaration of independence (March 2, 1836) were to receive a league and a labor of land, and all single men, a third of a league. The ad interim government extended this provision to cover settlers who arrived between March 2 and August 1, 1836, those colonists who served in the army and were honorably discharged, and the survivors of volunteers who died prior to December 14, 1837. These grants of land were called headrights of the first class.[75]

An act passed by Congress providing for the establishment of a general land office was vetoed by the President.[76] Houston felt that the unsettled conditions of the country would favor those holding false claims, and, though he favored the creation of a general land office, he wanted to defer the action to a later date. The legislators, however, did empower Houston to appoint agents at New Orleans to sell Texas land scrip at not less than fifty cents per acre. Some 700,000 acres were put up for sale, but the results were disappointing, and the government was forced to adopt other methods of raising money. An act was then passed which authorized the Executive to borrow five million dollars in foreign loans. Congress also united on establishing a land office over the President's veto.[77] Finally, the organization of a tariff system was provided for by an act of December 20, 1836. The law, which would become effective June 1, 1837, established ad valorem duties ranging from 1 per cent on breadstuffs to 50 per cent on silks, with an average of about 25 per cent on total imports. The act also placed a duty of twenty-five cents per

[74] Aldon S. Lang, "Financial Aspects of the Public Lands in Texas," *Southwestern Political and Social Science Quarterly*, XIII (1932), 57–58.

[75] Wooten, *A Complete History of Texas*, 253.

[76] Journal of the Senate, First Congress, First Session, 102.

[77] Miller, *A Financial History of Texas*, 55. Though the act establishing the general land office was passed on December 22, 1836, the actual opening of the office was postponed from time to time, and it was not officially opened until the spring of 1844.

62

ton on all foreign vessels of ten-ton burden or more arriving in Texas ports. Some direct taxes, such as a general property tax, a poll tax, and various license taxes, were included, but the emphasis was placed upon the tariff as the means of raising revenue.[78]

Houston, though he was adamant on the question of the land offices, allowed himself to be involved in speculation which in time had political repercussions. The Texas Railroad, Navigation and Banking Company was the creation of Austin, Branch T. Archer, James Collinsworth, Thomas F. McKinney, and James Pinckney Henderson. These men, every one of them high in the political councils of the nation, formed a corporation and secured a charter from the First Congress.[79] The charter stipulated that the company should have a capital of five million dollars, extensive banking privileges, and the right to connect the Rio Grande and Sabine rivers by canals and railroads. The capital stock should be divided into fifty thousand shares of one hundred dollars each. A bank would also be created with a specie capital of one million dollars. At the beginning of the bank's operations, the company should pay into the treasury of the Republic twenty-five thousand dollars in gold or silver, and thereafter 1½ per cent of the annual net profits of the canals and railroads and 1 per cent of the bank dividends. The charter granted the right of eminent domain and stated that the company might occupy a one-mile-wide strip through public lands. Also, the charter asserted that the President of the Republic should annually appoint a commissioner to examine the company and report upon the bonus due the government. The first bonus had to be paid within eighteen months from the passage of the act or the charter would be forfeited.[80] Houston signed the bill incorporating the company on December 16, and Congress adjourned soon thereafter.

In the interim between the adjournment of the First Congress and the meeting of the next in May, 1837, the fate of the company's charter became a vital political issue. The Jacksonian tradition of hostility to established banks and the fact that the company was the

[78] Robert E. L. Crane, Jr., "The History of the Revenue Service and the Commerce of the Republic of Texas" (Ph.D. dissertation, University of Texas, 1950), 12.
[79] *Austin Papers*, III, 472–73. The articles of incorporation are included in the Austin papers.
[80] Andrew F. Muir, "Railroad Enterprise in Texas, 1836–1841," *Southwestern Historical Quarterly*, XLVII (1944), 341.

POLITICAL HISTORY OF THE TEXAS REPUBLIC

project of leading politicians combined to cause strong distrust of the scheme. Thomas J. Green, a friend of the company in the House of Representatives, in a letter to Archer outlined the advantages that would result from the terms of incorporation:[81]

The privilege of discounting thirty millions of paper at ten per cent. per annum upon its ten millions capital stock; its *unrestricted* privileges to deal in bills of exchange; its *unrestricted* authority over the establishment of tolls, fees and charges of the works; the privilege of taking at the minimum government price, all the lands within half a mile of such works; its full and ample power to buy and sell all species of such property; . . . the right that foreign stockholders have to hold real estate in Texas not otherwise allowed to them, together with its *ninety-eight* years duration of charter are privileges . . . *beyond arithmetical calculation.*

This frank self-congratulation proved to be a bombshell, for the managers of the company foolishly allowed this letter to be circulated in its entirety in order to stimulate the purchase of the capital stock in Texas. The Houston *Telegraph and Texas Register*, whose editor, Francis Moore, Jr., had been strongly opposed to Houston on personal grounds, immediately protested against this form of monopoly:[82]

Let those HONEST legislators exult to behold ONE MILLION OF DOLLARS all accurately counted, and neatly arranged in high and shining piles; & when their avaricious eyes have feasted to satiety upon the delightful vision, may they stifle if they can, the bitter, bitter reflection, that this golden fruit of speculative legislation, like the forbidden fruit of Eden, is to entail an hereditary curse upon their posterity; that is to choke up every channel of enterprise throughout our land; control our currency; paralyze our commerce, destroy every germ of internal improvement, and finally, compel every class of citizens to bow down and do homage at the feet of a foreign, monied, aristocracy.

Such a castigation of the moneyed interests was certainly no foundation for the continued success of the monopoly. The Second Congress, which met in May, continued the onslaught upon the

---

[81] Thomas J. Green to Branch T. Archer, December 26, 1836, in Herbert Gambrell, *Anson Jones, the Last President of Texas,* 91. Green had extensive contacts in the United States and hoped to interest capitalists there in banking schemes in Texas.

[82] Houston *Telegraph and Texas Register,* July 29, 1837.

privileges of the company, but its demise came about in tame fashion. Because of the paper-money issues, the rate of exchange in Texas had fallen to about fifteen cents on the dollar. Hard times in the United States defeated the attempts to sell the company stock there, and only about $86,000 had been subscribed for in Texas. If the bank could save its charter it could print additional currency, but by the terms of the act of incorporation the $25,000 bonus had to be paid in hard money. Archer, who had lost his seat in Congress as a result of his association with the speculation, then paid to Secretary of the Treasury Smith the required amount in paper money. Smith, supported by the opinion of Attorney General John Birdsall, refused to accept the paper money, and no effort was made to open the bank or to test Smith's action at law.[83]

The sanction given to the banking company was the first real political issue in the Houston administration. It was the opinion of many that the President had favored the speculation and that he was the official power behind the five partners. Francis R. Lubbock, a clerk in the House at the time and a personal friend of Houston's, referred to the charter of incorporation as "perhaps the most sharply criticized act of Houston's first administration."[84] The political error of association with the company was not lost on the majority of its founders. Austin repudiated his connection with the company just before his death in December, 1836. Collinsworth and Henderson were assiduous in attempts to clear themselves of charges of complicity in the transaction, and in time the matter died. Actually, Houston had wholly agreed with Smith in his decision not to accept the paper money as the bonus payment, but the original act of incorporation was secured with the approval of the President.

Another vexatious problem facing the Hero of San Jacinto was the army. With the appointment of General Rusk as secretary of war, the command of the army was transferred to Brigadier General Felix Huston, one of the firebrands who arrived after the Battle of San Jacinto and who was instrumental in causing the detention of Santa Anna. The law partner of Seargent Prentiss, a prominent Whig politician in Mississippi, Huston came to Texas in search of adventure and military glory. The army found itself in a state of in-

[83] Gambrell, *Anson Jones*, 106.
[84] Lubbock, *Six Decades in Texas*, 91.

activity after the Mexican retreat was completed, and discord soon developed. Huston began to trumpet the old idea of a Matamoros campaign, and to the idle soldiers the prospect of adventure and plunder was alluring. To stay this threat the President offered the army command to General James Hamilton, former governor of South Carolina and an ardent friend of Texas, but he was unable to accept. Houston then appointed Albert Sidney Johnston commander, hoping that the removal of Huston would quiet the troublesome elements. Johnston, a graduate of West Point, had resigned his commission in the United States Army in 1834. Upon the death of his wife in August, 1835, he lived for a time in Louisville, Kentucky, and then came to Texas. Securing the backing of Houston and Rusk, he had attained the rank of colonel before he was offered the command of the Texas Army.[85] Johnston arrived in camp on February 4, 1837, and was quickly challenged to a duel by Felix Huston, who could not "submit to be overslaughed under humiliating circumstances."[86] The challenge was accepted, and on the sixth shot Johnston fell, seriously wounded. As a result, Huston retained control of the army, and the Matamoros scheme was in the air once again.

The President, however, persevered in his peaceful policy, and in March Felix Huston was writing to his recent adversary, Johnston, in a dejected tone:

I hope little from the war policy of the Administration. The facility of arriving at the same conclusions from the most opposite states of fact renders it entirely useless to argue or reason with the President on this subject. . . . As to our waging war, he will not hear of it. I am in very low spirits as to our prospects, and deem Texas in a very critical situation.[87]

Huston decided to attend the sessions of the Second Congress and propagandize his favorite project. His appearance at the capital in May gave Houston the chance to furlough the army. Accordingly, on May 18 the Secretary of War, William Fisher, ordered that the entire army, with the exception of six hundred men, be granted furloughs. The furloughs were unlimited but liable to revocation at any time. Of course, the soldiers were intent on getting out of Texas

[85] William P. Johnston, *The Life of General Albert Sidney Johnston*, 74–75.
[86] Felix Huston to Johnston, February 4, 1837, *ibid.*, 76.
[87] Huston to Johnston, March 28, 1837, *ibid.*, 81.

before the President could remand his order, which was the furthest thought from Houston's mind. Confronted with this *fait accompli*, Felix Huston returned to his law practice.[88]

The disbanding of the army was sharply criticized, especially in the west, though the measure was justified by the need to maintain the unity of the administration. In a despairing mood, Houston wrote to a friend: "We may yet save the country, but it will be a chance. Disorganization in the army heretofore has done all the evil. God avert the worst!"[89] In the United States the New Orleans *Picayune* strongly disagreed with the President's policy:[90]

The disbanding of the army by the president of the republic has given great dissatisfaction to the people of the whole country. The army became discontented because the people objected in vain to the president's refusal to gratify their wishes in an attack upon Matamoros. . . . The news from the interior of Texas is very unfavorable—anarchy, confusion, and all the beauties of discontent seem to prevail, to the dishonor of the Republic and the ruin of all the bright hopes of the thousands who have lately emigrated to that country. We never believed Gen. Houston to be the man for the high station he now occupies, and cannot believe that the country will long remain under its present administration.

Finance, land difficulties, and a discontented army were not the only problems of the first Houston administration, for the Indians also proved a constant menace. The Cherokees enjoyed title to their lands from Spanish grants which had been confirmed by Mexico at the time of its independence. In February, 1836, when the Texans needed their friendship, Houston, John Forbes, and John Cameron had been appointed by the provisional government to treat with the Indians. In return for their neutrality, the government had guaranteed to the Cherokees permanent title to their lands. But the First Congress refused to ratify the treaty, and the Indian lands were soon encroached upon by white settlers.[91] Houston advocated the cause of the Indians, both from a just view of the situation and from personal friendship, and would not consent to a wholesale war

[88] James, *The Raven*, 285.

[89] Sam Houston to Anna Raguet, August 2, 1837, *Houston Writings*, II, 134.

[90] New Orleans *Picayune*, June 24, 1837. This newspaper generally maintained a regular correspondent in Texas; thus, the majority of the reports concerning Texas were not reprints from local papers.

[91] Thomas C. Richardson, *East Texas: Its History and Its Makers*, I, 105–106.

against the Cherokees. For this policy he was severely censured in the western areas of the nation. The President's refusal to execute the laws of December, 1836, providing for a military establishment of 3,587 troops, as well as a chain of blockhouses, forts, and trading houses for the protection of the frontier, also later reacted against him. Houston suffered for looking at the situation in a practical fashion. How to pay for the recommended appropriations in anything but worthless paper money did not appear to concern the Legislature.

In the spring of 1837 the elected representatives of the nation rode into the sprawling town of Houston for the second session of Congress. The city had grown, and in 1837 was described by a traveler in this fashion:[92]

The main street of this city of a year extends from the landing into the prairie—a beautiful plain of some six miles wide & extending, with points and islands of timber, quite to the Brazos. On this main street are two large hotels, 2 stories, with galleries (crowded to overflowing) several stores 2 stories—painted white—one block of eleven stores (rent $500 each)—some two story dwelling houses—& then the capital—painted peach blossom about ½ mile from the landing. Other streets, parallel, & at right angles, are built on here & there, but chiefly designated by stakes. One story dwellings are scattered in the edge of the timber which form an amphitheatre round the prairie, according to the bend of the Bayou, which, being wider, would render this a most eligible town site. As it is, it is too inconvenient, besides being unhealthy.

The capital city was not a desirable place either to work or to live. One congressman wrote to his wife that Houston was "the most miserable place in the world."[93] And a young lawyer residing in the city has left this apt description:[94]

Took lodgings at Floyd's Hotel. . . . Rains, streets become very muddy in a few hours. Visit Billiard room, play game of Billiards, successful. In the same house are four Faro Banks in addition to which are a number

[92] Hatcher (ed.), *Mary Austin Holley Letters*, 70. The letter describing Houston appears on December 24, 1837, in the log of Miss Holley's first trip to Texas.

[93] Kelsey H. Douglass to his wife, September 27, 1837, Kelsey H. Douglass Papers.

[94] Andrew F. Muir (ed.), "Diary of a Young Man in Houston, 1838," *Southwestern Historical Quarterly*, LIII (1950), 284. This diary was kept by John Hunter Herndon, a native of Kentucky, who came to Texas in 1838. Herndon practiced law during the period of the Republic and resided in Richmond.

of others in the place, the greatest sink of dissipation and vice that modern times have known.

Despite depressed financial conditions in Texas, hopeful thousands continued to enter the country from the United States, where conditions were even worse. The Washington correspondent of the New York *Journal of Commerce* reported that "great numbers are going to the new *El Dorado* . . . where lands can be had for little or nothing, and where three crops of cotton can be made from one planting."[95] In this period, by far the largest number of emigrants came from Alabama, Tennessee, Mississippi, and Louisiana. This influx of settlers caused the population of Texas to swell considerably.[96]

Congress convened on May 1 and heard the President deliver his message. Houston called attention to the lamentable financial condition of the country and asked for adequate public-land legislation. He noted the need to draw the boundary on the northeastern frontier between the United States and Texas and, as a result of the undefined boundary, the duty of each nation to restrain its Indians. The President expressed his pleasure with the existing state of the army and recommended that the navy be strengthened. Finally, Houston observed that no change had occurred in the people's united sentiment for annexation.[97]

With this program before them, the congressmen set to work. As a solution to the lack of hard cash in the nation's coffers and to the failure of the land scrip sold in the United States to realize a sizable profit, the solons resorted to paper-money issues. The act of June 9, 1837, marked the beginning of this disastrous expedient. It authorized the President to issue government promissory notes to the amount of $500,000 in denominations of not less than $1 nor more than $1,000, payable twelve months after date and drawing interest at 10 per cent. There was pledged for their redemption one-fourth

[95] New York *Journal of Commerce,* quoted in *Niles' Weekly Register,* March 18, 1837.

[96] Barnes F. Lathrop, *Migration into East Texas, 1835–1860,* 39. In late 1836 the population of Texas consisted of some 52,670 persons, including 30,000 Anglo-Americans, 3,470 Mexicans, 14,200 Indians, and 5,000 Negroes. Also see Morfit to Forsyth, August 27, 1836, in Yoakum, *History of Texas,* II, 197.

[97] Report of the Proceedings of the House of Representatives, First Congress, Second Session (1837), 9–10.

POLITICAL HISTORY OF THE TEXAS REPUBLIC

of the proceeds of the sales of Galveston and Matagorda islands, 500,000 acres of land, all improved and forfeited lands, and the faith and credit of the government.[98] These notes were issued about November 1, and on December 14, 1837, Congress authorized the issuance of "change notes" or treasury notes of small denominations, to an amount not exceeding $10,000, and an additional issue of $150,000 of other treasury notes, if required. Customs duties were made payable only in specie or treasury notes. The amount of printed notes issued to January, 1838, was $514,500. They were not reissued, however, and experienced little or no depreciation. The excesses of paper-money issues were reserved for the next session of Congress.

By order of the President, the land offices were still closed, and a comprehensive land law was very much needed. The legislators did repeal all laws which allowed additional bounties to volunteers, for there was no great need for an army, and certainly no way to pay the soldiers at this time. With the passage of this act, Congress adjourned, having been in session little more than a month. This action aroused the ire of Francis Moore, Jr., later to be a Texas senator but then the influential editor of the *Telegraph and Texas Register:*[99]

In our humble opinion some mechanical means ought to be devised to induce our members of congress to hold longer sessions.—Such an obstinate disposition is manifested by some members to pop up and move an adjournment that they ought to be supplied by their constituents with seats of tough sticking plaster. They seem to be quite regardless of the lessons taught by the first legislators of America, who often convened in full assembly, "before the governor was stirring"—and more over were such thorough-going business men, that they spent as many hours in the legislative halls as they were accustomed to spend in their fields and workshops.

With no other alternative, Houston called a special session of Congress to deal with the land problem and other pressing questions. Feeling that to open the general land office would aid the speculators, the President had refused to comply with the law enacted at the first session of Congress, and so the matter remained virtually the same as it had been at the beginning of the administra-

[98] Miller, *A Financial History of Texas,* 67.
[99] Houston *Telegraph and Texas Register,* May 30, 1837.

tion. The crux of the entire question lay in drafting a bill that would please the veterans as well as the old settlers, for those who had fought in the battles of the Revolution felt that they were entitled to at least as much as those who had settled in Texas prior to the war but had not served in any of the campaigns. Only two weeks after the called session began, Kelsey H. Douglass, of Nacogdoches, introduced a bill for the benefit of the veterans.[100] William Gant, of Washington County, and General Thomas J. Rusk, representing the district of Nacogdoches, in turn presented bills dealing with the bounty question. The preoccupation with the land issue at the called session led the editor of the *Telegraph and Texas Register* to again chide the legislators:[101]

Most of the members of congress appear to be so fascinated by the new land bill that they have entirely forgotten the navy. Land, land, land, seems to engross their whole attention; if their disgraceful apathy should continue much longer, the thunders of the Mexican cannon pealing along our coast may announce to them the startling fact that the *title to the lands of Texas, is not yet secured.*

Debates on the land problem continued, with no apparent solution in sight. Finally, acts of December 4 and 14, 1837, provided that those veterans who had served for three months should receive 320 acres; for six months, 640 acres; for nine months, 960 acres; for twelve months or more, 1,280 acres. Additional grants were made to those who had participated in the war against Mexico and to all those who had become incapacitated for labor in the service of the Republic. The act did not provide for the division of the lands in sections of a mile square, as was guaranteed by the Constitution. This was the main point of contention while the bill was in the House and Senate, and those who voted against it pointed to the need to employ a surveyor in locating lands, the endless amount of litigation that would be involved, and the opportunities for speculation that would be presented.[102] In his veto message, Houston strongly emphasized the constitutional provision that the land be sectionized in "parcels of one mile square" and said that the

[100] Gambrell, *Anson Jones,* 115.
[101] Houston *Telegraph and Texas Register,* October 28, 1837.
[102] Report of the Proceedings of the House of Representatives, First Congress, Second Session, (1837), 115–23.

work of sectionizing could be completed in less than six months. He also objected to the provision of the bill which authorized the President to cause to be surveyed a sufficient quantity of land to meet all claims of land scrip previously issued by the government. Houston argued that the holders of the scrip themselves should be confirmed in their understood right to choose the location of their lands.[103] The joint acts were passed over the President's veto, though Houston remained steadfast in his refusal to open the land offices.

In relations with the United States, the Texas government continued to work for recognition of its independence. The United States Congress had empowered Jackson to send an agent to Texas to gather information concerning the political and economic condition of that country, with the prospect of favorable action on the question of recognition dependent upon the report. In compliance with this resolution, Jackson sent Henry Morfit, a clerk in the State Department, and the question lay dormant until the United States Congress resumed its sessions in December, 1836. In the interim Grayson and Collinsworth, the Texas commissioners in the United States, were recalled, and William H. Wharton was named minister to the United States. In his instructions, drafted by Secretary of State Austin, Wharton was told to claim independence on both a *de jure* and a *de facto* basis. Austin maintained that the fact of independence was proved by the failure of Santa Anna's invasion and by his admission that Texas was able to maintain itself. Santa Anna was en route to Washington and would impress these arguments upon Jackson. If negotiations reached the stage of a treaty of annexation, Wharton should press for the admission of Texas, with a boundary extending to the Rio Grande, on an equal basis with existing states. The treaty should recognize slavery with no other limitations than those imposed by the United States Constitution and should guarantee land titles without regard to the fulfillment of conditions which had formerly existed under Mexican rule. If Texas was to be required to pay its public debt, then Wharton should insist that the state was to retain its public lands. These were the public instructions to guide Wharton in his conversations with Jackson and Secretary of State Forsyth. Privately, the Minister was advised to con-

[103] "Veto of an Act Concerning Changes in the Law That Established the General Land Office," *Houston Writings*, II, 168–71.

er with the foreign representatives of England and France in Washington in the event that his mission proved to be a failure.[104]

Wharton departed on his task fully aware of the difficulties in his path. A letter written to Austin before he reached Washington gives evidence of an uncanny facility at prophecy:[105]

To be plain and candid, I believe the recognition of our independence will certainly take place, but I have not at present much hopes of our being annexed. That question when proposed will agitate this union more than did the attempt to restrict Missouri, nullification, and abolitionism, all combined. Already has the war violently commenced even on the prospect of our annexation. The Southern papers, those in favor of the measure are acting most imprudently. . . . The North must choose between the Union with Texas added—or no Union. Texas will be added and then forever farewell abolitionism and northern influence. Threats and denunciations like these will goad the North into a determined opposition and if Texas is annexed at all it will not be until after the question has convulsed this nation for several sessions of Congress.

Jackson addressed Congress on December 21 about the question of recognition. Using the Morfit report as his guide, the President observed that it had been the traditional policy of the United States to accord recognition on the basis of actual independence. The agent's report stipulated that Texas was independent, but a doubt existed whether the new Republic could maintain this state. In Jackson's words the situation resolved itself in this manner:[106]

It is true that with regard to Texas, the civil authority of Mexico has been expelled, its invading army defeated, the chief of the Republic himself captured, and all present power to control the newly organized Government of Texas annihilated within its confines. But, on the other hand, there is, in appearance at least, an immense disparity of physical force on the side of Mexico. The Mexican Republic under another executive is rallying its forces under a new leader and menacing a fresh invasion to recover its lost dominion.

Anastasio Bustamante had succeeded to the presidency in Mex-

---

[104] *Diplomatic Correspondence*, II, 127–40.
[105] Wharton to Austin, December 11, 1836, *ibid.*, II, 152–53.
[106] "Special Message to the Senate and House of Representatives of the United States," in James D. Richardson (ed.), *A Compilation of the Messages and Papers of the Presidents, 1789–1897*, III, 268.

ico upon Santa Anna's disasters in Texas, but Jackson seems to have overemphasized the danger of a Mexican invasion. Actually throughout Houston's first administration there was no significant military threat to Texas independence. However, Jackson reasoned that the uncertainties in Texas were enough to preclude recognition. The President also pointed out that recognition and annexation were virtually the same. It was his opinion that annexation would be the logical and speedy result of recognition, that this would place the United States in a bad light with the other major powers of the world, and that the United States would be suspected of land-grabbing and liable to the accusation of failing to maintain absolutely neutral standards. Also, the general consternation that annexation might cause in Europe, if accomplished in a precipitate fashion, must have been a factor in Jackson's mind.[107]

To the Texans, Jackson's message came as a complete surprise. In the United States, so pronounced an opponent of recognition as John Quincy Adams, now a member of the House from Massachusetts, was also taken unaware, but his sentiments were in direct contrast to the disappointment of the citizens of the Republic.[108]

A message was received from the President concerning the new republic of Texas—the recognition of her independence, and her application to be annexed to the United States. This message was in a tone and spirit quite unexpected to me, and certainly a large portion of the House —a total reverse of the spirit which almost universally prevailed at the close of the last session of Congress, and in which the President notoriously shared. This message discourages any precipitate recognition of Texas, and speaks with due caution and reserve of its annexation to the United States.

In his message, Jackson had pointed out that Congress traditionally exercised the right of recognition and that the final disposition of the matter would have to come from Congress, therefore, the

[107] In regard to the British reaction to the proposed annexation of Texas, the London *Times* had this to say: "We see in the late proceedings of the government and people of the United States a confirmation of the suspicion, long entertained in the best informed diplomatic circles, that the annexation of Texas to their already unwieldy territory is a favorite project. Texas would be a stepping stone to the acquisition of Mexico. . . . Meantime, will Europe be content to be a quiet observer of the progress of events!!!" London *Times*, in *Niles' Weekly Register* December 31, 1836.
[108] Allan Nevins (ed.), *The Diary of John Quincy Adams, 1794–1845*, 474.

discerning were not in despair over Jackson's policy. Houston, writing to Thomas Toby, the Texas land agent in New Orleans, commented: "I have read General Jackson's Message and think it is politic, but unfavorable. . . . How the U. States can get over our recognition, I can not conceive."[109] Wharton, far from being disheartened, expressed his opinion that "the administration expect to acquire Texas by treaty with Mexico soon and thus remove all cause of complaint. . . . Congress will probably recommend a recognition in the course of a week."[110] Though his spirits were not depressed by Jackson's rebuff, Wharton did become ill in Washington and indicated a desire to return to Texas. His wish coincided with the plans of Houston, who wanted to send to the United States a man who had been present at the sessions of the Republic's First Congress and who could give a true picture of the current political and economic conditions in Texas, as an antidote to the Morfit report. Thus, Memucan Hunt was named by the President as a special agent to the United States to act in concert with Wharton in the deliberations for recognition and with the understanding that he would assume the position of minister upon Wharton's return to Texas.[111] However, Wharton was besought to stay on at Washington until the inauguration of Van Buren, and he finally consented.

James Pinckney Henderson, who was appointed secretary of state upon the death of Austin in December, 1836, instructed Hunt to labor for recognition and for the admission of Texas into the Union by an act of Congress.[112] Meanwhile, the question of Texas' recognition had become the subject of debate in national politics. Robert J. Walker, the expansionist senator from Mississippi and the most devoted friend of Texas in the Senate, introduced a resolution on January 11, 1837, calling for the recognition of Texas independence. His move was opposed by the Jackson administration and passed the Senate with difficulty, only to fail in the House.[113] With Van Buren elected and Jackson about to leave the Presidency, Washington was in a state of transition, and the times were not favorable for

[109] Houston to Thomas Toby, January 27, 1837, *Houston Writings*, II, 41.
[110] Wharton to Austin, December 28, 1836, *Diplomatic Correspondence*, II, 159.
[111] Winkler (ed.), *Secret Journals of the Senate*, 55.
[112] Henderson to Hunt, December 31, 1836, *Diplomatic Correspondence*, II, 161.
[113] H. Donaldson Jordan, "A Politician of Expansion: Robert J. Walker," *Mississippi Valley Historical Review*, XIX (1932), 368–69.

negotiations required in handling so delicate a matter as the Texa question. Wharton gave a good account of the difficulties besettin him and Hunt in a letter to Houston:[114]

I will now tell you the whole secret of the reluctance of Congress act on this matter. I have made it my business to unravel the myster and I know that I have succeeded. Some of the members have open avowed to me their reasons for wishing to postpone our recognition unt the next Congress. It all proceeds from the Van Buren party. They a afraid that the subject of annexation will be pressed immediately aft recognition;—that annexation or no annexation will be made the test the elections for Congress during the ensuing summer;—that the Nor will be opposed and the South in favor of annexation, and that Mr. Va Buren will of course have the support of either the South or North mass accordingly as he favors or opposes annexation. The fear then throwing Mr. Van Buren into a minority in the next Congress induc his friends to desire a postponement of recognition at present, there keeping down the exciting question of annexation at the next electio and giving Mr. Van Buren more time to manage his cards and conso date his strength.

Wharton and Hunt were also embarrassed by the fact that t recognition and ultimate annexation of the Republic had become controversial national issue. The abolitionists seized upon the Tex Revolution as a diabolical plot of interested slaveholders to increa the slave area of the United States and to perpetuate that "peculi institution" at the expense of the North. Familiar charges were ba died back and forth, and Benjamin Lundy, perhaps the most voc Northern abolitionist, wrote a vehement pamphlet which attribute the Revolution to the "oppression of the Slaveholding interests."[1] Leading newspapers in both the North and the South editorialize on the Texas question and helped to foment the sectional disput A Virginia paper, the Richmond *Whig*, forcefully stated the Sout ern position:[116]

[114] Wharton to Houston, February 2, 1837, *Diplomatic Correspondence*, II, 17 80.

[115] Benjamin Lundy, *The War in Texas: A Review of Facts and Circumstan Showing That This Contest Is a Crusade against Mexico, Set on Foot and Support by Slaveholders, Land-Speculators, &c., in Order to Re-Establish, Extend, and P petuate the System of Slavery and the Slave Trade*, 2.

[116] Richmond *Whig*, quoted in Houston *Telegraph and Texas Register*, Janua 11, 1837.

76

Some of the Northern papers are beginning to take ground against the admission of Texas into the American Union, on the ground that it will strengthen the interests of the slave holding states. We shall soon hear the whole Northern phalanx in the cry, and the alarm will be sounded in every plausible form calculated to awake cupidity and fanaticism. . . . The coming sessions of Congress will develop signs which cannot be mistaken. The storm is gathering.

Meanwhile, in Washington, events proceeded at a rapid pace. Santa Anna reached the capital city and had an audience with the President, but Jackson despaired of accomplishing anything because the Mexican government had already repudiated the Treaties of Velasco. The famous Mexican prisoner was sent back to Mexico as a passenger on an American naval vessel. In Congress, Representative Linn Boyd of Kentucky moved that the independence of Texas be recognized, and the attempt of Churchill C. Cambreling, a staunch Van Buren man in the House, to sidetrack the issue by a motion to consider appropriations was defeated by a considerable majority. Writing to Rusk on February 12, Wharton surmised that the Committee on Foreign Affairs in the House would include in the general appropriation bill the expenses for a diplomatic mission to Texas.[117] This is precisely what happened. On February 28 the House adopted the twin resolutions of the Foreign Affairs Committee which provided for the recognition of Texas and directed that the bill for the civil and diplomatic expenses of the government should include provisions for an agent, appointed by the President, who would be sent to Texas.[118] On March 1 the Senate, by a vote of 23 to 19, enacted the resolution recommending legal recognition which Senator Walker had presented on January 11. The final step in the affair is told by Wharton:[119]

I have at length the happiness to inform you that President Jackson has closed his political career by admitting our country into the great family of nations. On Friday night last, at near 12 o'clock, he consum-

[117] Wharton to Rusk, February 12, 1837, *Diplomatic Correspondence*, II, 185.
[118] Debates in Congress, *Congressional Globe*, 24 Cong., 2d sess. (1836–37), 270.
[119] Wharton and Hunt to Henderson, March 5, 1837, *Diplomatic Correspondence*, I, 201. The newly appointed Chargé d'affaires, Alcée La Branche, had formerly served in the House of Representatives as a member from Louisiana. His appointment was confirmed by the Senate in its first session under the Van Buren administration, and he left for Texas in the fall of 1837.

mated the recognition of the Senate and the diplomatic appropriation bill of the Lower House, by nominating a Mr. Labranche of Louisiana chargé d'affaires near the Republic of Texas. He also sent for Genl. Hunt and myself and requested the pleasure of a glass of wine, and stated that Mr. Forsyth would see us officially on Monday.

In this fashion recognition was at last accomplished. The Texans had blundered at first in not concentrating all power in a single agent, or even in a single mission. In addition, Jackson would not act in hasty fashion, and the Van Buren supporters in Congress refused to encumber the presidential nominee with a definite stand on such a delicate issue as Texas. Add to these factors the presence of an emotional issue, the expansion of the slave system, albeit mistakenly involved, and it can be seen that the prize of recognition was difficult to attain.

In a political sense, recognition was an empty victory without the added factor of annexation. Colonel William Fairfax Gray, an accurate observer of public opinion, made this entry in his diary:[120]

. . . recognition does not give much pleasure to President and Cabinet of Texas. All persons are disappointed. Their hopes have been so highly raised of a speedy annexation to the United States by treaty with Santa Anna, that they can't at once be reconciled to the new state of things presented by recognition. Texas independent, and compelled to fight her own battles and pay her own debts, will necessarily have to impose heavy burdens [on] her citizens.

In addition to the charges of failure that were circulated against the Houston administration for the inability to secure annexation, the President was also accused of neglecting the military defense of Texas. In point of fact there was no significant military threat to Texas sovereignty, though the activities of the Mexican navy cruising off the Gulf were to be reckoned with. In particular, the capture and removal of Wharton from the Texas warship *Independence* upon his return from Washington (and his resultant imprisonment

[120] Gray, *Diary*, II, 219. Another contemporary observer has left this recollection of the failure to attain annexation: "The unsuccessful result of the diplomacy in 1837 was a painful blow to the people of Texas. Our finances were in a bad condition; our treasury was empty; it was a difficult matter to keep our army in the field, and our little navy afloat." Memoirs of John S. Ford, II, 198.

in Mexico City) did embarrass Houston.[121] The President's refusal to sanction an official rescue attempt led Secretary of the Navy S. Rhoads Fisher to order a cruise on his own responsibility, for which he was quickly dismissed. The entire incident was unfortunate, for it revealed the lack of harmony in the official family of the administration and led to the loss of some backing for Houston in Congress, where Fisher was popular. The fact that the Texas Navy consisted of three ships and that funds for more construction were not available did not dampen the ardor of some congressmen for a naval campaign against Mexico. The President, bringing to bear all his facility for practical judgment, remained hostile to any suggestion of offensive war.

With three sessions of the Republic's Congress already past, and with certain basic policies easily identifiable with the administration, opposition to Houston become concerted. In addition to political issues such as land, finance, treatment of the Indians, permanent location of the capital, appropriations for defense, and annexation, reports were current concerning the "Old Hero's" drinking and his over-all lack of personal decorum. These stories were undoubtedly exaggerated in many cases but contained enough truth for many to consider Houston unfit for the office he held. A friend of the President's was forced to write: "The P is so unpopular himself. Knowing how much you think of 'his Excellency' I will not tell you just how he does stand at this time."[122]

In a rebellious mood, Congress convened at Houston on April 9, 1838, and busied itself with the duties at hand. Finances called for the quickest attention, and the legislators began work on them first. The issuance of paper money in the form of interest-bearing promissory notes was continued, and on September 30, 1838, the amount of paper money in circulation was $684,069.59, or $34,069.59 above the amount which had been contemplated by the government; by November 3, 1838, the estimated amount in circulation was $812,-454. A bill to increase the issue to a million dollars was vetoed by the President on May 12, 1838, on the theory that such a large

[121] Jim Dan Hill, *The Texas Navy, in Forgotten Battles and Shirtsleeve Diplomacy,* 77.
[122] James Morgan to Samuel Swartwout, December 21, 1837, Morgan Papers.

79

amount of paper money in circulation would destroy the value of the notes and thus defeat the purpose. But by May 18 conditions were so bad that Houston signed a bill that provided for the continued reissue of the notes until an appropriation of $450,000 should be met.[123] Because of this course of action, Texas suffered from all the ills of an abnormal economy which lead to inflation. A letter from Ashbel Smith, then the surgeon-general of the Texas Army, to Henry Barnard, later to become famous as a leading American educator, throws some light on the times:[124]

Money is scarce here at the present time—it being in demand for the purchase of Land claims. These stocks in the Funded Debt have at least doubled in value since I left in January—as well as every other species of property. I purchased nearly a thousand dollars of the Funded Debt a few days since on our joint account, for 50 cents on the dollar. It is now worth 75 cents and is rising. In the meantime it is drawing 10 per cent on its face or 20 per cent on its cost.

As depreciation rapidly set in, caused by the paper-money issues of 1838, the notes continued to fall in value. By April the notes were worth but fifty cents on the dollar in New Orleans, while in Texas they were circulated at from sixty-five to eighty-five cents on the dollar. The inevitable result of this experiment with paper money was a public debt of about $1,942,000 accumulated in less than two years.

Another question that continued to occupy the attention of the congressmen was the permanent location of the capital. The legislators found much for which to condemn the city of Houston. Accommodations were poor, and the generally unhealthy atmosphere of the town was a leading factor in the desire to move to an inland site.[125] In June, 1837, the New Orleans *Picayune* had commented on the development of the city:[126]

The city of Houston, it is said, is falling faster than it has risen—that goods are there selling at auction at any price they will bring, and that for lots there is *no* sale. . . . Such a result must have been expected by

[123] Miller, *A Financial History of Texas*, 67–70.
[124] Ashbel Smith to Henry Barnard, May 6, 1838, Ashbel Smith Papers.
[125] Ernest W. Winkler, "The Seat of Government in Texas," *Quarterly of the Texas State Historical Association*, X (1906), 191.
[126] New Orleans *Picayune*, June 18, 1837.

reflecting, intelligent men; that a place without scarce any natural advantages should suddenly rise to such importance and maintain it, is certainly not to be expected.

At the previous session of Congress, a commission of five men had been selected by a joint vote of both houses to suggest a number of locations for the permanent capital.[127] The committee displayed a preference for the central and western areas of the country, nominating Bastrop as their first choice and indicating a preference for Washington, San Felipe, and Gonzales, in that order. In all, seven locations on or near the Brazos River were mentioned, while only three in the vicinity of the Colorado River received notice.[128]

Congress took no action on this report, and another commission was created in December, 1837, which was to report when the Legislature convened in April of the following year. This group, composed of members of Congress, recommended as its first choice a portion of the vacant lands near La Grange, on the Colorado. The distinctive factor about this report was that this time the sites on the Colorado River received the greater amount of attention, while Washington, which had been the strongest choice in the Brazos area, was dropped entirely. When Congress reconvened in April, the work of this commission was accepted and was sent to the President for his signature. Houston vetoed the resolution, basing his action on three points: (1) according to constitutional provision, the city of Houston was to remain the capital of the Republic until 1840; (2) the population of the country was rapidly shifting and increasing and any central location chosen in 1838 might not be at all centrally located in a few years; (3) the act deciding the location of a permanent capital might be repealed with ease by the next Congress.[129] The Legislature did not contest the President's veto, but a second bill was passed in which it was stipulated that, when designated, the name of the new capital was to be Austin, that twelve

[127] Lorena Drummond, "Five Texas Capitals: An Account of the Seats of Government in Texas since the Adoption of the Declaration of Independence," *Texas Monthly Magazine,* V (1930), 201. The five members of the commission, none of whom were members of Congress, were John A. Greer, John G. McGehee, Horatio Chriesman, J. W. Bunton, and William Scurlock.

[128] *Ibid.,* 202.

[129] Report of the Proceedings of the House of Representatives, Second Congress, Adjourned Session (1838), 162–65.

81

squares of land were to be reserved or purchased for the state, one of which was to be dedicated to a state university, and that Houston was to remain the capital until 1840. The bill received Houston's signature.

The capital problem temporarily settled, the solons turned their attention to land and Indian affairs. In a report presented to Congress, the Commissioner of the General Land Office, John P. Borden, suggested that a special land office be created to deal with the matter of conflicting patents caused by the faulty system of surveying. Borden's recommendation that a new general land law be enacted to supersede the law of December, 1837, which had been passed over Houston's veto, also went unheeded.[130] The final Congress under the Houston administration thus did nothing to modify the law of 1837, and the President continued to keep the land offices closed. The whole situation was replete with confusion, and the opportunities for speculation were great. The failure of the government to create an adequate land system and to legislate in a wise manner in this regard must lie with Congress rather than with the President. Houston constantly identified himself with the desire to administer a land law that was well defined and fair. His land policy remains one of the more admirable features of his first term in office.

In dealing with the Indians, Houston favored an honorable compliance with the various treaties negotiated with the tribes and also insisted that settlers were not to encroach upon Indian lands. The failure of Congress to ratify the treaties drawn by the ad interim government with the Cherokees and their allies (Caddoes, Shawnees, and Delawares) allowed the whites to move in upon the Indian lands in east Texas which, because of the failure of ratification, did not enjoy title at law. Houston tried to forestall a difficult situation by appointing agents to negotiate treaties with the individual tribes and by threatening the intervention of the United States if the Indians "should cut any capers" along the American border.[131] This failed, however, because the legislators refused to honor these individual treaties, and a troublesome, uneasy situation resulted. Houston took notice of this in a message delivered to Congress in May, 1838. The President deplored the fact that the treaties which

[130] Report of the Commissioner of the General Land Office, 30–31.
[131] Houston to Rusk, March 25, 1837, Rusk Papers.

were signed had not been ratified and then in forceful language continued:[132]

The Indian lands are the forbidden fruit in the midst of the garden; their blooming peach trees, their snug cabins, their well cultivated fields and their lowing herds excite the speculators, whose cupidity, reckless of the consequences which would ensue to the country, by goading these Indians to desperation, are willing to hazard everything that is connected with the safety, prosperity, or honor of our country.

The tense situation came to an unpleasant head in the summer and fall of 1838. Early in August, Colonel Henry W. Karnes with a company of twenty-one men was attacked by about two hundred Comanches near Béxar. The Indians were defeated and driven off, though the Texans did suffer some loss of life. More significant was a rebellion which took place at Nacogdoches also in early August. A number of Mexican citizens around Nacogdoches under the leadership of Vicente Córdova, a celebrated Mexican renegade, and Nathaniel Morris, the former alcalde at Nacogdoches, declared themselves opposed to the government and drew into their camp about three hundred Indian allies of the Biloxi and Hainai tribes. Houston, who was at his residence in Nacogdoches at the time, ordered General Rusk to disperse the rebels. Rusk took up the pursuit which led to the Cherokee village and, in direct contravention of the President's instructions, prepared to attack the Cherokees and the rebels who had just arrived there. Houston, allowing his predisposition for the Indians to sway him once again, censured Rusk for his contemplated action. Feeling that Rusk had betrayed his trust, Houston gave way to his troubled feelings in a letter to Jackson:[133]

I came from the seat of Government on a visit, as this is my residence, and had been here but a few days, when a commotion broke out which had long been preparing. The violence of the American character was one cause, and measures were taken without my knowledge or consent. Every man feels himself more capable than the constitutional head of the Government to control it.

This state of things has been brought about in part by the opposition which has existed to *Sam Houston,* not the President.

[132] "Message to the Texas Senate," *Houston Writings,* IV, 60.
[133] Houston to Jackson, August 11, 1838, *ibid.,* II, 270–71.

As Rusk made ready to attack the Indian village, the rebels fled; and because the Texas commander was delayed in following them, his pursuit was a failure. The significance of the incident to the country as a whole lay in the union of Mexicans and Indians in a general rebellion against the Republic. Barnard E. Bee, then secretary of war in the Houston cabinet, arrived at Nacogdoches and in a letter to Henry Smith stated his belief that the rebellion had been inspired by official Mexico and that the Mexican garrison stationed at Matamoros would march against Texas in the event the uprising was at all successful.[134] There is no proof of Bee's assertion of an alliance between the Mexican government and the Indians at this time; however, the likelihood of such an agreement was obvious to everyone. Rusk and Houston smoothed over their difficulties, and in October Rusk vanquished a combined force of Indians and Mexicans at the Kickapoo village. The Indian problem had resolved itself into a series of continuing encounters between the government and the various tribes. The President's conciliatory policy had been a distinct failure and had earned him the hatred of the western-frontier sections of the country.

A final problem, that of the renewed efforts to attain annexation, remained to trouble the first Houston administration. Upon the achievement of recognition in March, 1837, Wharton resigned his post, and Hunt was left in Washington as minister from Texas to the United States. After attending the inauguration ceremonies for President Van Buren, Hunt returned to Mississippi to attempt to secure a loan for Texas from capitalists of that state. Becoming ill, he remained at Vicksburg until July and then returned to Washington. In a communication to James Pinckney Henderson, Texas secretary of state, Hunt outlined his views on annexation:[135]

I believe the consequence of a failure to accomplish annexation will produce a dissolution of the Union That an exercise of such determination will be withheld however, as a dernier resort I likewise believe, and for us to be recognized as Independent by Great Britain with the expectation and belief on the part of these States that such relations would be entered into as to prevent forever our annexation to the latter

[134] Barnard E. Bee to Henry Smith, August 26, 1838, Barnard E. Bee Papers.
[135] Memucan Hunt to James P. Henderson, April 15, 1837, *Diplomatic Correspondence*, II, 208.

would at once make up the issue and our success or failure in accomplishing the desirable end of annexation be determined upon by this Government, and even Northern politicians sooner than see the consequences to which I had adverted, would perhaps advocate our connexion.

Hunt, though actively playing upon the fear of British recognition and perhaps ultimate annexation, was discerning enough to realize that the United States would not at that time risk war with Mexico by annexing Texas. The act of recognition, meeting with strong Mexican protests, had made the Van Buren administration particularly cautious. In late May Hunt was writing: "We must either whip Mexico into an acknowledgement of our independence, or procure its recognition by either England or France before we can hope for any definite action upon the subject by the United States."[136] The United States government was also embarrassed because Southern newspaper editors had adopted the cause of Texas as their own and would not let the issue die. In this respect, the New Orleans *Picayune* felt that "the admission of Texas into the Union, on an equal footing with the original states, should be made a Southern question; and every representative in congress from the south who is found to dodge the subject of admitting Texas should be hurled from his seat as a traitor to our best safety and interests."[137] The dilemma that confronted the administration was obvious, but Hunt determined to make a formal plea for annexation and thus force the hand of the Van Buren party.[138]

In June, 1837, Houston, with the consent of the Texas Senate, had appointed James Pinckney Henderson, his secretary of state, as roving minister to England and France. Henderson, who was selected mainly because his private means were such that he could afford the position, was instructed to work for recognition by England and France as well as for financial aid if such could be obtained. Hoping to use the Henderson mission as a lever, Hunt on August 4 submitted to Secretary of State Forsyth a formal petition for the annexation of Texas to the United States. In his application Hunt presented a brief history of Texas affairs from the early stages

[136] Hunt to Henderson, May 30, 1837, *ibid.*, 222.
[137] New Orleans *Picayune*, July 23, 1837.
[138] Justin H. Smith, *The Annexation of Texas*, 63.

of American colonization and petitioned for annexation on the grounds that the Texans were of the same blood as the citizens of the United States, held the Constitution of that country in great reverence, and had shared in the same type of democratic political development. Hunt also stressed that as a member of the Union Texas would aid in protecting the Western frontier of the United States and would assure the Union control of the Gulf of Mexico. On the other hand, if Texas were to remain independent she would become a formidable rival, and, because of conflicting tariffs and the very similarity of the two peoples and their political institutions, Texas would very possibly come to be involved in difficulties and collisions with her neighboring states. Hunt's formal application covered twenty pages in longhand and was presented in clear and concise fashion.[139]

Forsyth waited three weeks to reply; when he did, his answer constituted a thorough disavowal of the Texas pretensions.[140] Arguing at first that the United States had always recognized independence on the basis of fact and not on the considerations of right between the contending parties, the Secretary of State intimated that in his opinion the recognition which had been granted Texas in March, 1837, had been a hasty measure. The facts had been examined and they did not warrant the government's accepting the annexation proposal, if indeed it was at all constitutional for the United States to annex a foreign state. In conclusion, Forsyth pointed out that the United States was bound to Mexico by a treaty of amity and commerce and that annexation would be a direct repudiation of that agreement.[141]

Hunt's fears were more than realized in Forsyth's reply, which placed the emphasis on the failure of Texas to wring an acknowledgment of its independence from Mexico. But the Texas minister believed that there were other reasons for Forsyth's reluctance to accede to the annexation request. He suspected that the primary factor was the fear of endangering Van Buren's chances in the next election by a course of action that would be so offensive to the non-

---

[139] *Ibid.*, 64.
[140] Eugene Irving McCormac, "John Forsyth," in Samuel Flagg Bemis (ed.), *The American Secretaries of State and Their Diplomacy*, IV, 327.
[141] *Ibid.*, 328.

slaveholding states. Hunt felt that the danger of war with Mexico did enter into the government's reasoning, but in calling attention to the fear of party difficulties the Texas agent was closer to the truth.

With the refusal of annexation by the United States, the Houston government turned its attention to the efforts of Henderson in Europe. The British government had long shown an interest in the affairs of Texas. On August 5, 1836, only five months after Texas had declared its independence, the new nation was the subject of a debate in the House of Commons in which questions were put at great length concerning Texas. A fear that the United States would annex Texas and thus begin an aggressive policy in the Southwest was expressed. The principal consideration at issue, however, was the abolition of the slave trade; it was feared that if Texas established its independence this trade would be reopened. Viscount Palmerston, the foreign secretary, believed that the conduct of the United States in this matter had been entirely proper and that no action should be taken on the subject of the slave trade until it was certain that the Texas Revolution was successful. The government then instructed Alan Crawford, British consul at Vera Cruz, to make an inspection trip to Texas and report on general conditions in that country.[142]

After a tedious crossing, Henderson arrived in England, landing at Liverpool in early October, 1837, and was soon received by Palmerston. The Foreign Secretary appeared to take a sincere interest in Henderson's mission; but he was doubtful about the possibility of recognition, although he promised to lay the problem before the cabinet for consideration. Henderson, in a letter to Robert Irion, who had succeeded him as Texas secretary of state, explained that he was laboring for a commercial treaty and that Palmerston seemed favorably disposed to grant this in time. Henderson marshaled strong arguments on commercial and political advantages that would accrue to Texas as an independent nation and told Palmerston that the Texas Congress would not again let the annexation proposal be offered to the United States. He also pointed out that slaves could be taken into Texas only from the United States and

[142] J. L. Worley, "The Diplomatic Relations of England and the Republic of Texas," *Quarterly of the Texas State Historical Association*, IX (1905), 2–3.

that a law of the Congress of the Republic expressly forbade the African slave trade in Texas. Henderson concluded his interview with Palmerston by detailing the successful campaigns of the Revolution, dwelling upon the glorious victory at San Jacinto, and presenting forceful arguments on the established independence of Texas.[143] Palmerston took Henderson's plea under formal study, promising to submit it to the cabinet for general discussion.

The matter was put off from time to time, while Henderson was left to grumble and complain about the intolerable weather in England. Finally, on December 27, the Texas agent was informed that the British government could not recognize his country at this time. In another communication to Irion, Henderson reported that the ostensible reason for the British reluctance to recognize Texas was doubt of the Texans' ability to maintain their independence. Henderson believed, however, that the stated reason was a less important factor in determining the action of the ministry than were the uncertain political situation in England, the establishment of slavery in Texas, and the interests of the British creditors of Mexico, which made it undesirable to do anything that would jeopardize friendly English-Mexican relations. British commerce with Mexico was important enough that the government was unwilling to take any step which might lose British merchants their markets in Mexico. Henderson also thought that the cabinet had considered the likelihood of the ultimate annexation of Texas to the United States and that Great Britain felt it unnecessary to recognize the independence of Texas if that nation was likely to voluntarily surrender its independence through annexation. Henderson also reasoned that Palmerston was convinced that in recognizing Texas the British government would only be removing an obstacle to annexation.[144] Though Henderson continued to press for recognition in vigorous fashion, no success was forthcoming, and he decided to try his luck in France.

The roving diplomat arrived in Paris on March 23, 1838. He spent a month conferring with General Lewis Cass, the American minis-

---

[143] Henderson to Irion, November 5, 1837, *Diplomatic Correspondence*, II, 821–25.

[144] Henderson to Irion, January 5, 1838, *ibid.*, 839–42.

ter at Paris, about the course of action he should follow; thus he did not present his formal plea until the question of recognition had been given a thorough airing. Fortune was now with Henderson, for a dispute growing out of unpaid claims to French citizens in Mexico had caused the French ambassador there, Baron Deffaudis, to demand his passports. Finally, in April, 1838, diplomatic relations between Mexico and France were suspended. Learning that a blockade was to be established by the French on the Mexican coast, Henderson took advantage of the existing situation to present his claim.[145] Granted an interview with Count Molé, the French foreign minister, Henderson outlined the standard claims for recognition, stressing that Texas was independent, *de facto*, that France would have a trusted friend in Texas in the event of future difficulties with Mexico, and that France would receive favorable tariff concessions and trade rights in any commercial treaty signed with Texas. He also called attention to the poor economic condition of Mexico, its failure to live up to its treaty obligations with France, and the generally prosperous condition of Texas.

The results of Henderson's efforts in France during the Houston administration were culminated by the decision of the French government to send Alphonse de Saligny, one of the secretaries of the French legation at Washington, on an inspection trip to Texas. Count Molé informed Henderson that recognition could not fully be considered until De Saligny's report was received and discussed by the government. A commercial treaty was also left for further consideration, its settlement to be dependent upon the report from Texas. Henderson, writing to President-elect Mirabeau B. Lamar in late October, 1838, surmised that the French government would both recognize Texas and grant a commercial treaty upon the reception of De Saligny's recommendations. The Texas agent agreed to stay on at Paris, as requested by Count Molé, if this was in accordance with Lamar's wishes.[146] Since Lamar felt the need for a representative in France, Henderson was instructed to stay at Paris. The

[145] Herbert R. Edwards, "Diplomatic Relations between France and the Republic of Texas, 1836–1845," *Southwestern Historical Quarterly*, XX (1917), 210–13.

[146] Henderson to Lamar, October 28, 1838, *Diplomatic Correspondence*, II, 1230–31. Lamar was elected to the Presidency in September, 1838, though he was not formally installed in office until December 10 of the same year.

treaties of recognition and commerce that he eventually secured from France more properly belong in a consideration of the Lamar administration.

With Henderson working for recognition in England and France as a weapon to be used in negotiations with the United States for annexation, Houston prevailed upon Hunt to remain in Washington. In September, 1837, a month after Forsyth's refusal of the annexation petition, Peter W. Grayson, attorney general in the Houston cabinet, was sent to the United States as a special agent to aid Hunt in the cause of annexation. Hunt and Grayson labored in concert throughout the fall and winter of 1837 but met with little success. Grayson acknowledged that the question was one of extreme delicacy and that it had become entwined in party politics. In a letter to Secretary of State Irion, he explained his feelings:[147]

... there is *no solid foundation on which to build a hope that the measure can now be carried.* Without going into all the particulars that might be descanted on in relation to the matter, I will just observe that both parties here are afraid to move in the matter for fear of losing popularity in the North—in so critical and touchy a condition are they with respect to each other. I have indeed the strongest reason to believe that some of the most prominent men of both sides of politics here are heartily in favor of annexation, and would at once advocate the measure openly and freely but for the *scare crow* to which I have alluded, *the displeasure of the North.* This is the substance of what I have to say—on the subject—that the determination is to give the question the go-by for this session, until weighter matters can be adjusted, touching the future ascendency of the two belligerents—the Locofocos and Whigs.

With this record of continuous failure in the negotiations at Washington before them, the Congress of the Republic met in the spring of 1838 and debated a proposal to withdraw the offer of annexation. In the prolonged discussion certain significant reasons emerged to explain the desire to withdraw the petition: (1) the decision of the United States to refuse to consider annexation as long as Mexico laid claim to Texas; (2) England's indicated unwillingness to recognize independence as long as the annexation offer remained pending; and (3) the belief that Texas was able to maintain its independence and should rightfully enjoy the fruits of sepa-

[147] Grayson to Irion, December 7, 1837, *ibid.*, II, 273.

rate existence in favorable trade agreements with England and France. On the other hand, it was pointed out that the withdrawal of the offer would retard emigration from the United States and would discourage favorable sentiments in the United States Congress for annexation at some future, more auspicious, date.[148]

The question was referred to the Texas Senate Committee on Foreign Relations, which reported favorably on April 17, 1838, urging that the proposition be "unconditionally withdrawn" by the agents at Washington. Anson Jones, representing Brazoria, introduced a joint resolution in the House on April 23 which favored the adoption of the policy expressed in the committee report. His resolution was defeated on May 1 by a vote of 14 to 13 but was called up for reconsideration on the following day. Several amendments were then added, but the resolution was put down again by an identical vote. Congress adjourned on May 24, and on June 5 Hunt, considering his further presence in Washington completely useless, submitted his resignation. After Grayson declined the permanent appointment, Houston named Anson Jones minister to the United States, with specific instructions for formal withdrawal of the proposal for annexation. Jones did this on October 12, 1838, after the Houston administration had been repudiated at the polls; thus the matter stood when Lamar came into office.[149]

Although annexation had not been accomplished, there were two treaties of some importance negotiated between the United States and the Republic during the first Houston term. The first treaty, signed in Texas by La Branche, the American chargé d'affaires, provided for the settlement of certain damage claims held by citizens of the United States against the Republic. The second treaty, signed at Washington by Hunt and Forsyth, concerned the question of the boundary. Forsyth insisted that the Neches was the rightful eastern boundary, while Hunt maintained that, in accordance with the terms of the Florida treaty, the Sabine was the proper boundary. Hunt suspected Forsyth of attempting to describe the northwestern boundary so that Texas would be limited to the area which it had occupied as a Mexican state. The Texas agent was aware that such an alteration would aid the United States in any potential de-

[148] Joseph W. Schmitz, *Texan Statecraft, 1836–1845,* 61.
[149] Gambrell, *Anson Jones,* 130.

liberations for control of San Francisco Bay, and therefore lodged a strong protest. However, on April 25 Hunt and Forsyth concluded a treaty on the basis of the Florida treaty, leaving the remainder of the boundary question for further adjustment.[150] These two treaties represented the only noteworthy diplomatic accomplishments in the relations of the Houston government with the United States.

With a mediocre score of accomplishments in the problems of land, finance, and Indian relations, coupled with the failure to attain annexation in the sphere of foreign affairs, the Houston party could boast of no major political triumphs in its first term of office. The President had disregarded the will of Congress in refusing to open the land offices, in sanctioning treaties with the Indians that he well knew Congress would not honor, and in instructing Anson Jones, as minister to the United States, to withdraw the petition for annexation. Added to this, the Old Hero was as controversial a figure as ever before; and those who hated him still did so with a passion. Tales of his drinking made the rounds again, and his past life was held up to public ridicule. Commenting upon the political scene at this time, James Harper Starr, later secretary of the treasury under Lamar, observed: "If Texas is to be governed by such men as those now in power she will awaken from her dream of greatness ere long and find that she is not the greatest nation on earth or her government administered by the wisest and most virtuous men."[151] James Reily, a partisan of Houston's, put the case in a more forceful light: "Congress is decidedly Anti-Houston. I hope this remarkable man may escape our country without her limits being disgraced by the attacks which are now mediated against him. Dr. Archer has challenged the King Fishers & Felix Hueston intend to do [so]. . . . I trust he will refuse to accept any of their offers to fight."[152]

The Constitution of the Republic forbade a President to succeed himself in office, so Houston could not be considered a candidate in the election of 1838. Therefore, with the field wide open, the political maneuvering for the campaign of 1838 began early in the spring

[150] Thomas Maitland Marshall, *A History of the Western Boundary of the Louisiana Purchase, 1819–1841*, 210–11.
[151] James Harper Starr to Pamela O. Starr, June 2, 1838, James Harper Starr Papers.
[152] James Reily to Henry Raguet, November 20, 1838, James Reily Papers.

of 1837 in a letter Richard R. Royal wrote to Mirabeau B. Lamar. The Vice-President had returned to his native Georgia for a short trip and soon after arriving received this communication:[153]

I think you aught to Return to Texas as, soon as your Business will conveniently admit, you are Frequently spoken of *with much preference* as a probable Candidate for the office of Chief Magistrate at our next Election as it will be some time Before the Election; It would be well not to be announced before the Public for some time yet. But those things Require some Watching over the Public will and an Occasional suggestion from Friends.

On May 30, 1837, Senator Stephen H. Everitt, of the district of Jasper and Jefferson, implored Lamar to return "ere this Scrawl can Reach You. Houston worn-down by one continued course of Debauchery, is fast sinking under its effects and is at times Entirely unfit for business of Every Kind."[154] And on October 4, 1837, Robert Eden Handy, promoter of the town of Richmond, very significantly informed the Vice-President that "I saw Gen. Rusk a few days ago he *is not* and *will not be in* the field for the next President."[155] The Lamar boom received official sanction in December, 1837, when nine senators and two members of the House published an announcement in the Houston *Telegraph and Texas Register* expressing their desire that Lamar become a candidate for the nation's highest office.[156]

Though Lamar was popular with a majority of the congressmen, there was some doubt about his ability to win the election should General Rusk consent to be a candidate. Since personalities were of major importance in this election as in the preceding one, the popularity of Rusk was a factor to be reckoned with. A kindly man who was deeply loved and respected by his friends, Rusk had proved his bravery on the battlefield at San Jacinto and had since distinguished himself as secretary of war in the Houston cabinet, as a

[153] R. R. Royal to Lamar, May 7, 1837, *Lamar Papers*, I, 548–49.
[154] Stephen H. Everitt to Lamar, May 30, 1837, *ibid.*, 555.
[155] Robert E. Handy to Lamar, October 4, 1837, *ibid.*, 573.
[156] Houston *Telegraph and Texas Register*, December 9, 1837. The senators who signed the petition were Stephen H. Everitt, James S. Lester, Isaac W. Burton, William H. Wharton, Emory Rains, Albert C. Horton, John Dunn, Sterling C. Robertson, and George W. Barnett. Signers from the House were Daniel Rowlett and Edward T. Branch.

member of the House, and as a skilled Indian fighter. In the opinion
of John S. Ford, a contemporary and member of Congress in the
second Houston administration, Rusk "was the only man in Texas
who could show the shadow of a claim as the peer of Gen. Houston
in the esteem, admiration, and love of the people."[157] It was apparent to the Lamar supporters that the Rusk movement had to be
forestalled if their candidate expected to be successful.

Upon the publication of the congressional draft for Lamar, the
Georgian seems to have made up his mind about the Presidency.
Discerning enough to realize the threat that Rusk posed, Lamar
wrote to his former superior in the army before issuing a formal
reply to the draft movement. This was a galling task for Lamar, who
well remembered his humiliation after San Jacinto, when the army,
with the approval of Rusk, refused to accept him as commander.
But the Vice-President humbled himself. In his communication to
Rusk, Lamar expressed the desire for a meeting in order to determine Rusk's views on the approaching election. It was important
that harmony prevail at all times, more particularly now, when "any
violent contest for the Chief Magistry could not fail to be extremely
prejudicial to the peace and prosperity of the country."[158] Rusk declined the meeting "on press of business," stated that he would not
be a candidate because of "private affairs and domestic obligations
so long neglected," and admitted that he would be "pleased, dear
sir, to see your name before the people for the office of Chief Magistrate."[159] With this knowledge as security, Lamar consented to become the first official nominee in the campaign of 1838.

Although Rusk had declined in December, 1837, Houston and
many of his followers felt that the popular army man could be persuaded to run. Accordingly, the President made known his disposition for Rusk as his first choice for a successor, and the party supporters set to work. Francis R. Lubbock, who remained loyal to
Houston throughout the first term, was the guiding force behind a
meeting called in the middle of May, 1838, at Houston to put Rusk's
name in official nomination. Because the President had antagonized

[157] Memoirs of John S. Ford, II, 216–17.
[158] Lamar to Rusk, December 7, 1837, quoted in Asa K. Christian, "Mirabeau
Buonaparte Lamar," *Southwestern Historical Quarterly*, XXIII (1920), 169.
[159] Rusk to Lamar, December 9, 1837, *ibid.*, 169.

western Texas by refusing to open the land office and by his policy of Indian defense, and also because Houston was not overly popular in the middle or southern districts of Texas, three committees representing these two sections and the east were appointed to wait upon Rusk and learn his wishes. Some of the most prominent men in the Republic, including Congressmen Anson Jones, Joseph Baker, and Edward Burleson, as well as Thomas McKinney and Michel Menard, the two leading merchants of Galveston, and a delegation from the army, represented by Captain William H. Patton, attempted to convince Rusk of his duty to run. The general declined the honor again, however, pleading financial embarrassments, the fact that he had not attained the age of thirty-five, which by the terms of the Constitution was necessary in order to qualify as a candidate, and his earlier promise to Lamar that he would not allow his name to be used.[160] In his memoirs Lubbock records his belief that Rusk did want to run but that he did not want to risk any personal difficulties with Lamar. Feeling that if he did make the race it would rankle the old wound of the army's refusal to accept Lamar after San Jacinto, Rusk declined to permit his candidacy. It is Lubbock's impression that if Lamar had not indicated a wish to be a candidate Rusk would have been the candidate of the Houston party.[161]

With Rusk now definitely out of consideration, the Houston men were forced to act hurriedly in putting forward a nominee. The party agreed on Peter W. Grayson, attorney general in the Houston cabinet and later an agent in the United States working with the accredited minister, Memucan Hunt. Upon Hunt's resignation in June, 1838, the President had offered the appointment to Grayson; but Grayson had refused, and the position had gone to Anson Jones. Houston, wishing to keep Grayson in the United States and thus have him seem to run on the merits of the Houston administration, prevailed upon him to accept an appointment as a Texas naval agent commissioned to purchase ships for the Texas Navy in the United States. In Texas it was charged that Grayson was involved in the speculation of confiscated Mexican lands, that he had op-

[160] Covington, "Presidential Campaigns of the Republic of Texas," 93–94. Rusk was actually two months short of the constitutional age requirement at the time of the election; evidence indicates that the requirements would have been waived had he consented to run.

[161] Lubbock, *Six Decades in Texas*, 82.

posed the land law of December, 1837, and that he had not fought in any of the battles of the revolutionary campaign. Also, an unfortunate incident entered into the contest: In Kentucky Grayson had a reprobate cousin of the same name who had deserted his family, and the Lamar partisans were industrious in representing the doings of this cousin as Grayson's own conduct.[162]

The backers of Lamar, as the election approached, well realized the political importance of sectionalism in Texas. General Thomas J. Green, who had stirred up the army against Lamar in 1836 but defended him now because of his own passionate hatred for Houston, wrote to the candidate: "Let your friends watch *Sam Houston* in the east, he has much at stake in the election of Grayson, he is, rely upon it, the *primum Mobile* of the opposition, his traveling cabinet are the whippers-in."[163]

At the same time, Barnard E. Bee, former cabinet officer under Houston and a turncoat at election time, was imploring Ashbel Smith to visit eastern Texas and work for the success of Lamar.[164] These letters give proof of the popularity of Houston in the east and also point up the importance of the sectional vote in the election. Politically, east Texas included the original settlements of Nacogdoches and San Augustine, the entire section east of the Trinity River from Liberty in the south to Henderson and Crockett in the north, and the settlements along the Red River in the north. The political opinion of western Texas centered in the counties lying on the Brazos and Colorado rivers, and as far south as San Antonio. The Gulf Coast, including Galveston, Houston, and Matagorda generally favored Houston policies. Though this divergence of opinion was accentuated by the popularity of the President at San Augustine and at Nacogdoches, where he kept his private residence, it was actually a political legacy from the colonies established by Mexico. Houston's actions usually favored the east and gave offense to the west, and Lamar managers understood this important fact.[165]

The campaign began in earnest in the summer of 1838. Barnard

[162] Covington, "Presidential Campaigns of the Republic of Texas," 98.
[163] Thomas J. Green to Lamar, July 11, 1838, *Lamar Papers*, II, 181.
[164] Barnard E. Bee to Ashbel Smith, July 17, 1838, Bee Papers.
[165] George L. Crockett, "East Texas in the Politics of the Republic," in Eugene C. Barker (ed.), *Readings in Texas History*, 394–95.

E. Bee wrote to David Burnet, a candidate for the vice-presidency, that "where general suffrage prevails no stone ought to be left un- turned to enlighten the people," and the friends of Lamar actively worked at the process of enlightenment. They were handicapped, however, by certain elements in Lamar's character. The nominee, who was a widower, had allowed himself to become involved with Olivia Roberts, a friend from Mobile, Alabama, who had followed him to Texas upon his return in 1837. There does not appear to be any evidence of misbehavior on the part of either party, but rumors did abound concerning the conduct of the candidate. Edward Hall, a Lamar man, wrote to his chief from Columbia in a worried man- ner:[166]

On my way here I have seen a number of the Inhabitants & Voters of this Republic. the subject of the Presidential election has generally been introduced and I find more division in sentiment than I anticipated   The Talents, Patriotism & Bravery as well as the private Virtues of the Can- didates are pretty liberally canvassd. you stand conspicious for *Bravery & Honesty* but there is a great deal of gossiping about some *Picadillos* or *Amours,* which have a powerful influence among the *better halves* of many Families. Your talents have been pronounced of superior order in poetry. Your short residence in the Country has also been urged against you.

To counteract such accusations as these, Lamar was advised to base his platform on the following points: (1) protection of the frontier and a firm policy toward the Indians; (2) the attainment of a lasting peace with Mexico, based upon recognition of Texas inde- pendence; (3) adherence to the land law of 1837, including the opening of the land offices and the awarding of patents; (4) re- newed attempts to secure English and French recognition and a substantial foreign loan; (5) a free-trade policy and a disavowal of the existing tariff. The Matagorda *Bulletin* observed that the man who would "support a judicious Tariff, oppose the cash duty sys- tem, and endeavor to establish a better currency, would be the man of our choice,"[167] and other newspapers also adopted this stand. The platform consisted wholly of remedies for the mistakes that Hous- ton had made, and Lamar conducted his campaign on that basis.

[166] Edward Hall to Lamar, March 1, 1838, *Lamar Papers,* II, 39.
[167] Matagorda *Bulletin,* August 9, 1838.

At the height of the election race in July, 1838, the people of Texas were shocked to learn that Grayson had committed suicide. Traveling in Tennessee, he had stopped at Bean's Station, in the eastern part of the state, and on July 9 had blown out his brains with a pistol. Grayson was then about forty-seven years of age, and the reasons for his act have never been definitely ascertained. In a note left to the landlord of the inn where he stayed the night, Grayson attributed his action to the return of fits of melancholy, from which he had suffered as a young man and from which he had tried to escape in migration to Texas from Kentucky. Contemporary reports spoke of an unhappy love affair and of his bitterness at the reports which were being spread against him in Texas; however, the evidence would seem to point to the return of the mental illness from which he suffered.[168] The Houston faction then planned to run James Collinsworth, chief justice of the Texas Supreme Court and former commissioner to the United States. However, in a macabre development, Collinsworth also committed suicide late in July by jumping from a steamboat in Galveston Bay. In the case of Collinsworth, the cause was excessive drinking. Thomas F. McKinney, writing to his business partner, Samuel Williams, commented, "Collingsworth went exactly as you and B presumed. I was here and had been with him to Houston and we had returned and he was under the influence of Ardent Spirits for a week before hand."[169] Other contemporaries also agreed that drink had blurred the mind of the Chief Justice and had caused his suicide. The twin deaths made the election no contest; in the final tabulation of votes Lamar received 6,995 to 252 for Senator Robert Wilson, who had consented to make the formal race as the Houston party candidate but whose chances of winning were never seriously considered.[170]

The contest for the vice-presidency was a great deal closer, however, with David Burnet, the former President of the ad interim government, as a candidate on the Lamar ticket, running against Senator Albert Horton and Representative Joseph Rowe. Because of the unpopular treaties of Velasco negotiated with Santa Anna

[168] New Orleans *Picayune*, August 26, 1838.
[169] Thomas F. McKinney to Samuel Williams, October 13, 1838, quoted in Hogan, *The Texas Republic*, 44.
[170] Covington, "Presidential Campaigns of the Republic of Texas," 109.

(disliked because they had spared the Mexican general's life and because the Mexican government had repudiated them), and a suspicion of his participation in doubtful land transactions before San Jacinto, Burnet was victorious only by the narrow margin of 776 votes over the combined totals of Horton and Rowe.[171] Burnet had been identified with Lamar since the latter had served as his secretary of war in the ad interim government, and he was certainly helped in his race for office by the overwhelming victory of Lamar.

The election of Lamar must be taken as a repudiation of Houston's policies during his first term in office. It is doubtful that either Grayson or Collinsworth could have defeated the ultimate victor, and Wilson had not the faintest chance. Lamar came into the Presidency with a good opportunity to build a strong and permanent personal following by a successful administration where his predecessor had failed. Houston, victorious in the field, had found the political battles of government a far more taxing opponent than the Mexican army.

[171] *Ibid.*, 110–11.

Lamar Tries His Hand

GEN. LAMAR MAY MEAN WELL—I am not disposed to impugn his motives—he has fine belles-lettres talents, and is an elegant writer. But his mind is altogether of a dreamy, poetic order, a sort of political Troubadour and Crusader, and wholly unfit by habit or education for the active duties, and the every-day realities of his present station. Texas is too small for a man of such wild, visionary, vaulting ambition.[1]

MIRABEAU BUONAPARTE LAMAR, second President of the Republic of Texas, is as interesting a character study as Sam Houston, his predecessor in office. Born on August 16, 1798, near Louis-

[1] Anson Jones, *Memoranda and Official Correspondence Relating to the Republic of Texas, Its History and Annexation—Including a Brief Autobiography of the Author,* 34.

100

ville, Georgia, then the capital of the state, he was the second child in a family that was later to include four sons and five daughters. Mirabeau lived the typical frontier life while growing to manhood. He received a rudimentary education through the services of tutors and by himself developed a passion for reading. While not neglecting outdoor sports and activities, the young man also found time to prepare himself thoroughly in history and literature.

The active qualities in Lamar's personality dominated the contemplative traits in his character when he gave up a chance to enroll at Princeton and instead moved on to Alabama, determined to make his permanent home in that state. He tried his hand unsuccessfully at a mercantile establishment and then founded the Cahawba *Press*, which was also destined for a short life. However, after these setbacks, the restless Lamar found his true medium. His brother, Lucius Quintus Cincinnatus Lamar, already a promising young lawyer, was an active supporter of candidate George M. Troup in the Georgia gubernatorial election of 1823.[2] Upon Troup's election one of his first political debts to be paid was the appointment of Mirabeau B. Lamar as his private secretary.

Governor Troup's concept of state sovereignty and his successful defiance of the Supreme Court over his illegal acquisition of the Cherokees' lands are well known. Lamar's duties as private secretary were less dramatic in nature. He served as official greeter for the Troup administration, he submitted political tracts to the local Georgia newspapers, and he went on frequent speaking tours for his chief. On one of these speaking engagements Lamar chanced to meet Tabatha Jordan of Millidgeville, and after a determined courtship succeeded in making her his wife in January, 1826. In 1828 Troup suffered a defeat at the polls, and Lamar turned once again to the status of frontier editor, moving to Columbus, Georgia, where he established the Columbus *Enquirer*. In the main these were busy and happy years for the future President of Texas.

In 1829 Lamar decided to run for state senator on the Troup platform of states' rights and hostility to the Indians. Just at this time,

---

[2] Philip Graham, *The Life and Poems of Mirabeau B. Lamar*, 5. Mirabeau and his brothers were named by an eccentric bachelor uncle, Zachariah Lamar. The names he selected for his nephews reflected his reading habits: Lucius Quintus Cincinnatus, Mirabeau Buonaparte, Thomas Randolph, and Jefferson Jackson Lamar.

however, a great sorrow came in the death of his wife, a victim of tuberculosis at the age of twenty-one. The tragedy left Lamar grief-stricken, and he attempted to ease his sorrow by constant work and travel. He withdrew from the state election, but in 1833, having earned a certificate as a practicing lawyer in the interim, he ran, unsuccessfully, for the United States House of Representatives. The suicide in July, 1834, of his favorite brother Lucius, who suffered from extreme melancholia, acted as the capstone to Lamar's misfortunes; again he sought release in travel. In the middle of June, 1835, lured by the glowing accounts of a friend from his Columbus days, James W. Fannin, Lamar made a trip to Texas.[3] He soon returned to Georgia but upon the outbreak of the Revolution offered his services in defense of the new nation. He arrived just prior to the Battle of San Jacinto, and his bravery at that engagement was duly recognized, assuring his rise in Republic politics. Lamar served as secretary of war in the ad interim government and was elected vice-president in 1836. His triumph in 1838 was unanimous, and Texas looked forward expectantly to a release from the policies of the first Houston administration.

Public opinion in the United States also hailed the election of Lamar. The New Orleans *Picayune*, disgusted at the manner in which the national government had treated the annexation issue, observed:[4]

He appears to be unanimously popular with the people of this country, and will, no doubt, prove to be the best chief magistrate that could have been selected. It is certain that he is strenuously opposed to *annexation*. He wishes Texas to stand as she is—a free and independent Republic, alone and unconnected with any nation. He will also form an entirely new Cabinet; and it is expected that almost every thing will be changed for the better.

The new Executive, eager to justify the prophecies of success being made for his administration, debated at great length on the selection of his cabinet. However, in appointing to his official family men who had favored Rusk as their first choice for the Presidency,

---

[3] Philip Graham (ed.), "Mirabeau B. Lamar's First Trip to Texas," *Southwest Review*, XXI (1936), 369–70.

[4] New Orleans *Picayune*, December 19, 1838.

Lamar quickly antagonized some of his own strongest support. In naming Barnard E. Bee secretary of state, Lamar displeased many of his followers who thought the honor should have gone to Francis Moore, Jr., the editor of the Houston *Telegraph and Texas Register*. Moore had given Lamar his unqualified backing in the recent campaign, and neglecting to place him in the cabinet was a costly mistake.[5] For the office of postmaster general, Lamar retained the Houston appointee, Robert Barr, in direct contravention of the advice of Representative William E. Jones, a powerful Lamar supporter who referred to Barr as "one of the bitterest opponents you had in Texas."[6] The departments of war and navy were assigned to Albert Sidney Johnston and Memucan Hunt, eleventh-hour converts to Lamar's candidacy who had both held posts in the Houston administration. Richard G. Dunlap, formerly of Tennessee and a protégé of Jackson's, was appointed secretary of the treasury, and John C. Watrous, a recent arrival from Mississippi, was given the post of attorney general. Both Dunlap and Watrous had come to Texas after the struggle for independence, and Lamar was again censured for passing over those who had fought in the Revolution.[7] No reason can be found to account for Lamar's cabinet appointments; the majority of them proved extremely unfortunate.

The townspeople of Houston welcomed the inauguration of the new President as a major social event. On the appointed day, December 1, 1838, former President Houston appeared in colonial costume, complete with powdered wig, and delivered his "Farewell Address" in much the same fashion as did the man he was obviously imitating. Houston distracted attention from Lamar's prepared speech by forcing the assemblage to submit to a three-hour discourse on the past glories of the first administration. Upon the completion of the harangue, Lamar, utterly defeated by such tactics, ordered his private secretary, Algernon P. Thompson, to read his speech, and this was done, but in poor contrast to Houston's effort. Spirits ran high at the ball which followed the inauguration cere-

---

[5] Ashbel Smith to General Baker, December 30, 1839, Smith Papers.

[6] William E. Jones to Lamar, May 10, 1838, *Lamar Papers*, II, 156.

[7] Wallace Hawkins, *The Case of John C. Watrous, United States Judge for Texas: A Political Story of High Crimes and Misdemeanors*, 87.

mony. Reverend William Y. Allen, writing to Anson Jones, commented on the lively proceedings: "At the ball which wound up the *grand affair* 'tis said there was some excess of riot, and some shameful spreeing, towards the breaking of the day. One Hon. Representative, our friend from Jasper, had his nose pulled by a certain military dignitary."[8] Texans were looking to a new day, and, in their eagerness to forget the mistakes of the Houston administration, the strictest propriety was not at all times observed.

In his first message to Congress, submitted on December 21, 1838, the President outlined the policies that would guide his conduct in office. As if to emphasize the importance which he placed on the destruction of the Cherokees and their allies, the Indian question was taken up first. Lamar contended that the Indian tribes had never received patents to their lands from the Mexican government; that they had no rights under the treaties negotiated by the provisional government since the treaties had never been approved by a Republic Congress; and that they could expect no financial redress from the present administration. The President admitted that the speculation of certain land agents had perhaps forced the Indians into armed rebellion and that though this was to be regretted the nation must constantly maintain its Indian defenses.[9] As a corrective measure, Lamar recommended the creation of a line of military posts along the frontier to afford protection against the Cherokee raids. Thus from the outset the President clearly identified himself with a program of hostility to the Indian tribes within the Republic.

In the realm of finance, the area in which the Houston party had so badly floundered, Lamar came forth with some concrete suggestions. One was the creation of a national bank with an adequate amount of the public lands placed aside as security for the bank's capital. Another was the new administration's pledge to continue the government's efforts to secure a loan of five million dollars either in the United States or in Europe. This proposal was the more

[8] William Y. Allen to Anson Jones, December 19, 1838, quoted in Jones, *Republic of Texas*, 139.

[9] Message of the President of the Republic of Texas, Submitted to Both Houses, December 21, 1838, p. 11.

significant because the establishment of a bank was out of the question if the loan was not forthcoming. In addition, the new President voiced his displeasure at the great amount of paper money in circulation, the major part of which was worthless; but he presented no remedies to correct this evil.

In regard to foreign affairs, Lamar promised to prosecute the war against Mexico in active fashion and implied that he would favor the granting of aid to any of the rebellious Mexican provinces. He expressed the hope that Congress would see fit to make liberal appropriations for the upkeep of the army and navy and pledged that efforts would be made to strengthen the navy as a formidable wing of the Republic's fighting force. As for annexation, Lamar expressed his disapproval at the prior attempts which Texas had made in that area and declared that his administration would be hostile to the project. He made much of the point that Texas had been spurned in her earlier attempts to secure annexation and that national pride would only suffer if further requests were made. If left to its own devices Texas would surely prosper, and the President felt that no help need be forthcoming from the United States. Stressing the advantages in trade agreements that would result if Texas were to remain independent, Lamar implored Congress to let the annexation issue die of its own inertia.[10] The President had thus presented his objectives in his inaugural message, and more specifically in his first message to Congress; the outcome of the matter lay with the legislators.

In his farewell message Houston had requested the members of Congress to deal with Lamar in a more restrained manner than they had with his predecessor. The Third Congress, which met with the new President in December, 1838, was for the most part favorably disposed toward Lamar, though there were some members of the Houston party who had managed to retain their positions. In the Senate, Robert Wilson, representing the district of Harrisburg and Liberty, and Edward Burleson, of the district of Bastrop, Gonzales, and Fayette, continued to advocate Houston's policies. In the House, David S. Kaufman, representing the district of Nacogdoches, Isaac Parker, of the county of Houston, Louis P. Cooke of Bra-

[10] *Ibid.*, 11–15.

zoria, and Cornelius Van Ness, of Béxar, remained as principal Houston men.[11] The problem of legislating Lamar's many campaign pledges proved to be no easy matter.

In the area of domestic accomplishments, Lamar's Indian policy was the most notable feature of his term in office. Congress, in its first session under the President, passed three related acts for the protection of the frontier. The first of these provided for the creation of twenty-three companies to be stationed along the frontier at eight specified locations: at or near the Red River, at or near the Three Forks of the Trinity, at or near the Brazos, at or near the Colorado River, at or near the St. Marks River, at the headwaters of the Cibolo, at or near the Rio Frio, and at or near the Nueces River. At each of these outposts fortifications were to be constructed which might later become the center of later frontier establishments. As soon as the sites were provided, three leagues of land were to be laid off and surveyed into lots of 160 acres each. Two of the lots were to be reserved for the government for the purpose of constructing fortifications, one lot was to be given to the soldiers adhering to the term of enlistment, and the remainder was to be given in lots of 160 acres to bona fide settlers in fee simple who would agree to live there two years. The act further provided for the building of sixteen trading posts.[12]

On January 1, 1839, two other acts for the increased protection of the frontier were approved. The first authorized the President to accept eight companies of mounted volunteers for a period of six months and appropriated $75,000 to maintain that force. The second act provided $5,000 for the maintenance of a company of fifty-six Texas Rangers for a three-month period. A short while later another act was signed calling for the creation of three companies of militia for the defense of the frontier, and on January 24 the additional sum of $1,000 was set aside for frontier protection. Lamar had no grounds for complaint about his Indian program, for Congress had been prompt and liberal in making appropriations for frontier protection.

This Indian program now quickly came to the test, for even with

[11] Winkler (ed.), *Secret Journals of the Senate*, 112.
[12] Christian, "Mirabeau Buonaparte Lamar," *Southwestern Historical Quarterly*, XXIV (1920), 75.

the additional protection realized by the congressional acts settlers were reluctant to remain on the frontier. Writing in March, 1839, Senator John A. Greer gave a good account of the existing situation in a letter to John C. Watrous, attorney general in the Lamar cabinet:[13]

The frontier in this section [Robertson County] is in a miserable condition. They have been and are now on the eve of breaking up, at least those Who are able to get away, a great many are widows who are unable to get off others have had their horses stolen and are left without the means of moveing. I have urged them to stay assuring them that the Govt. would protect them as soon as practicable. They have determined to stay until the first of April if they have to stay in their houses, but if they do not get protection by that time they will break up they know they can not make corn without protection, they will move to a place of safety, you must try and have them protected, indeed if they had not hopes that the Comms. would locate the seat of Govt. at the falls they would have broken up long since.

Lamar, in the face of this serious situation, determined to act promptly. On February 14, 1839, Martin Lacey, an experienced Indian trader, was appointed agent to the Cherokees, Shawnees, and other Indian tribes.

The administration, which was eager to find a pretext that would justify a full-scale war against the Cherokees, found their excuse in May upon the capture of Manuel Flores, a renegade Mexican, and his band of Cherokee allies. Flores and his men, who were on their way from Matamoros to eastern Texas, were discovered while attempting to pass the Colorado River near the site which later became the city of Austin. General Burleson, commanding a detachment of Indian fighters, gave pursuit, and the rebels under Flores were soon overtaken. In the ensuing battle Flores was killed, but a diary found on his body revealed that he represented official Mexico and that that country had promised to lend aid to the Cherokees in the form of men and supplies to be used in a general war against the whites in Texas. The Cherokee difficulties around Nacogdoches in the Houston administration had been fomented by another Mexican outlaw, Vicente Córdova, but the trouble that occurred in the

[13] John A. Greer to John C. Watrous, March 2, 1839, *Lamar Papers*, II, 477–78.

Lamar administration stemmed directly from official Mexican aid. Lamar now had his reason for war and was quick to take advantage of the situation as it developed.[14]

Determined upon war, Lamar ordered Major Benjamin C. Waters with a detachment of soldiers to occupy a site of land bordering on the Great Saline. Ostensibly the men were supposed to guard against any disturbance, but they were occupying land which the Cherokees considered their own. The Indians, in the person of their chief, Bowl, protested against Lamar's action and threatened to make war if the troops attempted to construct a permanent fort on the disputed land. The President then issued a proclamation justifying his action on the grounds that the Cherokee lands had become the meeting place for conspiracies against the government and stating that the ultimate removal of the Indians was inevitable and would be accomplished either by peaceful means or through war. In reply, Bowl said that the Cherokees were willing to leave the Republic if the government would pay for the improvements on the land they were occupying. Lamar then assigned commissioners to oversee the proper assessment of the Cherokee property and to make the other arrangements necessary for the removal of the Indians.[15] It was understood that the larger portions of the debt thus incurred were to be assumed by the merchants of Nacogdoches and San Augustine and that the balance would promptly be paid in specie.

As commissioners to treat with the Cherokees, Lamar appointed his Vice-President, David G. Burnet; the Secretary of War, Albert Sidney Johnston; Thomas J. Rusk, who just prior to the start of the Indian difficulties had been elected chief justice of the Supreme Court; and two private citizens, James S. Mayfield and James W. Burton. In the event that the commissioners failed to arrange for the peaceful removal of the Cherokees, the Indians were to be expelled by force, and General Burleson and Major General Kelsey H. Douglass were instructed to hold their troops in readiness. The

---

[14] Anna Muckleroy, "The Indian Policy of the Republic of Texas," *Southwestern Historical Quarterly*, XXVI (1923), 136–37.

[15] Christian, "Mirabeau Buonaparte Lamar," *Southwestern Historical Quarterly*, XXIV, 75.

official report filed by Albert Sidney Johnston stated that Big Mush, the civil chief of the Cherokees, had favored removal, but that Bowl, who was then past his eightieth year, had convinced the tribes that aid would be forthcoming from Mexico and that victory against the whites was possible.[16] Negotiations were carried on for better than a week but failed to accomplish anything, and, believing that the Indians were only attempting to pass time in the expectation of Mexican help, the Texans finally attacked. Their success was complete, and in five days the Cherokees and their allies were dispersed. The troops finished the operation by laying waste to the Cherokee villages and by following the Indian retreat to the American border. Those Indians who escaped fled into Arkansas. Bowl was killed on the second day of the battle, and the sword which General Houston had given him in honor of their friendship was taken from his body in token of the Texas victory.

The expulsion of the Cherokees represented a qualified victory for the Lamar party. Its major importance was expressed by Ashbel Smith, who, observing that "Bowles the grand mischief maker is out of the way," pointed out to a friend that "this discomfiture of the Indians renders any hostile operations on the part of Mexico as exceedingly improbable for some time to come. For Mexico counted much it is believed on the cooperation of hostile tribes."[17] It was true that the Cherokee menace was removed and that the Mexican government had been deprived of a likely ally. However, there was at the same time an articulate body of opposition which contended that the Indian problem was not as serious as the administration had made it out to be and that the Cherokee War had been motivated solely for political purposes. The Houston *Morning Star,* which had been established by the party out of power to serve as the official organ of the opposition, expressed this feeling in eloquent fashion:[18]

The real object now is, when it is apparent to the friends of the administration that nothing short of some great and wonderful feat performed by them, will save their sinking reputation, to seize upon this as the most

---

[16] Johnston, *The Life of General Albert Sidney Johnston,* 110.
[17] Ashbel Smith to Memucan Hunt, August 9, 1839, Smith Papers.
[18] Houston *Morning Star,* April 13, 1839.

likely of all subjects, to make a reversion of public opinion in their favor. Hence it is, that our Indian difficulties are blazoned forth, and with them their own *extraordinary merits* in quelling them.

With the Cherokee problem settled, at least to the satisfaction of the administration, Lamar turned his attention to other matters. Although he had made no particular mention of the issue either in the inaugural address or in the first message to Congress, Lamar dealt next with the question of the permanent location of the capital. This question had proved troublesome to General Houston, and just prior to the completion of his term in office he had signed a bill creating commissions to recommend favorable sites for the capital of the Republic.

Faced with this situation and prodded by the President, the first Lamar Congress passed an act creating another commission to supersede those appointed during Houston's term. The act provided that five commissioners should be chosen by the Legislature from the membership of both houses. Accordingly, Alexander Horton, of Matagorda, and Isaac W. Burton, of Nacogdoches, were chosen by the Senate, and William Menifee, of Colorado, Isaac Campbell, of San Augustine, and Louis P. Cooke, of Brazoria, were selected by the House of Representatives—two from western, two from eastern, and one from central Texas.[19] By the terms of the act the commissioners were limited to the recommendation of a site "at some point between the rivers Trinity and Colorado, and above the old San Antonio road."[20] The act also stated that the name of the new capital would be Austin, and a supplementary act passed ten days later overrode the provision of the previous act which stipulated that the capital should not be removed from Houston until 1840. The purpose of the new bill was to remove the capital from Houston at all costs and to placate western elements by locating the seat of government in that section. The provision of the act which bound the commissioners to make their selections within a specified area effectively secured the bypassing of the city of Houston. The old San Antonio road crossed the Trinity at Robbin's Ferry, the Brazos near Tenoxtitlán, and the Colorado at Bastrop. The road formed the

[19] Winkler, "The Seat of Government in Texas," *Quarterly of the Texas Historical Association*, X, 220–21.

[20] Winkler (ed.), *Secret Journals of the Senate*, 129–30.

northern boundary of Austin's old colony, which was the settled portion of central Texas. In January, 1839, there were only a few villages located north of the road, and only the town of Bastrop could boast of a population of more than one hundred inhabitants. It was certain then that the Lamar party, realizing that the central and western sections of the Republic could be politically cultivated, because of Houston's bias for the east, meant to locate the capital in an area that would please those two sections.

After an intensive two-month search for an adequate location, the commissioners finally drafted their report on April 13, 1839. The finished report recommended the embryo town of Waterloo, a hamlet on the east bank of the Colorado about thirty-five miles above Bastrop. This site was particularly appealing to Lamar, who on an earlier hunting trip had referred to the area as a likely spot for a new "seat of Empire." However, the choice was not overwhelmingly approved by the Republic press. The Houston *Telegraph and Texas Register*, generally favorable to the Lamar party, said concerning the recommendation:[21]

In the report of the Commissioners appointed to locate the Seat of Government, it will be seen that the location has been made at Waterloo, an inconsiderable hamlet . . . on the extreme verge of the northern frontier. The country around this point is represented to be exceedingly fertile and beautiful, and the climate remarkably healthy. It is, however, almost entirely uninhabited, and what is worse probably, more exposed than any other point on the frontier to the depredations of the hostile Indians. Indeed within a few months past, parties of Indians have ventured many miles below it. As it will not therefore afford those conveniences of life and the security requisite for the purposes intended, we can hardly believe that the offices of Government will be removed during the present year.

Other objections were made to the proposed location of the seat of government, and protests were also voiced on the ground that it was a violation of the laws of the Republic to provide for the creation of the capital city before 1840. Commenting on this point, the Houston *Morning Star* observed:[22]

The idea of *permanently* locating the seat of Government by commis-

---

[21] Houston *Telegraph and Texas Register*, April 17, 1839.
[22] Houston *Morning Star*, April 12, 1839.

sioners appointed by Congress, seems to us entirely absurd—the only satisfactory way is to leave it exclusively to the people. That there must be a called session of Congress at this place in the fall seems inevitable— for the law at present in force designating the time for the removal of the different departments to the new Capital, cannot by any possibility be obeyed.

The act which had recently been passed for the permanent location of the capital also provided for the laying out of the site selected and for the sale of town lots. In accordance with these provisions the President appointed Edwin Waller government agent for the future capital of the Republic, empowered to supervise the sale of town lots at Austin beginning about August 1. The Cherokee War diverted popular attention from the new location, but the land sales went ahead as anticipated. The removal of the archives and other papers of the government was scheduled for October, and the final removals were completed in that month.

The frontier capital city, by the terms of the original bill, was named Austin and was expected to be a great improvement over the city of Houston because of greater natural beauty and an over-all healthier condition. To the local correspondent of the New Orleans *Picayune*, the capital presented this appearance:[23]

The state of society at Austin is at present, even in this incipient state of things, *very good*. There are, among our population, quite a number of respectable and intelligent females. It is in contemplation to organize a Presbyterian Church in a few weeks, there being a sufficient number of members of that denomination. A Sunday school is to commence next Sabbath. Two large and respectable Hotels, one 160 by 34 on Pecan st., and 93 feet on Congress Avenue. Both of these Hotels are to be conducted on temperance principles, both being owned and managed by the members of the christian church, and pledged to the temperance principle. Two of the principal merchants of the community are members of the church. The stores of the place are all closed on the Sabbath.

The removal of the seat of government to Austin represented another triumph for the Lamar party. It fulfilled a campaign promise and showed beyond a doubt the desire of the President to win the favor of the western and central sections of the Republic.

Though the Cherokee affair and the removal of the capital de-

[23] New Orleans *Picayune*, September 28, 1839.

112

noted successes for the administration, Lamar was not without his problems. Barnard E. Bee, Lamar's secretary of state, in a letter to Ashbel Smith soon after the election of 1838, had written that "Genl. Lamar will have a trying time of it—Every thing is expected of him—and what can he do without a Dollar."[24] Bee's observation sums up in very concise fashion one of the major problems that faced the administration. The Houston party had failed completely in the field of finance and had left Texas virtually two million dollars in debt, an unwelcome legacy inherited by the Lamar administration.

As an expedient to meet the emergency, the new President hoped to secure a loan of five million dollars in either Europe or the United States. He was particularly eager to get the loan in order to avoid the pitfall into which Houston had stumbled: the continual paper-money issues. As his first move toward obtaining the loan, the President submitted the name of James Hamilton to Congress for confirmation as a commissioner to negotiate in the United States and abroad.[25]

James Hamilton had served one term as governor of South Carolina, had represented that state in the United States House of Representatives from 1822 to 1829, and had organized an army in defense of nullification in 1832. His banking experience included the work of organizing, directing, and for a short time acting as president of the Bank of Charleston. His successful negotiation of a loan in Europe for his own state before coming to Texas well qualified him for the task at hand.[26] Hamilton was instructed to act in concert with Albert T. Burnley, who had been commissioned in the Houston administration and whose appointment had been honored by Lamar. It was understood, however, that Hamilton would handle the greater part of the negotiations in Europe. Although the appointment of Hamilton met with general approval, some discontent was voiced because the appointee could not qualify as an established settler of the Republic. The Houston *Morning Star* asked its readers whether Hamilton received his appointment "before he

---

[24] Barnard E. Bee to Ashbel Smith, September 19, 1838, Bee Papers.

[25] Winkler (ed.), *Secret Journals of the Senate*, 119–20.

[26] Joseph G. de Roulhac Hamilton, "James Hamilton," in Malone (ed.), *Dictionary of American Biography*, VIII (1932), 187–88.

even saw the country,"[27] but there was little difficulty in securing congressional ratification of the appointment. The agents were promised a liberal compensation on any loans they might secure and soon set about their task.

Because of the prevailing hard times in the United States, Texas agents there had fared very poorly in their search for financial aid, but Hamilton decided to call on Nicholas Biddle in Philadelphia in the hope of obtaining a loan. After considerable time and trouble, Hamilton was able to secure both a loan and the promise of Biddle's influence to aid him in his European negotiations. An agreement was made through Biddle with the Bank of the United States whereby the bank agreed to advance $400,000 in exchange for £94,000 in bonds bearing 10 per cent interest. Actually, the loan proved to be a disappointment, for the money, deposited in a bank in New Orleans, consisted of United States post notes. In order to turn these notes into currency the Republic was required to pay a 7½ per cent discount.[28] However, securing the loan was important as an aid to Hamilton in his European negotiations, for the Texas agent could now point to the support and influence of one of the most powerful banks in the United States.

In New York, Hamilton had the bonds engraved but concluded that it would be difficult to negotiate them as they were then made out—10 per cent bonds maturing in thirty years and secured only by government lands. He then wrote to Lamar suggesting that a sinking fund of $300,000 might be created as additional security for the bonds, but the President promised only to lay the matter before Congress for consideration. Hamilton and Burnley then left for England and arrived in London in August, 1839.

As the Texas agents proceeded to Europe, financial conditions at home became increasingly desperate. The Republic's currency was virtually worthless, and there seemed to be no avenue of escape from the steady paper-money issues. The Richmond *Telescope and Register*, leaping at a rumor that Hamilton had achieved the loan, described the perilous situation:[29]

[27] Houston *Morning Star*, April 13, 1839.
[28] William M. Gouge, *The Fiscal History of Texas; Embracing an Account of Its Revenues, Debts, and Currency, from the Commencement of the Revolution in 1834 to 1851–1852,* 97.
[29] Richmond *Telescope and Register,* July 3, 1839.

It is rumored that General Hamilton is about procuring the long talked of Loan. We much need it. The currency of Texas was never in so low a state, and a loan appears to be the only means of placing it at par valuation. Should General Hamilton be the agent of bringing about the removal of so critical a crisis in our financial affairs, Texas will be under obligations to him, she can never repay.

Though they presented their case in vigorous fashion, the Texas agents met with failure in England. To Lamar, Hamilton explained that the unfavorable English harvest of 1838 had caused the export of about seven million pounds of bullion and that the resulting unfavorable exchanges had forced the Bank of England to borrow two million pounds sterling from the Bank of France. The best English securities were of doubtful validity at this time, and Hamilton doubted that he would be able to borrow against Texas securities. Financial conditions in England made it impolitic to bring forward the idea of a loan.[30] Hamilton then requested permission to move on to France and to work for French recognition in harmony with the Texas representative there, James Pinckney Henderson. Hamilton believed that once recognition was accomplished the prospect of a French loan would be increased and that an example set by France might cause an English loan to be rapidly forthcoming.

At the close of the Houston administration, James Pinckney Henderson was at Paris in his capacity as Texas minister to England and France. When Lamar assumed the Presidency of Texas, the French government agreed to commission one of its secretaries at the Washington legation to make an inspection trip to the Republic and to submit a report on the political and economic conditions there. Accordingly, Alphonse de Saligny was sent to Texas and was present there at the commencement of the Lamar administration. While in New York before embarking for England, Hamilton had met with De Saligny and had encouraged him to draft a favorable report concerning his impressions in Texas.[31] When Hamilton arrived at Paris, De Saligny had just returned from his mission and was pre-

[30] Hamilton to Lamar, August 29, 1839, *Lamar Papers,* III, 83–84. Prior to his departure for England, Hamilton had written to the British minister at Washington, Henry S. Fox, requesting British mediation to secure a lasting peace between Texas and Mexico. The proposal at this time was not acted upon. See Hamilton to Fox, May 20, 1839, *Diplomatic Correspondence,* II, 867–68.

[31] Hamilton to Lamar, July 8, 1839, *Diplomatic Correspondence,* II, 459.

paring his report. Lamar, believing that Hamilton could be of assistance to Henderson in his efforts at recognition, gave Hamilton official permission to join the Texas minister at Paris.

In the interim between December, 1838, and August, 1839, or since the beginning of the Lamar administration, Henderson had not been lax in working for recognition. In November, 1838, he had been informed by Anson Jones, the Texas minister to the United States, that the Republic Congress had voted to withdraw the petition for annexation and that Henderson was therefore left free to strive for French recognition and perhaps a commercial treaty, unencumbered by any binding agreements between the Republic and the United States. During Henderson's stay at Paris, conditions between Mexico and France continued to grow worse as a result of unpaid damage claims owed by the Mexican government to certain French citizens residing in Mexico. In February, 1839, the Mexican government issued letters of marque and reprisal which further aggravated relations with the French government. With matters in this state, recognition seemed to hinge upon De Saligny's report, which was expected daily. Henderson wrote home that the government was disposed to recognize Texas because of the Mexican difficulties and would do so quickly if the report was favorable.[32]

In June, Baron M. Pontois, French minister to the United States, arrived in Paris on a leave of absence. Pontois informed Henderson that De Saligny had left Texas before the first of May and that he would deliver his report in person. It was Pontois' opinion that the government would recognize the independence of Texas, and in an interview with the King he strongly advised that policy. By July the Foreign Office had received De Saligny's report, which stated that Texas was in fact independent and recommended recognition. On the basis of the report, Pontois, who had remained in Paris, was commissioned to treat with Henderson. The slavery problem was mentioned as a source of possible friction by the French diplomat, but Henderson contended that the international slave trade was prohibited in Texas and that, since slaves could not be brought into the Republic except from the United States, the number of slaves could not be increased, though their geographical position might be changed. The Texas agent then concluded his argument in rather

[32] Henderson to Bee, February 27, 1839, *ibid.*, 1242.

abrupt fashion by pointing out that slavery in any case was a matter of domestic policy and not the concern of foreign nations.[33]

In the negotiations which followed, Pontois suggested that France might prefer a treaty of amity and commerce and in the same treaty would accord recognition. Henderson wanted France to recognize the independence of Texas first so that the Republic might enter upon the deliberations on an equal basis with the French government; otherwise, it might seem that Texas had entered into the treaty under restraint and had given up privileges which it would not have surrendered in any other case. Pontois took Henderson's request under consideration, but Count Molé, the French foreign minister, would not yield the point. He insisted that recognition must be by treaty rather than by separate act, and negotiations proceeded on that basis.[34]

The terms of the treaty were discussed throughout August. Difficulties arose over the rates on French wines, silks, and ready-made clothing such as shoes and hats. Pontois wanted the silks and wines to enter Texas on the same footing that they entered the United States. As the silks were admitted duty-free at American ports and the wine at a nominal duty, this would represent a major concession on the part of the Lamar government. Henderson felt that he would be compelled to agree to some reduction of the duties imposed in Texas upon French wines and silks, but he would try to secure in return a like reduction by France of the duties on Texas cotton. In a communication to Burnet, then acting secretary of state, Henderson informed his government that Pontois had promised to speak with the ministers of commerce and finance about the proposed reduction of duties on Texas cotton coming into French ports. Henderson was hopeful that the treaty talks would be successful and that recognition would immediately follow.[35]

While some of the final difficulties of the treaty were being adjusted, the French Foreign Office gave indications of delaying the

---

[33] Edwards, "Diplomatic Relations between France and the Republic of Texas," *Southwestern Historical Quarterly*, XX, 220–21.

[34] Schmitz, *Texan Statecraft:1836–1845*, 76.

[35] Henderson to Burnet, August 5, 1839, *Diplomatic Correspondence*, II, 1265. Burnet was acting secretary of state for a short while in place of Barnard E. Bee, who had been commissioned as a special agent to Mexico in an attempt to effect a treaty of peace.

negotiations. This was due to Pontois' information from De Saligny that Hamilton, who had recently arrived in Paris after his unsuccessful efforts to negotiate the British loan, was empowered to offer greater inducements than Henderson and that Hamilton had plenary powers in the treaty deliberations. Henderson felt some natural resentment at Hamilton's arrival and was very perturbed over De Saligny's interference at a point when negotiations were proceeding smoothly. Henderson expressed his chagrin in a letter to Burnet:[36]

... I was not pleased at that speech of Mr. Saligney but reflecting that I was not acting for myself in this business and that a diplomatist ought *never* to evince the slightest anger in the discussion of a Treaty, I contented myself by assuring him that he [Hamilton] had no instructions for me or he would have informed me of it long since as he knew that I would be engaged ere this in discussing the Treaty and moreover I informed him that your despatch did not mention that such was the case.

Hamilton's position was a difficult one. He was primarily interested in the loan, and, believing that the success of his mission depended upon recognition, he was willing to sacrifice some commercial advantages in order to further the chances of a loan. Prior to Hamilton's arrival the French government had agreed to a 25 per cent lower duty on Texas cotton if Texas reduced its tariffs 40 per cent on French wines, 50 per cent on French silks and 20 per cent on French brandies. Hamilton strongly urged Henderson to withdraw the concession on Texas cotton but to retain the corresponding privileges that had been allowed the French products. Henderson protested at first and said that the negotiations should begin again on an entirely new basis, but he finally yielded to Hamilton rather than delay the matter until he could write home for the advice of the President.[37]

The treaty was signed on September 25, 1839, and stipulated that Texas cotton entering France was to pay a duty of twenty francs per one hundred kilograms. French manufactured articles, the principal commodity being silk, were to enter Texas ports at one-half duty, French wines at two-fifths, and French brandies at one-fifth.

[36] Henderson to Burnet, August 20, 1839, *ibid.*, II, 1269.
[37] Edwards, "Diplomatic Relations between France and the Republic of Texas," *Southwestern Historical Quarterly*, XX, 223.

NOTICE.

EACH Emigrant who has removed ... to this Colony, as a part of the Colonists, which I am authorized ... ble, under my contracts with Go-vernment, as Empresario, and ... has not received a title, is notified to present himself ... to me, after the 1st day of December next, and hand in a list in writing ... comply with the 3d article of the Coloni-zation Law, containing the name and ages of the head of the family, his wife, the names and age and sex of each child, the number of depend-dants, or servants, his occupation or trade where removed from, and the date of arrival in this colony with his family, which list must be signed by the applicant.—Single men will also present themselves and hand, in the above list, so far as it is applicable to them. The said list must be made out before ... the office, ... the recommendations, according to the Christianity, morality and ... habits of the applicant, as is required by the 5th article of the said law, must be presented at the same time, in order that if the applicant should be received as a settler by me, his name may be registered, the oath prescribed by the 3d article of the said law administered, and a certificate to that effect issued to him or her. Two dollars must be paid to the Secretary on receipt of such certificate, fifty dollars ... to me, ... of it on the receipt of title and the balance one year thereafter; and ten dollars must be paid to the Sec-retary, five of it on presenting the petition, in form, to the Commissioner, and five on receipt of title.—Notes for these sums must be executed before the above certificate will be issued in which notes all the benefits of law No. 70, approved 23d January 1823, exempting lands, &c. from the pay-ment of debts must be renounced. The above is a compensation for the labor ... of bringing ... the title for the applicant, which I am not bound to do as Empresario; the fees paid for it, the Law, how-ver, does not extend to ... ing land for the settler, each one must do that for himself, under such regulations as may hereafter be established by the Government. Commissioner ... alone is authorised by law, to survey lands and issue titles; the above sums are in payment of the Commission-er's legal fees.—Also, thirty dollars must be paid to the Government on each quarter of a league, in four ... of six years, from date of title and quarter leagues in proportion, besides the stamp paper.

I am daily expecting the Commissioner, and therefore, wish all those who have removed and have their families in the country, to present them-selves as above stated, as soon as possible, after the 1st of December next, in order that they may have their certificate of reception ready to present to him. None, who cannot present satisfactory recommendations and who have not actually removed with their families to this colony, need apply.

The certificate of reception may be declared null and void, any time before the title is issued, should it appear that the applicant had attempt-ed to deceive me by false recommendations or false statements of any kind, or should he remove out of this Colony, or fail to present himself to the Commissioner, within one month after public notice is given to that effect, or should he refuse to comply with the terms of payment herein stated.

I also reserve the right of changing or modifying the terms of payment above stated, any time after the 1st of February next. No attention will be paid to any application, unless made by the applicant in person, and in the manner above stated, for it is evident that no other can take the oath but the applicant.

In order to have uniformity, applicants will use the following form:—

To Mr. S. F. Austin, Empresario—I have emigrated to the Colony, ... as one of the colonists, which you are authorised by Government to intro-duce, and I request that you will examine my recommendations, and if found satisfactory, be so good as to register me under your contracts with the Government. I agree to the terms published by you, of the 20th November, 1829; and am ready to take the oath prescribed by the Coloni-zation Law.

[Here the ... and other particulars, stated in the first paragraph of the above notice, must be inserted in regular order, and also whether the ap-plicant is married or single, widow or widower.]

(Date and Signature.)

S. F. AUSTIN.

Town of Austin, 20th November, 1829.

Stephen F. Austin's empresario notice, 1829

Courtesy of the Texas General Land Office

Santa Anna captures the Alamo, March 6, 1836

Courtesy of the Texas State Library

ARMY ORDERS.

———— ✳ ————

CONVENTION HALL, WASHINGTON, MARCH 2, 1836.

War is raging on the frontiers. Bejar is besieged by two thousand of the enemy, under the command of general **Siezma**. Reinforcements are on their march, to unite with the besieging army. By the last report, our force in Bejar was only one hundred and fifty men strong. The citizens of Texas must rally to the aid of our army, or it will perish. Let the citizens of the East march to the combat. The enemy must be driven from our soil, or desolation will accompany their march upon us. *Independence is declared*, it must be maintained. Immediate action, united with valor, alone can achieve the great work. The services of all are forthwith required in the field.

SAM. HOUSTON,

Commander-in-Chief of the Army.

P. S. It is rumored that the enemy are on their march to Gonzales, and that they have entered the colonies. The fate of Bejar is unknown. The country must and shall be defended. The patriots of Texas are *appealed to, in behalf of their bleeding country.*

S. H.

Broadside issued by Houston as commander-in-chief of the Texas Army
Courtesy of the University of Texas Library

TEXAS!!

Emigrants who are desirious of assis
ng Texas at this important crisis of he
ffairs may have a free passage and equi
ments, by applying at the

NEW-YORK and PHILADELPHIA
HOTEL,

n the Old Levee, near the Blue Stores.

Now is the time to ensure a fortune in Land
To all who remain in Texas during the War w
be allowed 1280 Acres.
To all who remain Six Months, 640 Acres.
To all who remain Three Months, 320 Acres.
And as Colonists, 4600 Acres for a family a
1470 Acres for a Single Man.

New Orleans, April 23d, 1836.

Call for Texas Army volunteers

Santa Anna surrenders to Houston after the Battle of San Jacinto

From a painting in the Texas State Capitol

STEPHEN F. AUSTIN
From Homer S. Thrall, A Pictorial History of Texas, *1879*

WILLIAM H. WHARTON
From Abner J. Strobel, The Old Plantations and Their Owners of Brazoria County, Texas, *1926*

JAMES PINCKNEY HENDERSON
From an old photograph, the University of Texas Library

JAMES HAMILTON
From National Cyclopedia of American Biography, *XII*

Leading political figures of the Republic

DAVID G. BURNET

SAM HOUSTON

MIRABEAU B. LAMAR

ANSON JONES

Presidents of the Republic
From Homer S. Thrall, A Pictorial History of Texas, *1879*

Hall of Independence at Washington-on-the-Brazos

Capitol at Columbia

Capitols of the Republic
    *Drawn by Malcolm Thurgood from originals in the Texas State Library
    and the University of Texas Library*

Capitol at Houston

Capitol at Austin

Capitols of the Republic
    *Drawn by Malcolm Thurgood from originals in the University of Texas
    Library*

View of Austin about 1839

"Redback" issued by Lamar's administration (front above, back below)
Courtesy of the Texas State Library

Texas Navy schooner San Antonio
Courtesy of the University of Texas Library

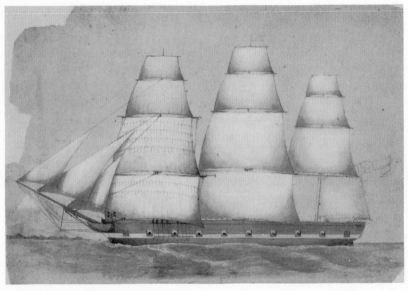

Texas Navy sloop-of-war Austin
Courtesy of the University of Texas Library

Houston delivers inaugural address, 1841
From Charles E. Lester, The Life of Sam Houston, *1855*

Mrs. Eberly saves the archives
From an old print, Courtesy of Texas Parade

Mexican troops capture San Antonio, 1842
From London Illustrated News, *November 5, 1842*

"Mier Expedition—Drawing of the Black Bean," by Frederic Remington
Courtesy of the Hogg Collection, Museum of Fine Arts of Houston

29th Congress, } Begun and held at the city of Washington, in the District of Columbia, on Monday
1st Session. } the first day of December, eighteen hundred and forty-five.

Joint Resolution for the admission of the state of Texas into the Union.

Whereas, the Congress of the United States, by a joint Resolution approved March the first, eighteen hundred and forty-five, did consent that the territory properly included within, and rightfully belonging to the Republic of Texas, might be erected into a new state, to be called The State of Texas, with a republican form of government, to be adopted by the people of said republic, by deputies in Convention assembled, with the consent of the existing government, in order that the same might be admitted as one of the states of the Union; which consent of Congress was given upon certain conditions specified in the first and second sections of said joint Resolution: And whereas, the people of the said Republic of Texas, by deputies in Convention assembled, with the consent of the existing government, did adopt a Constitution and erect a new state, with a republican form of government, and in the name of the people of Texas, and by their authority, did ordain and declare, that they assented to and accepted the proposals, conditions, and guarantees contained in said first and second sections of said resolution: And whereas the said Constitution, with the proper evidence of its adoption by the people of the republic of Texas, has been transmitted to the President of the United States, and laid before Congress, in conformity to the provisions of said Joint Resolution:— Therefore

Resolved by the Senate and House of Representatives of the United States of America in Congress assembled, That the state of Texas shall be one, and is hereby declared to be one, of the United States of America, and admitted into the Union on an equal footing with the original states, in all respects whatever.

Section 2. And be it further resolved, That until the representatives in Congress shall be apportioned according to an actual enumeration of the inhabitants of the United States, the state of Texas shall be entitled to choose two representatives.

John W. Davis   Speaker of the House of Representatives

Geo. M. Dallas.   President of the Senate.

Approved December 29th 1845 —

James K. Polk

Joint resolution for the admission of Texas into the Union, 1845
Courtesy of the Texas Memorial Museum

Henderson, at Hamilton's urging, had given up almost every concession that Texas had desired, but the Republic did gain the recognition of a major European power. The administration hoped that the French action would in time influence the British government to act in the same manner and the example of recognition by France would show the United States the Republic's importance as an independent power.

With recognition accomplished, Henderson found time to marry and then returned to England. His efforts for a treaty comparable to the one he had negotiated in Paris were not successful in London, and he soon returned to Texas, arriving at Galveston in January, 1840. Hamilton, meanwhile, turned his attention to procuring a loan in France. He felt that with recognition accomplished a loan would be easier to negotiate, but the Texas agent was doomed to disappointment again. While in Texas on his tour of inspection De Saligny had implied that a French loan might be realized if part of the sum were used to strengthen the Republic's frontier and thus ensure a plan by which French manufactured goods could reach the Mexican trade through Texas ports. Hamilton made the most of this point in his talks with French capitalists and government officials, but the depressed money market at the time also had its repercussions in France, and success again eluded the agent. Failing to accomplish his mission, Hamilton returned to Texas via England and arrived home late in the fall of 1839.[38]

With prospects of the loan dimmer than ever, the administration was forced to find some expedient for its grave financial problems. The mistakes made by the Houston party in the issuance of paper money was apparent to all, but the Lamar clique was forced to the same solution as a last resort. Also, to further depress conditions, the President displayed his lack of practical sense in financial affairs by allowing the expenditures of government to increase far beyond those during Houston's term of office. Appropriations for civil purposes skyrocketed from $192,000 under Houston's last Congress to $555,000 under Lamar's first. This was not because of an increase in existing salaries but because of the hiring of additional department clerks, the increased requirements of the postal service, and the

[38] Schmitz, *Texan Statecraft: 1836–1845*, 85.

costs incidental to the removal of the capital from Houston to Austin.[39] In addition, expenditures for the army and navy increased from $881,000 under Houston's final Congress to $1,523,445 under the initial Lamar Congress, which adjourned in late January, 1839.

The outstanding circulation in paper money at the close of the Houston administration had been $800,000. Houston had vetoed one bill calling for an increase in the circulation of paper money, and he never did sympathize with the reckless policy adopted by Congress. Lamar, in contrast, failed to make any attempts to stop the flow of worthless paper. From January, 1839, to September of the same year, the Third Congress of the Republic issued $1,569,-010 in paper-money notes. By September, 1840, $1,983,790 more in paper notes had been issued—a total, not including reissues, of $3,552,800. The estimated amount in circulation on September 30, 1839, was $2,013,762 and on September 30, 1841, was $2,920,-860.75.[40] The first issues of paper money, or "redbacks," as they were called, were valued at only about 37.5 cents on the dollar, and by November, 1840, they had fallen to 16.66 cents. The reckless policy of the administration in sanctioning these expenditures of Congress, coupled with the charge of excessive patronage because of additional appointments, resulted in increased opposition to the government. The Houston *Morning Star* confessed itself disgusted with the President's policy and poured forth its invective:[41]

. . . Already since the inauguration of Gen. Lamar, our money, on account merely of the extravagant issues, has decreased in value about forty cents on the dollar; and still his cry is that of the horse leech, "Give! Give!" The truth is, that His Excellency has too lively an imagination to be successful in his attempt to "economize the public resources." The inexhaustable mines of the San Saba valley are too constantly present to his mind, and lead him to act and talk as though their boundless wealth was already in his grasp. Else how could he talk of standing armies, lines of military posts, the invasion of Mexico, &c. &c. We conclude that his flowery language on these subjects must be "all for talks sake" and to show what mighty schemes may be engendered in the brain of a very ordinary man; or else as we hinted above, that the San Saba gold mines have turned his head.

[39] Miller, *A Financial History of Texas,* 21. [40] *Ibid.,* 70.
[41] Houston *Morning Star,* November 27, 1839.

The failure to attain the loan in Europe and the resulting financial plight in Texas constituted the first major disappointments for the Lamar group. Texas was in sore financial straits from which no remedy appeared to be forthcoming.

In the field of foreign affairs, Lamar, in accordance with his campaign promise, made a definite attempt to secure an honorable peace with Mexico. In his inaugural address, Lamar indicated that the Republic would not renew the annexation discussions with the United States and that Texans should devote their energies to building up the nation's internal resources.[42] In accordance with this general plan, James Pinckney Henderson had been ordered to remain at Paris, and James Hamilton was commissioned as the Republic's financial agent to both England and France. Henderson had succeeded in gaining French recognition, and though Hamilton had returned empty-handed there was hope for the future. However, the government most passionately desired peace with Mexico. The failure of Mexican recognition had impeded Hamilton's efforts in Europe and also had forestalled the annexation negotiations. Lamar reasoned that if a legitimate peace was obtained with Mexico, in which the recognition of Texan independence must be *sine qua non*, the prospects of aid from abroad would increase immeasurably. Therefore, the President decided to humble the nation's pride and make the initial overture in the peace deliberations by appointing a special agent to Mexico.

Lamar decided to try for peace at a time when Mexico was undergoing another period of internal strife. The government of France had declared war after arbitration attempts had failed to secure payment of the claims due French citizens residing in Mexico. Santa Anna, because of his heroic conduct at the battle of Vera Cruz, was once again a national hero.[43] Upon the completion of the "Pastry War," as the difficulty with France was later referred to, Anastasio Bustamante, the leader of the Centralists and the established President of the nation, was forced to surrender the government to the reinstated hero. Then the wily Santa Anna, realizing the financial problems that he would face, made a great show of

[42] The Inaugural Address of Mirabeau B. Lamar, President of the Republic of Texas," in *Lamar Papers*, II, 319–20.
[43] Schmitz, *Texan Statecraft: 1836–1845*, 89.

121

allowing Bustamante to return to office four months later. He was only too happy to allow Bustamante and his party to flounder in office while ruling from behind the scenes.[44] The attention of Mexico was thus occupied with the abortive war with France and the rapid settlement of internal differences, certainly not with matters pertaining to Texas. Lamar decided to act, feeling that Santa Anna would assume the reins of the presidency when the moment best suited him and that the Mexican leader would be favorable to peace negotiations.

The President's peace plan consisted of two major points. An envoy would be sent directly to Mexico to press for terms, and at the same time a minister would journey to the United States to attempt to secure the mediation of that country. Thus, efforts would be made simultaneously from two sides. Richard Dunlap, who had been serving as secretary of the treasury, was sent to Washington to manage affairs there. Dunlap in his youth had been a personal protégé of Jackson's, and it was felt that this closeness to Van Buren's mentor would aid him in his deliberations with the United States. He was instructed to solicit the good offices of Secretary of State John Forsyth to bring about the desired end. Forsyth had proved himself consistently hostile to Texas pretensions, leaving Dunlap an extremely difficult task. The Texas representative was instructed to use his discretion in approaching the Mexican minister at Washington if Forsyth proved reluctant to recommend the mediation of the United States. Finally, Dunlap was told that his and Bee's commissions were of equal importance and that the two agents should keep in constant touch with each other and work in perfect harmony.[45]

Dunlap proceeded to Washington and took possession of the archives of the legation. He broached the subject of mediation during his first interview with Secretary Forsyth, and the reaction of the American government was to offer to sponsor the mediation proceedings should Mexico prove to be willing. Accordingly, Forsyth instructed Powhatan Ellis, the United States minister to Mexico, to stand ready to interpose the good offices of the United States between Texas and Mexico if and when the latter nation asked for

44 *Ibid.*, 91–92.
45 Webb to Dunlap, March 13, 1839, *Diplomatic Correspondence*, I, 368–72.

them but meanwhile to observe a strict neutrality.[46] Dunlap then busied himself with the unsettled boundary question between the United States and Texas and anxiously awaited word of Bee's success at Mexico City.

The instructions to Bee, drafted by James Webb, who had become secretary of state upon Bee's appointment as special agent, were more explicit in nature. It was assumed that Bee would not be received as an accredited minister from the Republic to Mexico, for that would imply the recognition of Texas independence, and therefore the envoy was given separate credentials as a special agent. The final decision was left to his discretion, but Bee was advised not to make known his higher functions as a minister until he had sounded his way as an agent and ascertained whether or not the Mexican government was disposed to treat with him in either capacity. His powers as a special agent were plenary, and he was fully authorized to negotiate a treaty of peace. Bee was bound by only two provisions of his instructions. He was to sign no treaty which did not unconditionally recognize Texas independence, and he was to insist upon the settlement of the Texas-Mexican boundary at the Rio Grande rather than at the Nueces. Other than his instructions on these two points, both of which were made absolutely essential to any permanent treaty signed with Mexico, the Texas agent was left free to use his discretion in all cases.[47]

On his way to Mexico, Bee arrived at New Orleans in April, 1839. He remained there nearly a month and conferred with General Hamilton, who was about to depart for Europe on his first quest for the loan. While in New Orleans, and through the intervention of Hamilton, Bee met with the representatives of the British commercial house of Lizardi and Company, one of the chief bondholders of the Mexican debt to Britain, which in 1839 amounted to about fifty million dollars. In accordance with his instructions, Bee was prepared to pay up to five million dollars for the recognition of Texas if the boundary dispute over the Nueces and the Rio Grande was settled at the Rio Grande. The agents of the commercial house now proposed that Richard Pakenham, the British minister to Mex-

[46] Schmitz, *Texan Statecraft*, 92.
[47] Webb to Bee, February 20, 1839, *Diplomatic Correspondence*, II, 433–34.

ico, persuade that nation to satisfy its obligations to the British bondholders to the extent of five million dollars by locating land for them in the territory claimed by Texas. In return, Mexico would receive the sum of five million dollars from Texas and agree to the Rio Grande as the boundary line. If the plan was a success then Mexico would fulfill part of its obligations to the British bondholders and receive a large cash amount in addition. Also, Texas would receive the boundary line it claimed, with the prospect of British settlers, and the bondholders would collect what was considered to be a bad debt.[48] The plan was outlined in a communication to Pakenham at Mexico City, and he was informed that Bee would present it upon his arrival.

Bee sailed from New Orleans on the United States schooner *Woodbury* and arrived at Vera Cruz on May 8. He was received by a ranking Mexican military officer, General Guadaloupe Victoria and was treated with all courtesy. Victoria had been instructed to look upon Bee as a private citizen and to get a written statement from him setting forth his objectives. If the Texas agent came as a commissioner from one of the many rebellious provinces within Mexico, his proposals might be considered; but if he came to treat for recognition of independence, he would not be granted a hearing and Victoria should ask him to depart.

Actually, Bee was asking the impossible, for no Mexican party could afford the blow to its popularity that official recognition of an agent from Texas would mean. The Vera Cruz *Censor*, in its comments on Bee's mission, serves as an index to popular opinion in Mexico at the time:[49]

We do not know which most to admire, the audacity of those brigand in sending us their pedlar, (marchante,) to ask us to allow them the quiet and pacific possession of their robbery, or the answer the commandant general gave to the individual who appraised him of the arrival of this Quixotic ambassador. From the tenor of the reply, it appears that if he lands, he will be accommodated with lodgings at the prison Nevertheless, the supreme government will designate what definitely ought to be done. The commandant says, he is not aware of the exist

[48] Schmitz, *Texan Statecraft: 1836–1845*, 92.
[49] Vera Cruz *Censor*, quoted in Houston *Telegraph and Texas Register*, June 5 1839.

ence of a nation called the republic of Texas, but only a horde of adventurers in rebellion against the laws of the government of the republic.

The Mexican government, upon learning from General Victoria the true nature of Bee's proposals, refused to receive the Texas emissary. By the end of May, Bee realized that he would accomplish nothing by remaining in Vera Cruz. In a letter to James Webb, Bee stated that the negotiations should have first been opened at Washington before an attempt was made to secure recognition from Mexico. The Texas agent believed that if he was given permission to continue on to Washington and meet with the Mexican authorities there his efforts might result in some success. Bee reasoned that the good will of the United States might be used for mediation if negotiations were commenced at the American capital.[50]

In a despairing mood Bee sailed for New Orleans on June 1, 1839. At just about this time Pakenham received correspondence from Lizardi and Company about the proposed scheme whereby British bondholders would receive lands in the disputed boundary area. In an interview with Manuel Gorostiza, the Mexican foreign minister, Pakenham urged the recognition of Texas independence at an early date. The Foreign Minister admitted the general advisability of recognition but added that the government dare not risk such an unpopular act. Furthermore, he indicated that a settlement of the boundary dispute at the Rio Grande was out of the question. Despite the unfavorable outcome of the interview, Pakenham felt that if the offer of five million dollars was actually made it would prove too tempting to resist. The British Minister also felt that the reconquest of Texas was an impossibility and contended that Bee's failure was without significance for with proper management success could be attained. He advised an armistice as a preliminary move, though Bee's opposition to that policy was well known.[51]

Bee's commission to go to Mexico in the character of a minister and not as a secret agent destroyed his effectiveness. This was the opinion held by many who were conversant with the Mexican character. Here the sentiments of Joel Poinsett, formerly United States minister to Mexico, are enlightening. Samuel A. Roberts, secretary

---

[50] Bee to Webb, May 28, 1839, *Diplomatic Correspondence*, II, 449.
[51] Ephraim D. Adams, *British Interests and Activities in Texas, 1838–1846*, 26–28.

of the Texas Legation at Washington, in writing to President Lamar, gave this account:[52]

Great interest is felt by the Government here in regard to the proposed treaty of amity between Texas & Mexico—We had first heard of Col. Bee's departure from Vera Cruz which being mentioned gave Mr. Poinsett an opportunity to go somewhat at length into the subject & as he expressed himself freely and as I thought very sensibly and in a statesman like manner I particularly noted what passed. . . . He in the first place condemned the *policy* of sending a *public* minister to Mexico at all—and gave some of his reasons that Santa Anna or who ever might be at the head of the Govt. could not receive him in his *public capacity* without first acknowledging the very thing which was the *object* of the mission Viz—The Independence of Texas—thereby *concluding* the Treaty before it was begun!! He hinted also that the agent selected was too *fussy*, too fond of show, to conduct *secretly* a business of this magnitude & importance,—and I believe he knows him well. . . . It is Mr. Poinsett's opinion that a *secret* agent might have effected the object of the mission.

When Bee reached New Orleans he found a letter from Colonel Juan Almonte, an influential friend of both Santa Anna and Bustamante, informing him that the government had reconsidered and was now willing to listen to the propositions of the Texas government. At this point the involved negotiations took on a cloak-and-dagger aspect. Some time before Bee left Vera Cruz he had met an Italian, John Vitalba, who was acting as Santa Anna's secret agent under instructions to communicate with any representatives of Texas. On his way to New Orleans, in accordance with his mission, Vitalba learned of Bee's presence in Vera Cruz and called on him. The Texas agent, having once failed in his attempt to establish communication with official Mexico, was not particularly eager to meet with Vitalba. However, in the overtures of Santa Anna's agent, Bee sensed a disposition on the part of the Mexican authorities to negotiate. Vitalba's instructions involved too much secrecy to suit Bee's taste, and he felt that it would be wiser to deal openly with the Mexican government. Vitalba far from being discouraged, sailed for New Orleans on the same boat with Bee.[53]

[52] Samuel A. Roberts to Lamar, July 9, 1839, *Lamar Papers*, III, 36.
[53] Bee to Webb, May 13, 1839, *Diplomatic Correspondence*, II, 445.

The Lamar government found their next agent in the person of James Treat. The prospective appointee, a merchant with offices in New York, was interested in the affairs of Texas. He was friendly with Samuel Swartwout, who had business connections in the Republic, and had kept in fairly regular correspondence with James Morgan, an agent of Swartwout's and one of the early settlers of Galveston. Treat had spent a large part of his life in South America and had resided in Mexico for seven years, during which time he had made the acquaintance of Santa Anna and other Mexican leaders. He also spoke Spanish well and had been in correspondence with Vitalba, whom he regarded as a good friend. After receiving a communication from Vitalba, Treat became convinced that the situation in Mexico was ripe and that, if secret overtures were made and the right persons reached, the recognition of Texas might result.[54] Treat communicated his views to Morgan, who then wrote to Lamar recommending that Treat be sent as a secret agent to Mexico.[55] The President, with Bee's failure before him, was not overly impressed by Morgan's suggestion, and the matter was allowed to rest for some time.

Meanwhile, Treat continued to correspond with Morgan and spoke of his desire to proceed to Mexico. In June, 1839, Treat met with General Hamilton in New York, after which Hamilton made inquiries concerning Treat's character and general fitness for any mission he might undertake. With his own doubts satisfied, Hamilton next wrote to Lamar suggesting that Treat could be of assistance to Bee in further talks with the Mexican government. Hamilton wrote Bee that Treat was on his way to New Orleans to confer with Vitalba, that he should join them both there, and that he would find Treat of great service to him in his efforts to secure peace.[56]

Treat arrived in New Orleans on July 9, 1839, and at once set about to convince Bee of the propriety of his proposed undertaking.

---

[54] Schmitz, *Texan Statecraft: 1836–1845*, 97.

[55] Morgan to Lamar, December 27, 1839, Morgan Papers.

[56] Hamilton to Lamar, June 28, 1839, *Diplomatic Correspondence*, II, 453. See Bee to Webb, July 5, 1839, *ibid.*, 457. Hamilton and Bee did not meet in New Orleans, and Hamilton erroneously assumed that Bee would return to Mexico to make another attempt at recognition, thus the reference to Treat as being willing to assist Bee in any further negotiations.

The New Yorker felt that a secret agent having the right connections in Mexico and empowered to pay a fee to bring the right influences to bear would meet with success. Bee confessed himself impressed with Treat's reasoning and recommended to the government that his plan be adopted. In submitting the plan Bee was fully aware that as the negotiations progressed the "way would have to be paved with gold,"[57] and he supposed that the whole project would involve the spending of from half a million to a million dollars. It was his opinion, however, that the necessary money could be taken out of the five million dollars he was authorized to spend in fixing the boundary and that a sufficient balance would still be left to settle the dispute. As their acquaintance ripened, Bee came to place complete trust in Treat's ability to accomplish the mission and urged him to proceed to Austin and present his plans in person to President Lamar.

In a message delivered to the Senate and House of Representatives on December 10, 1839, the President expressed his belief that a secret mission to Mexico would be successful. Lamar stated that he had the assurances of Bee and Pakenham that a secret agent would be received by the Mexican government.[58] Congress expressed no objections to the scheme, and the President, favorably impressed with Treat as a result of a series of personal interviews, decided to commission Treat a private or confidential agent of the Texas government. Treat's instructions were similar to those which had previously been issued to Bee. The recognition of independence and the Rio Grande boundary were again required in any treaty negotiated. Treat was allowed to spend five million dollars to secure the boundary settlement, and any money that might be used as bribery must be taken from that sum. Also, the agent was empowered to spend an additional thousand dollars for whatever agents or assistants he might require after his arrival in Mexico. Treat was authorized to call upon the United States Minister at Mexico City, Powhatan Ellis, if he thought the good offices of the United States could be used in any plans for mediation. Finally, Treat was instructed to negotiate treaties of amity and commerce if

---

[57] Bee to Webb, July 9, 1839, *Diplomatic Correspondence*, II, 461.
[58] Winkler (ed.), *Secret Journals of the Senate*, 148–49.

he was successful in settling the questions of independence and boundary.[59]

Though the times appeared auspicious for Treat's mission, developments in Mexico prior to his departure were to hinder his work. In one of the constant revolutions against the Centralist government, the Federalist party had succeeded in establishing independent settlements along the Rio Grande. The Lamar party favored the Federalist cause, and early in 1839 the President issued a proclamation opening trade with the Republic of the Rio Grande. In an attempt to secure a binding alliance, the Federalist leaders, Generals Pedro Anaya and Antonio Canales, came to Austin and asked for aid to the revolutionary states of Mexico, which they asserted included Tamaulipas, San Luís Potosí, Zacatecas, Jalisco, Nuevo Leon, Coahuila, Durango, Sinaloa, Chihuahua, New Mexico, and the Californias. The government maintained a neutral policy, but General Canales successfully recruited a force of Texans without the consent of the administration.

The recruits crossed the border with Canales and later took part in some sporadic fighting. Lamar, realizing that Treat's mission was being endangered because of the aid that the Federalists were receiving, issued an official announcement of neutrality and enjoined all citizens of Texas to refrain from participating in any acts of hostility. Then, in order to announce the President's proclamation to the Texans who had joined the Federalists, Colonel Benjamin H. Johnson with a small force crossed the Rio Grande to the camp of the Federalists. On their way back the entire party was captured and put to death. The administration, though outraged, contented itself with a formal protest to the Mexican government, thus indicating Lamar's willingness not to embarrass the Treat negotiations.[60]

Treat arrived in Mexico in late December, 1839, and immediately commenced activities which he hoped would lead to recognition of Texas independence. He had decided to effect his aims through the intervention of his friends in Mexico, and if that failed he would negotiate through the ministers of England and the United States.

[59] Ibid., 156–59.

[60] Hubert Howe Bancroft, History of the North Mexican States and Texas, I, 328.

Treat explained that by the use of this method he would be enabled to "reserve a *shot* or *two* in the *locker,* so that my *first defeat* shall not be *exactly* final."[61] Despite Lamar's disavowal of aid to the Federalists, the Mexican government resumed a hostile attitude toward Texas. Treat arrived in time to find the Mexican Congress considering two measures to cope with the Federalist uprising and the aid that might be forthcoming from Texas in defiance of Lamar's proclamation. One act petitioned Congress for special powers to levy taxes to support a war against Texas, and the other proposed to make it treasonable for anyone to write or speak in favor of Texas.[62] Originally Treat felt that the act asking for appropriations to levy war was desirable, for he was of the opinion that, upon the Texas victory, an unconditional recognition of independence would be the basis of any peace treaty. But as the session of Congress lingered on and nothing was accomplished, the envoy's patience began to wear thin. Suffering from tuberculosis, and in general ill-humor because of the apparent failure of his plans, Treat outlined his difficulties in a communication to Lamar.[63]

. . . If I had *only* to *convince a majority* of both Houses of Congress—a *majority* of the Cabinet and the President—and more than *half* the *Sensible men* who *besides the above,* are in office, and the *same proportion* of *intelligent men out of office* whose opinions would be *worth something, of the policy advantages,* nay, the *necessity* of an amicable arrangement now, I would say to you, Sir, "I will accomplish your wishes, *only give me a little time,*" I should *honestly* believe I could make *good* my word. But when *all this* is *done,* then comes the fears, doubts, and *apprehensions,* of *consequences—whether* it will prove *unpopular, whether* the Cabinet will be broken up and lose *their places*—and whether a Revolution, *might not* be the Consequence, etc., etc., *Hence* the *necessity* of *dividing up* the *responsibility* beginning with *Congress,* and placing the *Executive* and *Cabinet* in an *easy position to act,* while the public and even *Congress itself may be* ignorant of *what is really going on.* It is only *thus, we trust,* they will be able *to get over* the *anticipated* difficulty.

After much delay, and finally through the intervention of Paken-

[61] Treat to Hamilton, December 16, 1839, *Diplomatic Correspondence,* II, 511.
[62] Schmitz, *Texan Statecraft: 1836–1845,* 116–17.
[63] Treat to Lamar, January 1, 1840, *Diplomatic Correspondence,* II, 526.

ham, Treat secured an interview with the Secretary of State, Juan Cañedo. Though the meeting was conducted on a friendly and informal basis, Cañedo objected to the irregularity of Treat's credentials. Treat had been furnished with an official, signed set of instructions, but he had not been given separate credentials independent of the instructions. The Secretary of State contended that without the separate document to establish the validity of Treat's powers the talks could not proceed because President Bustamante and others would object to the irregularity. Cañedo then insisted that Pakenham guarantee the validity of Treat's credentials before the negotiations could be allowed to proceed. Pakenham did so early in February, 1840, but then Cañedo maintained that deliberations could not commence unless Pakenham gave a formal and official guarantee that his government would acknowledge any stipulations Mexico and Texas might enter into in the course of the negotiations. This highly unusual demand could not be complied with, and Treat was again rebuffed.

It was apparent that the Mexican government was chiefly concerned with putting Treat off but at the same time not confronting him with an absolute refusal. Cañedo and Bustamante were aware that an unequivocal refusal might drive the Texans into an alliance with the Federalists and that the recognition of Treat's demands would surely prove very unpopular in Mexico. Confronted by this dilemma, the government could only negotiate in complete secrecy. Treat was willing to accept these conditions because he believed that the government might soon become stable enough to hear his proposals regardless of the wishes of many of the people. However, in Treat's thinking the wish was father to the thought, for he wrote to Lamar that both Bustamante and Cañedo were well aware of the commercial benefits that would follow hard upon recognition; that the Mexican government realized it could never again reconquer Texas; and that as soon as the government was bolstered up to the point that it could negotiate in defiance of popular sentiment secrecy could be dispensed with, allowing the deliberations to proceed at a speedy tempo. Treat did admit that any policy was subject to political considerations, but he was sanguine in the belief that official recognition would soon take place.[64]

[64] Treat to Lamar, February 15, 1840, *ibid.*, 566–68.

On February 13, 1840, Treat submitted a memorandum to the Mexican government setting forth his aims. As a result, he was granted an interview with Cañedo, who stated that his government could not negotiate on the basis of Texas independence but that there was a chance that Mexico would consider an armistice, since this would not involve the surrender of any sovereignty. Taking this report as a favorable omen, Treat, through Pakenham, then submitted the definite propositions for recognition and the boundary settlement at the Rio Grande for an indemnity not exceeding five million dollars. In the meantime, Treat's official credentials arrived, and in May, 1840, the propositions which he had submitted were brought before the executive council of the government, a department in the executive branch of the Mexican government independent of the cabinet. After much deliberation the council agreed to the steps taken by Cañedo, and the complete papers were handed over to Congress in July. This policy was followed because the secret negotiations had now become a matter of public concern, and Congress demanded the right to debate the issue. As submitted to the Mexican legislative body the subject required a simple affirmative or negative vote. A negative vote would end the whole affair, and Treat could start back for Texas. On the other hand, an affirmative vote would not necessarily indicate ultimate success; it would mean only that the way for negotiations would be open and that Treat's propositions would be officially considered.[65]

Treat expected Congress to act quickly upon the question but was again disappointed. The Federalist party in Yucatan, rebelling against the exorbitant tax rates imposed by Mexico City, succeeded in capturing the Yucatan Peninsula from the armies of the Centralists early in June, 1840. The Federalists then set up a sovereign government, though remaining ostensibly loyal to the Mexican constitution of 1824. The situation was similar to that of Texas at the time of the Revolution, and it was well known in Texas that a declaration of complete independence on the part of the Yucatan Federalists was wholly dependent upon outside aid. Lamar had failed to take advantage of a possible alliance with the Federalists of the Republic of the Rio Grande, and had been sorely tried by the constant trickery of Cañedo and Bustamante. Feeling that Treat might accom-

[65] Schmitz, *Texan Statecraft: 1836–1845*, 117.

plish nothing, the President now determined to embarrass the Centralists by effectively giving aid to the Federalists in Yucatan. The administration knew that an alliance with Yucatan, separated from Texas by the Gulf of Mexico, would not be so likely to lead to subsequent clashes of territorial interests as an alliance with the Republic of the Rio Grande would certainly have been. This attitude was well founded, for Canales, as President of the rebel republic, claimed all of northern Mexico, including the Californias and present-day Arizona and New Mexico—regions which the Texas Republic hoped in time to claim.[66]

After much deliberation, Lamar decided to send the skeleton navy on a cruise in the Gulf. Commodore Edwin W. Moore, the ranking Texas naval officer, was instructed to prevent a blockade of Texas ports by the Mexican navy, to establish communication with the Federalists of Yucatan, and to communicate with Treat, who was expected to have finished his mission by this time. Lamar's decision to send the navy on a cruise and his attempts to ally with the Yucatan Federalists met with unanimous approval in Texas. A campaign against Mexico was always popular, and even the Houston *Morning Star*, which had constantly been in violent opposition to the principles of the administration, joined in the general cry of approval:[67]

That the efficient aid which these vessels could render the malcontents, and the loss and terror they could inspire among the Centralists, would contribute in an eminent degree to bring the Mexican government to terms with us, we think no one who has reflected upon the subject can doubt. The commerce of Mexico is already nearly prostrated; Yucatan is revolutionized; the north and east is in arms, and the cause of Federalism in Tampico and in several other towns upon the coast, though partially smothered, is far from being extinguished. All that is wanting to complete the overthrow of the Central authority are union among the disaffected, and the efficient cooperation of our navy. The former can easily be brought about by diplomacy and by the promise of such cooperation, and, as our navy is now fortunately situated, the latter can be granted with little or no sacrifice. . . . Beyond a doubt, captures and contributions can be made more than sufficient to meet all addi-

[66] Hill, *The Texas Navy,* 125.
[67] Houston *Morning Star,* July 18, 1840.

POLITICAL HISTORY OF THE TEXAS REPUBLIC

tional expenditures which have been incurred, if not to cover the whole outlay.

Lamar informed Treat of the new policy through a communication sent by the Secretary of State, Abner Lipscomb, who had succeeded Webb in January, 1840. The President indicated that the nation was weary of the Mexican negotiations and that if in Treat's opinion further deliberations would prove futile the envoy should return home immediately. However, Treat was instructed to stay on at Mexico City if he thought he would be successful in later meetings. Lamar also stated that, if a treaty of peace should prove impossible to negotiate, an armistice should be arranged for as long a period as possible—from one to three years with a six months' cancellation notice, if such could be obtained. The government felt that an armistice might be preferable to a treaty, for it would enable the Republic to dictate any terms at the expiration of the armistice, so confident were the Texans that their military strength would in time be respected. Also, Lamar felt that a treaty at the present time, when the Republic was soliciting for it, would of necessity entail many sacrifices.[68]

The message from the President was sent to Treat by Commodore Moore, who was under orders to station himself in Vera Cruz waters and wait thirteen days for an answer from Treat. If the negotiations were to cease, Treat would quit his post and inform Moore, who would then regard the information as an order to prey upon Mexican commerce.[69] The new instructions to Treat were dated at Galveston on June 13, 1840, and though Moore dispatched them from Vera Cruz through the British Minister, Pakenham, they were so delayed that Treat did not receive them until August 13. Therefore, the period of time during which Moore was to wait for an answer had already expired when Treat received his instructions. Since Treat did not know whether Moore was still waiting for him, and because his new instructions authorized a truce, Treat decided to exercise his discretion and continue the talks, estimating that a month or less would be required to negotiate a truce.

Upon receiving his new instructions, Treat informed Pakenham

[68] Abner Lipscomb to Treat, June 13, 1840, *Diplomatic Correspondence*, II, 643–45.

[69] Lamar to Moore, June 20, 1840, *ibid.*, 651–52.

that he was now seeking an armistice if a lasting peace treaty could not be obtained. The British Minister concurred in this plan and advised Treat on the formulation of a new statement of the Texas position. This document, which Treat submitted to Cañedo, placed emphasis on the peaceful and neutral attitude which Texas had maintained toward the Republic of the Rio Grande and set forth the conventional arguments concerning the established independence of Texas, the recognition of that state by both the United States and France, and the inability of Mexico to reconquer Texas. Finally, the envoy stated that since a treaty of peace was out of the question the Republic would content itself with an honorable armistice.[70]

After prolonging his vigil for several additional weeks, during which time there was no answer from the Mexican government, Treat decided to bring matters to a head. On September 5, 1840, he addressed another communication to Cañedo stating that he had been in Mexico for the past nine months and could report nothing of a favorable nature to his government. Treat contended that conditions were very urgent and stated that, unless he received some assurance before September 18 satisfying him of the true intentions of the Mexican government, he would be forced to ask for his passports and withdraw from his post.

The waiting period expired without any official action on the part of Mexico, and on September 21 Treat requested his passports. At this point Pakenham proposed to bring forward the matter of an armistice, and a document drawn up by Treat setting forth the Texas terms was now submitted by the British Minister. In his final attempt at a settlement, Treat demanded a truce for a period of three or four years, with the Rio Grande as the boundary line. However, the Mexican government definitely objected to the Rio Grande, and on September 29 Treat was given his passports. The envoy wished to depart immediately, but upon the insistent urging of Pakenham he decided to remain a week longer.

As matters developed, however, the additional delay accomplished nothing. Pakenham urged the Mexican government to give consideration to an armistice, but he finally conceded defeat and wrote to Treat, telling him that further attempts would be useless.

[70] Schmitz, *Texan Statecraft: 1836–1845*, 124–25.

135

In the British Minister's opinion, Mexico would not act in a reasonable manner concerning the armistice and had absolutely refused to consider it. Pakenham felt that the government would never officially negotiate with Treat and that if an armistice were to be considered possible the Mexican authorities would insist that the line of separation be the San Antonio River rather than the Rio Grande. Faced with such basic and irreconcilable differences, Pakenham believed that Treat should leave the country.[71]

Treat made final preparations for his leave-taking, but ill-health detained him a short while longer. Upon his departure he promised that if Texas took up arms against Mexico the Republic would not attempt to extend its boundary beyond the Rio Grande. He also gave his promise to counsel the Texas authorities to follow a policy of peace, which was completely in accord with the British Minister's sentiments.[72] On his part, Pakenham gave his word to continue in his role as mediator and to be ready at all times to communicate to the Mexican government any overtures that the Texans might think proper to make.[73]

Treat was never able to relay these matters to the authorities at home, for he died of consumption on board the schooner-of-war *San Antonio* on November 13, 1840. John Vitalba, who was traveling with him, took charge of his official papers and forwarded them to the government of Texas. The mission had been a failure and had cost the agent his life. The Texas populace, saddened at the death of Treat and disgusted at the lack of any effective settlement of the Mexican difficulties, united in the clamor for war. The Houston *Morning Star*, accurately reflecting the general will, observed that "forbearance on account of pending negotiations is no longer necessary; and the late hostile active operations of our navy render a resort to arms imperative."[74] Bee and Treat had failed; an alliance with Yucatan was in the offing; and a gloomy atmosphere pervaded the Republic.

[71] Adams, *British Interests and Activities in Texas*, 47.
[72] Vitalba to Lamar, December 8, 1840, enclosing letter from Treat to Pakenham, October 14, 1840, *Diplomatic Correspondence*, II, 722.
[73] Adams, *British Interests and Activities in Texas*, 49.
[74] Houston *Morning Star*, November 28, 1840.

One Failure After Another

THE SOLE OBJECT of Lamar is to insure, to secure, his reelection. And the country has to pay for his experiment; but he ought not to presume too far upon the forbearance of an injured, an oppressed people. We are to adjourn on Thursday next, so say both Houses of Congress. God knows we are doing no good by staying here. Congress meets too often and does too much. The printing of Congress would break any nation, and when it is done the country has paid for a beautiful batch of lawsuits.[1]

IN ADDITION TO the financial plight of the nation, the inability to achieve an honorable peace with Mexico further discredited the Lamar party. It was true that while the removal of the capital to Austin and the expulsion of the Cherokees were generally

[1] Houston to Anthony Butler, February 2, 1841, *Houston Writings*, II, 366.

popular with the people of Texas yet even those measures had made enemies for the administration. Lamar's position was made still more delicate by the deterioration of his relations with Congress. His term had begun harmoniously; every advantage had been given the President so that he would not follow in the dismal steps of his predecessor. Congress had granted Lamar extensive powers in military affairs and finance, and he had been allowed to exercise a wide jurisdiction.[2] Because of this auspicious debut, Lamar's failures were especially galling to his friends and particularly pleasing to his enemies. The *Brazos Courier*, which generally was not unfavorable to the administration, summed up the existing situation in May, 1839:[3]

The present administration has in no wise met the expectations of its friends, nor afforded any decided cause for gratulation to the patriotic of any party. No man, perhaps, ever assumed the Government of a Nation surrounded with such a host of friends, or possessed of such facilities of effecting good, as Gen. Lamar.—At the opening of the last session of Congress, he found the legislative influence, with rare unanimity, ready to sustain and enforce Executive action. How he has improved these advantages, let us learn from the decided and emphatic expression of disappointment that may be heard from every homestead.

In July, 1839, as accurate a political observer as Ashbel Smith commented in a letter to Memucan Hunt: "There is a very strong opposition to the Administration and apparently increasing."[4] Hunt, writing from New Orleans, communicated his fears to Lamar and entreated the party chieftain to play the astute politician:[5]

Your political career since your occupancy of the Executive chair, is, so far as I have had interchanges on the subject, in this city, universally popular. Yet I hear every day that you are losing your popularity, and upon inquiring the cause, I am informed that almost every one coming from Texas says so. I express my surprise that such should be the case, without a just cause, and am informed that you are cold and repulsive in your manners, &c. I plead the constant occupancy of your mind and important matters of State and the impossibility of those courtesies

[2] Houston *Telegraph and Texas Register,* January 30, 1839.
[3] *Brazos Courier,* in Houston *Morning Star,* May 3, 1839.
[4] Ashbel Smith to Memucan Hunt, July 25, 1839, Smith Papers.
[5] Memucan Hunt to Lamar, June 5, 1839, *Lamar Papers,* III, 14.

138

which seem to be looked for when your mind is thus engrossed &c&c. It is however very little trouble to ask a man when he reached the city, &c, &c, &c, and I will take the liberty of recommending to you to tax yourself in this respect.

If Lamar was not at home wooing the public, the same condition was unfortunately true of members of his party. There was a laxity of political organization, and as Lamar could not make capital of personal magnetism, as Houston had, the party suffered at the polls. A partisan of the Lamar faction eloquently expressed the troublesome situation, after his defeat in the congressional elections of September, 1839:[6]

Gen L's friends dont work as they ought. Why on earth, when truth, justice, patriotism & talent too are all in his favor why I ask are there not more able and lucid articles in the papers—He seems to me to drag the whole load without even a friendly 'god speed ye' to encourage him—It's well for him he has so much constitutional firmness.

Policy failures and the absence of effective electioneering tactics were culminated in the congressional elections of September, 1839. Opposition to the government was current throughout the Republic, and the most faithful partisans of the party were aware of the danger signs. In August, Branch T. Archer had written to the President advising him that "the suffering condition and heavy complaints, of our Northern, and Western, fellow citizens are all charged as you know, (whether right or wrong,) to Executive neglect or indifference."[7] In the same vein Thomas J. Green, a bitter enemy of Houston, after imploring Lamar to make an electioneering trip to Velasco, observed: "I am no politician if the reaction does not commence with this letter and your *coming home* to see your old friends here would be most favourable."[8] The Lamar party was certainly well aware of the importance of the congressional election, and their anxiety served to reflect the great unpopularity of the President.

Although opposition to the administration was general, in the realm of party politics it came to center in Sam Houston. Immedi-

---

[6] Kelsey H. Douglass to ?, n.d., in Gambrell, *Anson Jones,* 174.
[7] Branch T. Archer to Lamar, August 7, 1839, *Lamar Papers,* III, 58.
[8] Thomas J. Green to Lamar, August 15, 1839, *ibid.,* 66.

ately after Lamar's inauguration, Houston had left Texas for a triumphant tour of the South. The "Great-Ex" was feted everywhere he appeared, and the cause of Texas suffered no harm.[9] Concluding his trip with a sojourn at "The Hermitage" as the guest of Andrew Jackson, Houston slowly made his way back to Texas, arriving in the summer of 1839. His friends quickly gathered around him and began to point to Houston as the obvious candidate to succeed Lamar in the next general election. This plan was not intended to be secret, as can be seen in an excerpt of a letter to Lamar from Stephen H. Everitt, a senator devoted to the Lamar party: "You are aware perhaps . . . that Gen Houston will be a candidate at the next presidential Election and his friends are now Laying their plans and Electioneering to secure the Vote of the people."[10] Therefore, by the summer of 1839 the Houston party was reincarnated as the active opposition to the principles of the administration.

The expulsion of the Cherokees was the one act of the Lamar faction that was a complete denial of the principles of the Houston party. Lamar hoped to gain political support because of his Indian policy, and a follower of the President's accurately gauged the political scene by observing: "Hope Rusk will take Bowles [sic], it will knock old Sam, out of the next Presidency with the people if he does."[11] However, upon his return Houston began his campaign for a seat in Congress with a speech directly attacking the treatment of the Cherokees and generally condemning Lamar's Indian policy. Houston had always received strong backing from the Nacogdoches area, and though his attack against Lamar's action cost him the support of Rusk, Henry Raguet, and other influential citizens of Nacogdoches the Old Hero of San Jacinto was elected to the House of Representatives as a member from San Augustine. Houston's victory at the polls was a testimonial to the continuing popularity of the first President of the Republic and a warning to the party in power.

Antiadministration sentiment was also responsible for the elec-

[9] Memucan Hunt to Lamar, July 13, 1839, *ibid.*, 41–42. In a letter posted from Jackson, Mississippi, Hunt wrote: "General Houston was received with considerable attention at Columbus in this State, and on my reaching there, I was surprised to find how favorable an impression he had made." This type of reception characterized Houston's entire tour.

[10] Stephen H. Everitt to Lamar, May 6, 1839, *Lamar Papers*, II, 563.

[11] H. Thompson to Lamar, August 18, 1839, *ibid.*, III, 73.

tion of Anson Jones to fill the Senate seat which had become vacant upon the death of William H. Wharton.[12] The President had named Richard G. Dunlap minister to the United States to replace Jones, and the consequent loss of office nettled this highly sensitive man, who felt that he had acquitted himself well. It is true that Jones had done an admirable job as the representative of Texas in the United States, and upon his return one can be sure that he bore no feelings of good will toward the party in power. Samuel A. Roberts, the secretary of the Texas legation at Washington, wrote to Lamar advising him to cultivate Jones upon the latter's return and to make the necessary advances, but characteristically the President did not consider the matter important enough, and Jones was allowed to drift back into the Houston camp.[13]

With Houston and Jones as the spearheads of the anti-Lamar feeling, the President lost the backing of another of his followers, James Pinckney Henderson. This diplomat, who had labored long at his own expense in Europe, also had his particular grievance against the administration. Henderson believed that his French mission had suffered because of the last minute interference of General Hamilton, the Texas agent empowered to raise a loan in Europe. The disappointed envoy felt that if left alone he could have secured favorable trade concessions from the French government as well as a treaty of recognition, and he blamed Hamilton's anxiety to negotiate a loan as the factor which forced him to moderate his demands upon the French government. Also, Henderson believed that Hamilton would succeed him in France and that his return to Texas would be viewed as a surrender of his post.[14] Just prior to his departure for home, Henderson wrote to friends indicating his desire to run for Congress in opposition to the administration, though the former diplomat arrived too late to be an eligible candidate in the election of 1839.[15]

By hard work and constant campaigning, the anti-Lamar forces were highly successful in the congressional election. When the tabulation was completed, it was clear that only ten of the congress-

[12] Gambrell, *Anson Jones*, 172. William Wharton was killed in an accident; withdrawing his pistol to examine it prior to riding, he accidentally shot himself.
[13] Samuel A. Roberts to Lamar, September 24, 1839, *Lamar Papers*, III, 116.
[14] Moses Austin Bryan to Parents, n.d., 1839, Moses Austin Bryan Papers.
[15] Ashbel Smith to Memucan Hunt, June 10, 1839, Smith Papers.

men elected with Lamar in 1838 had been returned to the Fourth Congress. Thirty newly elected men, the majority of whom were sworn followers of Houston, were in control of the House, and four new opposition senators were also elected. This success definitely represented public reversion from the policies of the Lamar government. In the House, Houston, Samuel P. Davis, representing the county of San Augustine, and Samuel May Williams, representing the county of Galveston, constituted the leadership of the antiadministration group. In the Senate, the Houston men were led by Anson Jones, from the district of Brazoria, and James Seaton Lester, from the district of Fayette, Bastrop, and Gonzales.[16] William H. Jack, member of the House from Brazoria, continued as the nominal head of the Lamar group in Congress. The New Orleans *True American* commented on the political situation in Texas in the following fashion:[17]

Politics of Texas—It appears that the Houston party in Texas is the opposition. They give President Lamar no credit for any act of his administration. The great principle of the opposition is, that Lamar is unfit to the task of presiding over the Republic. We do not find any distinction made between the creeds of the two parties. Both are good democratic creeds, and they only differ as to measures.

With Houston and his cohorts controlling the House and exercising an important influence in the Senate, the opposition could both effectively embarrass the administration and push through legislation of its own making. In characteristic fashion, the leading oppositionists determined to strike at the President's Indian policy, and after many speeches devoted to attacks on the Cherokee War Houston drafted a bill to sectionize the Indian lands. The bill, as introduced by Houston, contended that the Cherokees had been the rightful owners of their lands prior to the expulsion and that now the lands should be sectionized and sold. Houston attempted to prove that the Indians had been the legal owners of their lands on the basis of two prior enactments: (1) the decrees of the state of Coahuila and Texas which authorized the privilege of citizenship for those Indians who might forsake their savage habits and culti-

---

[16] Winkler (ed.), *Secret Journals of the Senate*, 134.
[17] New Orleans *True American*, n.d., in Houston *Morning Star*, February 18, 1840.

vate the soil, and (2) the resolutions of the Consultation of 1835 which empowered Houston and other commissioners to negotiate with the Indians as a sovereign people for a treaty of peace.[18] However, the administration was able to secure a report from the Committee on Indian Affairs, whose chairman, Senator Isaac W. Burton, was an avowed Lamar man, stating that the Cherokees had never complied with the resolutions of the Mexican government and thus did not enjoy rightful title to the land.[19]

The provisions of Houston's bill were of great practical importance because if the administration was able to prove that the Cherokees had no valid claims to their lands then the area in question was originally and still remained the property of the Republic. If the lands were public property, all headrights and other certificates located in the area were valid, regardless of previous congressional acts. However, if it could be proved that the lands belonged to the Cherokees, then all locations made before the confiscation of the lands by Congress were null and void because the lands were still private and not public domain.[20] In short, if the Cherokees had legal title to their lands, then all allocations made before their confiscation by Congress were void. If, on the contrary, the Indians had enjoyed no such title, the lands had always been public property and the State could rightfully appropriate the land for its own use.

The Houston party marshaled its forces and in the face of the adverse committee report was able to prove that the Indians had enjoyed the undoubted right of occupancy of the lands in question, though the right of absolute ownership could not be clearly established. Therefore, it was maintained that the Cherokee lands could not be considered vacant and liable to location in accordance with any law establishing a general land office after the date of the Cherokee War, which occurred in April, 1839. In this form the Cherokee Land Bill was passed by Congress in January, 1840, the words "reserved for and occupied" substituted in the Senate for the words "owned and occupied" by the Cherokees. By effecting the passage of the bill the Houston party opened up the lands for private sale,

[18] Houston *Telegraph and Texas Register,* January 1, 1840.
[19] Winkler (ed.), *Secret Journals of the Senate,* 77–78.
[20] Austin *City Gazette,* January 22, 1840.

expecting to bring a total income of over three thousand dollars into the public treasury by the time they hoped to be in the administration again. Also, Houston had successfully championed his favorite cause in having the Cherokees' rightful ownership of their land, before their unwarranted expulsion, written into the laws of the Republic. The entire affair represented a striking victory for the Houston-led opposition.

Finding themselves victorious in their attack on the administration's Indian policy, the Houston forces decided to snipe at some of the other Lamar enactments. The removal of the capital to Austin and the woeful plight of the country's finances provided more than enough ammunition for a concerted attack. The complaints against the location of Austin as the capital of the Republic were more than justified. The site chosen by Lamar was not centrally located, and the area selected for the new "seat of empire" had proved unfortunate in every respect. Writing to his friend Anna Raguet, Houston gave a clear account of the inconveniences associated with life in Austin:[21]

This is the most unfortunate site upon earth for the Seat of Government, between water, cold region, indifferent and sparce timber. It is removed outside of the settlement, and not a house between this and Santa Fe. Our eating is very plain, and no society to enjoy in this place, and I do not visit "court." It is said to be rather fine—so it should be from what appears on our financial records.

In addition to unpleasant living conditions at the capital, it was common knowledge that certain speculators close to the government had made large sums of money on the original sales of town lots in Austin.[22] This factor and the always-present danger of an Indian raid on what was virtually a frontier outpost combined to give the opposition a point of attack in the hasty removal of the seat of government from Houston to Austin. Soon the anti-Lamar newspapers took up the cry, and in tongue-in-cheek fashion the Houston *Morning Star* commented on the prevailing danger of an Indian raid:[23]

[21] Houston to Anna Raguet, December 10, 1839, *Houston Writings,* II, 322.
[22] San Augustine *Journal and Advertiser,* November 12, 1840.
[23] Houston *Morning Star,* March 11, 1841.

The way the married ladies in Austin attend balls and parties is a beautiful commentary upon the security of "the city of seven hills"—they always take their children with them—put them in the next room, and dance with fear and trembling—otherwise they might return and find their sucklings minus a scalp.

The above are facts too well known for contradiction; and in view of them, we would respectfully ask, is Austin thus situated forty miles beyond the settlements, and in the heart of the Indian range, a proper, a convenient, and a safe place for the seat of government?

The Houston men were unable to secure the removal of the capital, but the party members did identify themselves with a pledge of removal upon the victory of their candidate in the next presidential election.

The financial condition of the nation proved to be the weakest point in the administration's armor. Hamilton had failed to negotiate the anticipated loan of five million dollars and had succeeded only in earning the hatred of James Pinckney Henderson. With the loan not forthcoming, the government had been forced to rely upon the constant issues of paper money, and by 1840 the notes had fallen to as low a rate of exchange as 16.66 cents on the dollar. In addition to the resulting inflation, Lamar made the mistake of increasing the civil list of the Republic at precisely the time when the government should have been practicing the strictest economy. The President continued to authorize the issue of promissory notes for the support of the phantom Texas Navy and generally displayed a lamentable inability to understand the financial problems besetting the nation.

Times were terribly severe in the Republic. James Morgan, writing to his friend Samuel Swartwout about a projected business deal, described the financial plight:[24]

... I will go ahead in this matter & do all that I can do and if times were not so d——nable here you should not want—I cannot sell a foot of land —no money in the Country—We'r perfectly drained & times awfully hard indeed in the money way—property valued two yrs. ago by Swoon appraising at $55,000 in the town of Houston sold lately under the hammer at Sheriffs sale for $800!! All owing to the deficiency of Capital.

In much the same manner, W. B. Dewees, a settler in Austin's

[24] James Morgan to Samuel Swartwout, July 6, 1840, Morgan Papers.

original colony, in a letter to a friend sketched the ills to which Texas had fallen heir:[25]

In the beginning of our revolution Congress issued a species of money called Texas Promissory Notes; these notes for a time were at par; but they at length commenced decreasing in value, little by little, till at the beginning of this year, they were worth not more than ten or twelve cents on the dollar. Those of us who had disposed of much of our property for the Texas money when it was at par have lost a great deal, and some have lost their all by its decrease in value. We are obliged to pay one hundred, or one hundred and fifty dollars for a barrel of flour, and other things are in like proportion. This, of course, causes a great deal of distress. In addition to this, our crops have fallen short this year on account of the dry season, so that we have suffered greatly for want of food. We have been barely and scantily supplied with the necessities of life; luxuries we have had none.

The continual attacks against Lamar's financial policy began during the sessions of the Fourth Congress, which sat from November 11, 1839, until February 5, 1840. Though this Congress was controlled by Houston men, the opposition was still unable to write into law any effective curbs to the extravagant spending of the administration. However, the Fifth Congress, which was elected in November, 1840, contained a greater majority of Houston supporters, and this group quickly began to put into effect a policy of retrenchment. Salaries were lowered for many government positions, and some officers holding government posts were released outright: The salary of the chief justice of the Supreme Court was decreased from $5,000 to $3,000, the office of the secretary of the navy was abolished, and the duties of that office were placed upon the secretary of war. The position of postmaster general was also abolished, and the burdens of that department fell to the secretary of state. In addition, various minor offices in the treasury department and in the military and naval departments were outlawed. In all, the appropriations of the Fifth Congress for civil purposes amounted to about $450,000, compared to $550,000 by the Third Congress. Finally, no sums were pledged for the maintenance of the regular army, and the President was refused the power to issue additional promissory notes for the support of the navy. Therefore,

[25] Dewees, *Letters from an Early Settler of Texas*, 236.

the total appropriations for the upkeep of the Republic's army and navy amounted to only $211,050, compared to $1,581,369 allowed by the Fourth Congress.[26]

The Houston faction continued their obstructionist tactics in Congress by refusing to ratify the appointment of General Dunlap as minister to the United States, thereby forcing his return from that country. The antiadministration forces also made political fodder out of some financial irregularities that were found to exist at the Galveston customhouse, and, since the collector at that place, Samuel Roberts, was appointed solely on the basis of his friendship with Lamar, the government suffered accordingly. The President was forced to remove Secretary of the Treasury Asa Brigham in the wake of the scandal and to appoint the supposedly nonpartisan James Harper Starr in his place.[27] These sniping tactics and others of the same nature that characterized Houston and his party were well described by Anson Jones, himself generally a reluctant participant: "Gen. Houston, I fear, does not care how completely L——r ruins the country, so that he can hide the errors, the follies, and wide-spread ruin of his own past administration, and have it to say, 'I told you so; there is nobody but old Sam after all'."[28]

Because of the constant attacks to which the administration was being subjected, Lamar and his partisans attempted to redeem themselves in other fields of governmental action. When news of the failure of Treat's negotiations reached Texas early in December, 1840, Lamar immediately recommended that the armed forces of the Republic be ordered to compel Mexico to acknowledge Texas independence.[29] The President's recommendation was taken under consideration by both the House and Senate, and a joint committee was created to consider the advisability of a declaration of war against Mexico. Houston, though personally opposed to war at this time, was unable to maintain his party intact, and many of his followers joined the Lamar men in favor of war. At this point President Lamar, completely worn down by the cares of state and suffering

[26] Miller, *A Financial History of Texas*, 22–23.
[27] Crane, "The History of the Revenue Service and the Commerce of the Republic of Texas," 51.
[28] Jones, *Republic of Texas*, 36.
[29] Christian, "Mirabeau Buonaparte Lamar," *Southwestern Historical Quarterly*, XXIV (1920), 138.

from an intestinal disorder, asked Congress for a leave of absence to journey to the United States for treatment. By a joint resolution of Congress he was granted leave on December 12, 1840, and the reins of the Presidency were placed in the hands of Vice-President David G. Burnet.[30]

In taking notice of the recent development of affairs, the Houston *Telegraph and Texas Register* stated that Burnet "assumes the government under the most dark and inauspicious circumstances,"[31] and such substantially was the truth. As early as 1839 Burnet had been spoken of as the logical successor to continue the principles of Lamar in office, and the former vice-president was well aware that a good showing in office was an absolute requisite for his future plans. Accordingly, in his first official act as President, Burnet sent a jingoistic message to Congress stating that Mexico was gathering her armies for an invasion of Texas and that prompt and decisive action by Texas was imperative. Burnet observed that "Texas proper is bounded by the Rio Grande—Texas, as defined by the sword, may comprehend the Sierra Madre. Let the sword do its proper work." He then submitted a plan of military campaign which called for an invasion of Mexico by way of the lower Rio Grande.[32]

In the face of inflamed public sentiment to the contrary, Houston and those of his men who remained loyal objected to an offensive campaign as one more needless drain on the finances of the country. The opposition contended that defensive measures were more consistent with the state of the treasury, and Congress wrangled over the two plans for several weeks without taking any decisive action. News then came from England that General Hamilton had negotiated a treaty, the purpose of which was to bring about an early peace between Mexico and Texas. The merits of this plan were quickly recognized, and Congress postponed action on a definite stand toward war until Hamilton's labors could be fully investigated.

General Hamilton was in Paris when France accorded recognition to Texas. He then returned to England, and, though his pri-

---

[30] Graham, *Mirabeau B. Lamar*, 60.

[31] Houston *Telegraph and Texas Register*, December 23, 1840.

[32] Proceedings of the House of Representatives, Fifth Congress, First Session, December 16, 1840, 293.

mary concern was to negotiate a loan, he considered himself the ranking Texas envoy in Europe upon the departure of James Pinckney Henderson. Hamilton felt that the times were favorable for a renewal of the attempts to achieve British aid in any peace negotiations between Texas and Mexico. In January, 1840, he was hopeful of success and was very concerned lest the few Texas ships under Commodore Moore blockade the Mexican ports and interfere with the profitable trade between Great Britain and Mexico. Hamilton wrote to Burnet, then serving as acting secretary of state in addition to his duties as vice-president, imploring him to "keep your fleet at home until you hear from me from London. A single indiscreet movement would destroy all prospect of peace and negociation."[33] However, as the talks progressed and Hamilton found Lord Palmerston unwilling to use the offices of the British government to effect peace, the Texas diplomat determined to use a new method of approach. After Lamar signified his intentions of entering into an alliance with the Federalists of the Yucatan area and of dispatching the navy to aid the revolt in Yucatan, Hamilton, in turn, confronted Palmerston with a change of tactics. In a note addressed to the Foreign Secretary, Lamar's envoy summarized the consequences that were likely to follow if Great Britain failed to arbitrate between Texas and Mexico:[34]

1st. In sixty days from this day (October 14, 1840) Vera Cruz, Tampico & Matamoros will be blockaded by the Texian Squadron, which consists of one Corvette, two Brigs, three schooners & one naval Steamer, now off the Coast of Mexico, while Mexico is destitute of all naval force whatsoever.

2nd. If Texas is informed that Great Britain will not recognize her Independence & that consequently there is no hope of peace with Mexico, she will forthwith join the Federalists, revolutionize the northern provinces of Mexico & make such additions to her Territory as the laws of war would justify under the usages of civilized nations.

3rd. Great Britain has an obvious interest in avoiding a discriminating duty which will be levied against the productions of all nations which have not recognized Texas & formed Commercial treaties with her on or before the 1st of Feby. next.

[33] Hamilton to Burnet, January 5, 1840, *Diplomatic Correspondence,* II, 878.
[34] Schmitz, *Texan Statecraft: 1836–1845,* 129–30.

4th. If Her Majesty's Government should decline recognizing I must avail myself of the present situation of public affairs in Europe & make the most beneficial arrangements I can with some continental nation giving it exclusive commercial advantages for a valuable equivalent.

5th. Texas greatly prefers a friendly alliance with England from all those considerations which are connected with a common origin—But if Great Britain refuses all international companionship with her, she will be driven to seek friendly & profitable associations elsewhere.

Palmerston, in the face of Hamilton's threats, soon consented to listen to the Texan's proposals. By November, three treaties had been drawn up by the two governments. The first, signed on November 13, was a treaty of commerce and navigation, embodying the usual provisions of treaties of this nature and providing for an increased amount of trade relations between the Republic and Great Britain. The second treaty, signed on November 14, was in the nature of a convention concerning the public debt which the Mexican nation had contracted before the Texas Revolution. By the terms of this treaty it was stated that Great Britain had offered her mediation between Texas and Mexico, that Texas had accepted that offer, and that in case a successful mediation with Mexico was accomplished and a treaty of peace signed within six months after the convention was communicated to the Mexican government Texas would assume one million pounds sterling of the foreign debt contracted by Mexico before January 31, 1835. The third treaty, which provided for the suppression of the African slave trade, was signed on November 16 and provided for the mutual right of search by a certain limited number of cruisers of each nation, with the additional limitation that such right of search could be exercised only when specific warrants had been issued to the commanders of the ships indicated.[35] Burnet submitted the first two treaties to the Senate in January, 1841, and they were quickly ratified. The treaty concerning the abolition of the slave trade did not arrive from England until after Congress had adjourned.

By the terms of the negotiations it was stipulated that if the treaties were ratified within six months then Great Britain would accord official recognition to the Republic. It is apparent that Palmerston had concluded that there was no immediate danger of

[35] Adams, *British Interests and Activities in Texas*, 58–59.

American annexation of Texas and that the Republic itself wished to remain independent of the United States. Also, British bondholders were anxious to see Texas independent and prosperous and were fully disposed to make good a large part of the old Mexican debt. Finally, in regard to the slave trade, Palmerston was eager to bring pressure to bear upon the United States in order to wring at least a limited right of search from that government. Throughout the two years preceding the treaties the slave traders had consistently abused the American flag at the same time that American irritation at British interference was on the increase. The matter was fast approaching a crisis, and Palmerston hoped to use the slave-trade treaty with Texas as an example of what the American government ought to be willing to concede.[36]

Thus assured of British aid in any negotiations which might be instituted, the administration decided to make one last effort to realize a peace with Mexico. The government felt that a treaty of peace with Mexico would assure some glory to the party in power and therefore decided to humble its pride for the last time. Lamar returned to Austin in late February, 1841, his health restored, and in March it was decided to send James Webb, then serving as secretary of state, as an envoy to Mexico commissioned to negotiate for peace. Webb had served as justice of the Supreme Court in the Lamar government and had also served as secretary of state for a short while. He was thoroughly familiar with the views of the administration, and it was hoped that he would succeed where Bee and Treat had failed.[37]

Webb's instructions, dated March 22, 1841, were basically the same as his two predecessors', though he was empowered to confer freely with the British minister, Pakenham, and to take the latter into his confidence whenever the occasion might warrant it. Webb's instructions revealed the government's chagrin at the rude reception which had been accorded to Bee and Treat, and in the event Mexico continued its refusals, Webb was to inform the Mexican government that the Texans had made their final offer. In addition, if the Mexican Foreign Office refused to begin peace talks, Webb was to return to Texas by way of Yucatan and ascertain if the rebels

---

[36] Smith, *Reminiscences of the Texas Republic*, 33.
[37] Schmitz, *Texan Statecraft: 1836–1845*, 131–32.

there would be willing to take part in a war which Texas might be compelled to wage against Mexico.[38] Webb was not authorized to enter into any express treaty stipulations with the Federalist government of Yucatan, but he was authorized to pledge the friendship of Texas and to suggest to the authorities of Yucatan the propriety of sending an agent to Texas with full powers to negotiate for a treaty of alliance. The administration hoped to emulate Hamilton's success by holding the club of an alliance with the Federalists over the head of the Mexican government.

Rebuffed twice by Mexico, the people of Texas were not overly hopeful that Webb's mission would be successful. It was felt that the government had held out the olive branch long enough. Totally disregarding the financial state of the Republic, the *Brazos Courier* gave its opinion of the forthcoming mission:[39]

Judge Webb was about leaving Galveston for Mexico in the schr. of war San Bernard, in search of peace. How much better it would be if the Government had appointed Commodore Moore, to go down as minister, accompanied by the whole fleet. We could then have *treated* and *coerced* alternately, according to circumstances.

Webb left Texas early in April and proceeded at once to the harbor of Sacrificios, near Vera Cruz. Upon his arrival he forwarded a letter to the Mexican commandant general at Vera Cruz, informing him of his mission and requesting official permission to land and be furnished with passports to Mexico City. The Mexican official replied that he had no authority to grant the request, and the Texas envoy was thereby confronted with the first evidences of official Mexican opposition to his mission.

In accordance with his instructions, Webb next addressed a note to Pakenham, explaining the purpose of his visit and soliciting the British minister's help in obtaining an interview. Webb enclosed copies of all the pertinent documents relating to his mission in the hope that the information would prove valuable to Pakenham in his attempts to arrange the interview. The Texas envoy then expressed his hope that Mexico would consider at length this final overture made by the Republic. In his communication to Pakenham, Webb

[38] Mayfield to Webb, March 22, 1841, *Diplomatic Correspondence*, II, 735.
[39] *Brazos Courier*, n.d., in New Orleans *Picayune*, April 18, 1841.

observed that there could be no affront to the national pride of Mexico because the petitioner for peace was, by all practical circumstances, an independent nation. The envoy concluded his note by pointing out that since his position in the harbor of Vera Cruz might lead to trouble he would put out to sea for ten days and then return to find out whether Pakenham had been successful in his efforts to arrange the interview.[40]

On June 8, 1841, Pakenham dispatched a note to the Mexican government announcing the arrival of Webb and soliciting an interview in his behalf. He received a reply on the same day which refused any meeting with an agent from Texas. Pakenham, in communicating the Mexican refusal to Webb, advised the envoy that Texas should forbear from any reprisals against Mexico at this date and that the question of peace should be allowed to remain suspended until an opportunity presented itself to reopen negotiations on a more favorable basis. If Mexico was forced to take up arms once more against Texas, Pakenham believed that all hope for an ultimate peace between the two countries would be lost.[41]

Webb received this note in the middle of June and explained to Pakenham that the continuation of a pacific policy on the part of the Republic would be extremely difficult. The Texan pointed out that the overtures which were constantly being made by the Federalists in Yucatan were becoming increasingly harder to resist and that the national honor of Texas demanded relief from what had become an intolerable situation. These were the arguments which Webb dwelt upon in his correspondence with Pakenham; in a communication to President Lamar the envoy gave other reasons for war:[42]

I think if active steps are taken, the War may be renewed, and consequences most important to the Nation be achieved by it, before your administration closes. At all events, the War can be renewed, and placed upon a footing by you as will preclude your successor from discontinuing it, and your administration will have the Credit of it. Should Genl. Houston succeed in the Presidential Canvass (and of this there is now

[40] Webb to Mayfield, June 29, 1841, *Diplomatic Correspondence*, II, 751–52. This letter was written after the mission had already proved to be a failure.

[41] Pakenham to Webb, June 10, 1841, *ibid.*, 756.

[42] Webb to Lamar, June 29, 1841, *ibid.*, 764.

the strongest possibility) I understand that he will be opposed to a renewal of the war. Unless therefore it is done in your time, we may expect an additional three years of doubt, difficulty, and embarrassment.

The Republic had complied with the treaties signed with Great Britain by sending Webb as an envoy, and the failure to establish peace could only be traced to the arbitrary conduct of the Mexican government. If the Texas government had had the financial means to prosecute a war, it is certain that the action would have brought credit to the Lamar group. The Houston *Morning Star* continued its opposition tactics by ridiculing the administration's vacillating policy:[43]

It is said that nothing as yet has been definitely determined upon by the administration, with regard to the manner in which the late scathing insult offered to the nation by Mexico shall be received. One thing is certain—there is no "lower depth" in national humiliation to be reached, than the point to which this *second* repulsion of pacific advances has reduced us. Our feverish anxiety for peace has betrayed us into steps, which, in the eyes of the world, may be considered as prompted by fear rather than foresight; such a construction has doubtless been put upon the movements by our enemy; and thus the very means which Texas has used to effect a pacification, will result in rendering the consummation still more remote.

After receiving Pakenham's note, Webb started for Yucatan to comply with his original instructions. However, an accident at sea in which the foremast of the *San Bernard* was destroyed forced the cancellation of the trip, and Webb therefore proceeded directly to Galveston, arriving on June 28, 1841.

In the report which he submitted to the government, Webb expressed his belief that further negotiations with Mexico were useless. If conditions were allowed to remain in an indefinite state, great harm would result, for foreign nations would quickly lose confidence in the ultimate stability of Texas, and the financial credit of the Republic would sink to even lower depths. Therefore, Webb advised the government to recognize the independence of the states of Yucatan and Tabasco and jointly with those countries to declare total war against Mexico. In the proposed military campaign the

[43] Houston *Morning Star*, August 5, 1841.

154

Republic would furnish the naval forces and the rebel states of Yucatan the troops. Webb believed that half the people in the towns would leap at the chance to throw off the despotic Centralist government and that without the necessary revenue and commerce from this area the government at Mexico City would quickly collapse.[44]

Upon receiving Webb's report, Lamar was so enthusiastic about the proposed scheme of action that he hastened to Galveston for a conference with his former envoy. As a result of a discussion, the President forwarded a letter to Governor Miguel Barbachano of Yucatan proclaiming that the Texas ports were open to the commerce of Yucatan on the same terms extended to a most favored nation. Lamar then invited the people of Yucatan to enter into a permanent alliance with Texas and to send an agent accredited to the government so that the details of a formal alliance might be worked out.[45] Responding to the invitation, the Governor of Yucatan sent Martin Peraza to Texas with full powers to negotiate a treaty of alliance. Peraza arrived at Austin in late August, 1841, and in a short time signed a treaty with the government of the Republic.

The treaty, signed on September 17, 1841, pledged the co-operation of the Texas fleet with the naval force of Yucatan in preventing a Centralist invasion of that state. The administration agreed to provide three or more vessels for the protection of the Yucatan coast, and it was further agreed that the prizes taken should be the possession of the country making the capture. Money which might be derived from seizing merchantmen, tolls, customhouses and the like would be equally divided between the two governments. Finally, it was stipulated that, in return for the assistance which Texas rendered, Yucatan was to advance eight thousand dollars in order to get the Texas fleet ready for sea and an additional eight thousand dollars each month for as long as the fleet remained in active service.[46]

Commodore Moore's instructions were soon made out, but the fleet did not sail for some two months. Arriving at the Yucatan port of Sisal early in January, 1842, Moore learned that a tentative con-

[44] Webb to Mayfield, June 29, 1841, *Diplomatic Correspondence*, II, 752.
[45] Lamar to the Governor of Yucatan, July 20, 1841, *ibid.*, 792–93.
[46] Hill, *The Texas Navy*, 145.

vention had been signed between Mexico and Yucatan on December 28, 1841, but that ratifications had not yet been exchanged. Moore was informed that Santa Anna had once again assumed the presidency of Mexico and that that wily leader, rather than attempt the military conquest of Yucatan, had negotiated with the province. Since Santa Anna had insisted only on a nominal connection between the rebellious state and the central government, the people of Yucatan enjoyed a quasi-independent political existence. In an interview with Moore, Governor Miguel Barbachano justified his action on the ground that there was no violation of any promise to Texas, for Lamar had entered into the agreement knowing that Yucatan had not at that date formally declared her independence. However, the Governor stated that as the ratification of the treaty with Mexico had not as yet occurred the Texas fleet was welcome to remain in Yucatan waters, and Moore, deciding to take advantage of this offer, gave the command to lay over for a short while. When the Texas officer did leave, it was with the understanding that if the treaty was not ultimately ratified he was welcome to return.[47]

Moore's fruitless expedition to Yucatan finished Lamar's attempts to negotiate for a peace with Mexico. James Harper Starr, who served for a short time as secretary of the treasury in the Lamar cabinet, clearly indicated the Texas sentiment toward Mexico in a letter to a friend: "I think the administration will try to strike a blow at Mexico before their term expires—we of the West are only waiting for the word to go down on the Rio Grande settlements, like the 'Wolf on the fold'."[48] James S. Mayfield, a member of the Lamar party representing Nacogdoches in the House of Representatives, assured Lamar that all would be well if peace could be realized with Mexico, and further reminders of this same nature only served to magnify the size of his failure in Lamar's own eyes.[49]

Before the President could make his most spectacular attempt to wring an honorable peace from Mexico through the tragic Santa Fe expedition, other matters came to the fore to plague the luckless administration. Upon the consummation of Henderson's treaties

[47] Alexander Dienst, "The Navy of the Republic of Texas," *Quarterly of the Texas State Historical Association*, XIII (1909), 30.

[48] James H. Starr to W. J. Jewett, July 15, 1841, Starr Papers.

[49] James S. Mayfield to Lamar, June 7, 1841, *Lamar Papers*, III, 534.

with France calling for favorable trade relations and the recognition of Texas, the French government had named Alphonse de Saligny its first minister to the Republic of Texas. De Saligny, while serving as a secretary of the French legation at Washington, had been sent on an inspection trip to Texas, and it was on the basis of this experience and his favorable report on conditions in Texas that France had accorded recognition to the new Republic. De Saligny, because of his supposed enthusiasm for the cause of independence in Texas and his familiarity with conditions there, was the logical choice to represent his country at Austin, and his appointment was received with genuine approval by the administration.

From the beginning, however, the French minister displayed an uncanny ability for embroiling himself in one difficulty after another. To begin with, he brought popular suspicion upon himself at his arrival in Austin when he knowingly passed counterfeit money on the local teamster who had transported his luggage and household equipment. De Saligny explained that the money had been given to him in New Orleans, but he was forced to admit that he knew it was counterfeit before he passed it on the teamster. In addition, when the complaint was made De Saligny refused to take the money back or to give any redress, and the government of the Republic was forced to make good the carrying charges of the irate teamster. The affair caused a great deal of excitement in the rude frontier town of Austin, and the natural disposition in frontier communities to ridicule any act associated with monarchial pretensions had a thorough airing at the expense of the newly arrived minister from France.[50]

However, it was a matter of greater importance that set the administration against De Saligny. The diplomat arrived with a plan, believed to be the personal creation of Louis Philippe, for the establishment of colonies of French settlers along the frontier of Texas. Perceiving the existing political situation in the Republic, De Saligny successfully induced Houston to propose a bill to Congress embodying the basic provisions of the French plan for colonization. By the terms of the bill, which Houston sponsored in the House, it was proposed that the Legislature of the Republic grant to a corporation of French capitalists three million acres of land (in sec-

[50] Schmitz, *Texan Statecraft: 1836–1845*, 154–55.

tions scattered over the western areas of the country) upon which the company was to locate at least eight thousand French immigrants by January, 1849. As an inducement to migrate, the French settlers were to have the right to import whatever they chose, free of duty, for a period of twenty years. Moreover, the land settled by the company was to be free of taxation until 1848. The French company, on its part, was to establish a line of at least twenty forts along the western frontier from the Red River to the Rio Grande and maintain them for a period of twenty years. As soon as eight thousand settlers were actually located in or near these forts, the company was to receive full title to the three million acres of land. In addition, the French company was to enjoy certain other substantial privileges. It was given the right to work all the mines found in the ceded area during the twenty-year grant, provided that 15 per cent of the annual proceeds was given to the treasury of the Republic. Exclusive rights of trade with the towns of upper Mexico were also granted to the company, and it was stipulated that for twenty years no other colonists or companies would be granted land in the area ceded to the French corporation.[51]

The Franco-Texienne Bill, as introduced by Houston during the sessions of the Fifth Congress, immediately stirred up a hornet's nest of controversy. The antiadministration newspapers lined up in favor of the proposal, but the Houston *Morning Star*, while expressing its hope that the bill would receive a fair hearing, was forced to admit that it was "a *monopoly* the Congress has no power to grant."[52] Houston's dedication to the bill left the former President open to bitter political charges. The Lamar clique in Congress hinted that Houston stood to realize a valuable profit from the passage of the bill and generally decried his partnership with the French minister as an attempt to despoil the Republic of its choicest lands.

The congressmen also objected to De Saligny's personal interference in a domestic matter. That this charge was valid cannot be denied. The French minister brought all his old-world charm and hospitality to bear in an attempt to carry his favorite project. De

---

[51] Bernice B. Denton, "Count Saligny and the Franco-Texienne Bill," *Southwestern Historical Quarterly*, XLIV (1941), 138.
[52] Houston *Morning Star*, January 14, 1841.

Saligny's graciousness as a host and eagerness to entertain members of Congress at private dinners can be illustrated in the reactions of congressmen who attended his parties. Isaac Van Zandt, member of the House from Harrison County, whose vote on the impending measure was considered doubtful, wrote to his wife concerning a dinner at the French Legation in Austin:[53]

> I was yesterday at a dinner given to a few of the members and prominent men about the city by Mr. Saligney, the French Minister. It was the most brilliant affair I ever saw, the most massive plate of silver and gold, the finest glass—and every thing exceeded anything I ever saw. We sat at the table four hours—I was wearied to death but had to stand it with the Company—We had plates changed about fifteen times.

The Franco-Texienne Bill also gave the frontier editors supporting the administration a chance to display their humor at the expense of Minister De Saligny. The Frenchman was closely compared with Citizen Genêt, and more than one friend of the government called upon the people to remember the wisdom implicit in Washington's parting address and avoid entangling alliances. The most poetic effort, however, was attained by the editor of the *Texas Sentinel,* printed at Austin. Referring to the bill in question as the "Bill of Abominations," the editor lamented the fact that certain influences were industrious in serving *"French wines, Principe cegars, West India sweet-meats, and lusty promises."* The editor then sorrowfully recounted that so powerful were De Saligny's methods of persuasion that those who were against the bill and resisted it with "master eloquence" did so to no avail. "Their truths were wasted upon the desert air—for *the thing was arranged over the fuming bottles* and smoking dinners of M. Saligny."[54]

In the face of all this editorial brilliance, the Houston party was hard pressed to achieve favorable action on the bill. At times the vote on the issue crossed party lines when western members, looking to the protection of the frontier, lined up in support of the bill. But De Saligny's favorite project met defeat in the Senate in February, 1841. The debate continued throughout the summer, and the ultimate passage of the bill became a campaign promise of the

[53] Isaac Van Zandt to his wife, December 6, 1840, Isaac Van Zandt Papers.
[54] *Texas Sentinel,* July 7, 1841, in Schmitz, *Texan Statecraft: 1836–1845,* 157.

Houston faction in the presidential election in the fall. However, upon the return of the Houston party to office, the whole matter was allowed to drop.

Meanwhile, long before the Franco-Texienne Bill became a dead issue, the French Minister involved himself in the greatest of his misfortunes while representing his government in Texas. Upon arriving at Austin, De Saligny made Richard Bullock's hotel his legation headquarters. Relations between landlord and tenant were cordial until De Saligny refused to pay his rent on the grounds that the rates were exorbitant. Bullock then accused the French Minister of bad faith in the payment of his personal debts and freely circulated his opinions to the people of Austin. The government realized that this was purely a private matter, but when Bullock continued to insult De Saligny publicly the administration was forced to interfere and protect the Minister. Having no legal way to compel Bullock to abstain from expressing his contempt for the Frenchman, the government passed a law specifically intended to protect De Saligny, making anyone liable to punishment if guilty of "slanderous words, maliciously written or spoken" against any foreign minister.[55]

Bad feeling between Bullock and De Saligny continued to exist, and the trouble culminated in the famous "pig incident." De Saligny had left Bullock's hotel and had established himself next door. At this location the Frenchman kept the beautiful horses which were his pride and stored the corn which he used for feed. As it developed, Bullock raised pigs and was not particularly concerned about keeping them enclosed, a prevailing delinquency in any frontier town. When some of the pigs intruded into De Saligny's stable and consumed the corn intended for the Minister's horses, De Saligny's servant, Eugene Pluyette, retaliated by killing twenty of the pigs. This was too much for Bullock's sensibilities to bear, and upon catching Pluyette after a lengthy chase the landlord administered the servant a sound thrashing. The enraged De Saligny then had Bullock arrested for assault while claiming a diplomatic immunity for his servant. In a communication to the Texas Secretary of State, James S. Mayfield, De Saligny admitted that he had given express orders to his servant to destroy the pigs but that he had given the

[55] *Ibid.*, 159.

order only after some of the swine had broken into his room, destroyed his papers, and devoured his linen.[56]

James Morgan in commenting on the affair observed that De Saligny "got so mad he cut off his *beautiful beard.*"[57] While the French Minister indulged his temper, the newspapers in the Republic contended that the entire incident was consistent with the habits of European governments. The San Augustine *Journal and Advertiser* asserted: "This business, however, is somewhat illustrative of the habit of monarchial representatives regarding their wishes in whatever concerns them as beyond the pale of any restraint, and the haughty temper in which they discharge their official relations with republican governments. Go it Texas! *Viva la pigs!*"[58] The citizens of Austin continued to have a hearty laugh at the expense of the discomfited De Saligny, while the Minister continued his lengthy and verbose protests to the government.

To add insult to injury, James Harper Starr, at the time a cabinet official, furnished bail for Bullock's release. Once free, the innkeeper renewed his assault on De Saligny's character, and the affair was brought to a climax when De Saligny, intending to call on George Flood, the American representative in Texas who lodged at Bullock's hotel, was forcibly restrained by Bullock from entering. The French Minister quickly reported this latest outrage to the government, claiming diplomatic protection for his person, and demanded instant punishment of Bullock. In a note to Secretary of State Mayfield, De Saligny accused the administration of complete negligence in bringing the landlord to justice and demanded immediate satisfaction or the granting of his passports.[59] Mayfield, though he was weary of the whole matter and also had some reason to suspect that De Saligny had objected to his appointment as secretary of state, answered the Minister in courteous fashion and attempted to make amends.[60] However, the government refused to place Bullock, by now a popular favorite in the city, in jail once again, and after an ex-

---

[56] De Saligny to Mayfield, March 21, 1841, *Diplomatic Correspondence*, II, 1303–1304.

[57] James Morgan to Samuel Swartwout, April 22, 1841, Morgan Papers.

[58] San Augustine *Journal and Advertiser*, May 20, 1841.

[59] De Saligny to Mayfield, March 25, 1841, *Diplomatic Correspondence*, II, 1306–1308.

[60] Mayfield to James McIntosh, May 12, 1841, *ibid.*, 1326.

change of notes did not effect his desired object De Saligny broke off diplomatic relations with the Republic and asked for his passports.

The De Saligny episode, though ludicrous, had some very serious effects on financial affairs in Texas. General Hamilton was still in Europe, and after the negotiations with Lord Palmerston which led to the signing of treaties with England he hastened to Paris in an attempt to secure the five-million-dollar loan which the Republic so desperately needed. Writing to the President shortly after his arrival, Hamilton informed Lamar that the French money market was being subjected to severe pressure because of unstable financial conditions throughout the world, but he expressed hope that he would be successful in getting the loan from a French private banking house, Lafitte and Company, thus bypassing the need for governmental sanction.[61] Precisely when Hamilton had the greatest hopes of success, De Saligny besieged the French government with reports about the treatment he had received at Austin and informed the French Foreign Office that he had officially broken off diplomatic relations with the Republic. The French Prime Minister, Guizot, learning of De Saligny's case, became decidedly unfavorable toward Hamilton's project, and in a short while the Parisian newspapers supporting the Guizot administration took up the cry against the loan. The editorial in *La France* dealing with the Texas question indicates the tone of public opinion at the time:[62]

Let us see if the French capitalists may rely on the preference offered them by these young republicans—these colonizers, *par excellence*—this energetic and industrious race! The Texan race has absolutely the same constitution, moral and physical, as that of the United States; and he must be very ill-informed who does not know that in New Orleans, as on the frontiers of Canada, the people of French origin are not the most beloved.

Not long after the appearance of this and other similar editorials, the French Minister of Finance, Humann, who was De Saligny's brother-in-law, issued a semi-official note which was hostile to the proposed loan. The banking house of Lafitte and Company, realiz-

[61] Schmitz, *Texan Statecraft: 1836–1845*, 161.
[62] *La France,* June 9, 1841, in N. Doran Maillard, *The History of the Republic of Texas,* 400–401.

ing the feelings of the government, then refused to consider Hamilton's proposals further, and the diplomat was forced to admit another defeat.

The populace in Texas was understandably enraged over this latest turn of events. The loan was sorely needed, and the failure this time was particularly galling when Hamilton had been so close to success and when his failure could in large measure be attributed to the petty conduct of De Saligny. The Houston *Morning Star* certainly expressed the feelings of the newspapers throughout the Republic in commenting: [63]

It seems that the French Minister of Finance has published an official notice that the government will give no countenance to the negotiation of the Texian loan; the whole tenor of the note being hostile to that negotiation. It requires no great penetration to ascertain what influence it is that has caused so sudden a revulsion of feeling in the French Cabinet. The most amicable terms existed between them and our minister but a short time before the publication of that official note, and every inclination appeared on their part to favor the interests of Texas. But about the time M. De Saligny's despatches reached Paris, a change became manifest. Is it possible that a petty quarrel between that hotheaded young man and a sturdy "boniface" in Austin, *all about a pig*, has so suddenly revolutionized the policy of a great nation like France? Are not her statesmen above influences so trifling? Is it possible that an innocent "little grunter" the summit of whose offending was "rooting up the ground" of a particular garden, has brought to bear against us the wrath of thirty million of Frenchmen? We can scarcely believe it, though circumstances and appearances favor such belief.

Having failed in France but determined to make one final effort toward securing the loan in England, Hamilton crossed the Channel again. The Texas agent had several conferences with both Prime Minister Aberdeen and Lord Palmerston, but again to no avail. To strengthen his position Hamilton submitted a plan that would link England and Texas in close trade relations. The scheme called for preferential trade concessions in ship timber from the Texas forest lands. In emphasizing the advantages of this agreement to the British government, Hamilton stressed the danger of annexation on the part of the United States and the absolute need of prompt and de-

[63] Houston *Morning Star*, June 19, 1841.

cisive action on the part of Great Britain to avert it. However, Hamilton argued in vain, for Palmerston's action in signing treaties with the Texas government was under fire in the British press. Parliament had not yet ratified the treaties, and the treaty dealing with the slave trade had not been approved by the Texas Senate. The London *Morning Herald* voiced its opposition to the manner in which the Foreign Secretary had conducted the negotiations:[64]

Lord Palmerston's successful Diplomacy!—When the late Foreign Secretary signed the treaty recognizing the independence of Texas, which has not yet been ratified, although Lord Palmerston illegally appointed a consul-general to Texas, he contemporaneously signed a convention with the Texas envoy, stipulating terms on which peace should be concluded by the intervention of Great Britain between Texas and the mother-state, Mexico, and the independence of the former recognized by the latter. Nearly twelve months have since elapsed, and not only have peace and the recognition not been concluded between Mexico and Texas, but war is on the point of breaking out afresh, and British mediation is wholly repudiated even by imbecile Mexico. The Texan powers, to ratify the treaty of recognition and commerce, have been in London six months, and the ex-minister never ratified a document of which he boasted in the House of Commons; yet Lord Palmerston has the vanity to talk of his successful diplomacy!

Hamilton had several additional interviews with the Prime Minister, but on October 4, 1841, Aberdeen finally refused to entertain Hamilton's proposal any further, and the matter was concluded on a note of failure.

The administration, for all its attempts, had failed completely to make peace with Mexico and to find a solution to the unsettled financial conditions. This discreditable situation explains why the President was eager to grasp at straws and to sanction any scheme, quixotic as it might be, which might afford some relief to the nation. Looking about for some expedient, Lamar decided to attempt to win the trade of the Santa Fe region of New Mexico for the Republic. The trade with Santa Fe netted merchants of the United States an average of five million dollars a year, and the administration hoped that this revenue could be directed into the empty coffers of

[64] London *Morning Herald*, October 4, 1841, in Maillard, *The History of the Republic of Texas*, 416.

the Republic. Lamar believed that the people of Santa Fe would be receptive to commissioners from Texas and would eagerly declare their independence of Mexico. The Houston *Morning Star,* observing that several private mercantile companies in the Republic were considering the possibility of trade relations with Santa Fe, enthusiastically commented:[65]

Trade of St. Louis—The arrival of steamboats at St. Louis during the last year, has been 1589. Nearly half the trade of that city could be diverted and turned to this country by a small share of exertion, capital, and enterprise—We mean the Santa Fe trade. Instead of carrying it on by land carriage, over four thousand miles, as it is necessary with the traders from St. Louis, our merchants in this city could reach Santa Fe by traveling a distance of only five or six hundred miles. We can obtain from Europe, cloths, fancy stuffs, and all manufactured articles at much less cost than their market price in St. Louis; and at this time, unsettled as the more southern parts of Mexico are, Santa Fe offers no obstacles to a free and undisturbed trade. This subject is every day engaging more and more of the attention of our capitalists and enterprising merchants. Those who first enter into this trade, will gather not only a rich harvest of wealth, but the gratitude and admiration of every citizen who has at heart the prosperity of Texas.

As early as 1839 Lamar had seized upon the Santa Fe trade as the panacea for all the ills which beset the Republic. Informed by Representative William E. Jones that the only tie the Centralist government had with the province of Santa Fe was through taxation and that the "revolutionary spirit is warm in New Mexico," Lamar tentatively submitted his proposal to commence trade relations with the region in his second annual message to Congress, delivered in November, 1839.[66] Congress, which was at that time controlled by the administration, refused to sanction the plan because of the expense involved and because of a genuine doubt that the residents of Santa Fe were eager for independence, and the President allowed the matter to rest for a time. However, Lamar did make contact with two Americans, Captain William G. Dryden and John Rowland, who had permanent residences in Santa Fe, and upon receiv-

[65] Houston *Morning Star*, March 17, 1840.
[66] "Second Annual Message to Congress, November 12, 1839," *Lamar Papers*, III, 181–83.

ing their favorable reports concerning the possibilities of great wealth to be derived from the trade the Chief Executive again took the matter under official consideration. Under Lamar's spur the attempt was made to win support for the plan in the sessions of the Fifth Congress, but the failure was even more pronounced this time because of the strength of the Houston bloc in both the House and Senate. Congress adjourned in February, 1841, and the President, realizing that rapid steps would have to be taken in order to launch the plan during his administration, decided to act upon his own responsibility, without the sanction of Congress. Accordingly, he obtained the necessary drafts to finance the expedition from the Secretary of the Treasury, John C. Chalmers, and over $89,000 was removed from the treasury.[67]

Once having determined to act, Lamar proceeded to put his plan into operation in rapid fashion. On June 5, 1841, the President addressed a proclamation to the citizens of Santa Fe announcing the outfitting of an expedition that would leave Texas shortly. Lamar stated that the purposes of the Texas mission were peaceful, that his nation was interested in furthering trade relations with the people of Santa Fe, and that the Republic of Texas would welcome the citizens of Santa Fe as allies if the yoke of Mexican Centralism was pressing too heavily upon the backs of the citizens of that territory.[68] The President called attention to the fact that the caravan upon leaving Texas would be forced to travel through Indian country and that the members of the party would be armed against a possible Comanche or Cayuga attack; but Lamar gave his assurances that the expedition was not to be construed as hostile in nature. Four commissioners were selected to accompany the mission, one of whom was Antonio Navarro, a native Mexican of San Antonio, who was selected to emphasize the sympathy of the Texans for the people of Santa Fe. In their instructions, drafted by Acting Secretary of State Samuel Roberts, the commissioners were told that little opposition was expected to their project. Roberts emphasized that force was not to be used unless the commissioners found that the authorities in Santa Fe were attempting to forestall the political desires of the inhabitants. In that case, and if the commis-

[67] Memoirs of John S. Ford, 248.
[68] "Address to the Citizens of Santa Fe, June 5, 1841," *Lamar Papers*, III, 488–95.

sioners learned that the people were willing to give aid to the Texans, the expedition was authorized to use force against the Mexican officials, but under no circumstances whatsoever were the members of the party to attempt to coerce the people themselves.[69]

As the caravan prepared to depart, an air of excitement was felt at Austin. Many looked upon the journey as a lark and a capital chance for adventure. George Wilkins Kendall, the fiery editor of the New Orleans *Picayune,* whose account of the trials suffered by the Texans during the ill-fated expedition has since become a classic of frontier literature, has described the scene at Galveston just before its departure:[70]

At Galveston I found every one talking of the proposed Santa Fe Expedition. It was looked upon as nothing more than a pleasant hunting excursion, through a large section of the country, much of which was unknown to the white man. Such portions of the route as had been previously explored were known to abound with buffalo, bear, elk, antelope, and every species of game, besides fish and wild honey. The climate was also known to be dry and salubrious; in short, until a point high up on Red River should be gained, the trip promised to be one of continued interest and pleasure. But beyond that point the country was a perfect *terra incognita,* untrodden save by wild and wandering Indians, and all were eager to partake of the excitement of being among the first to explore it.

Continuing in this light vein, Kendall's newspaper stated that the editor's trip would be "full of novelty and delight, and unmingled with opposing inconveniences."[71] However, before his adventures were over, Kendall and his fellows were to be subjected to innumerable "opposing inconveniences."

Five companies, totaling 265 men under the command of General Hugh McLeod, left the Bushy Creek encampment near Austin on June 18, 1841. The commanding officer was a graduate of West Point and had endeared himself to Lamar because of his skillful command of the major regiment in the President's Cherokee War. But now, in command of a motley array of soldiers, traders, pleas-

[69] Samuel Roberts to Cooke, Navarro, Brenham, and Dryden, June 15, 1841, *Diplomatic Correspondence,* II, 737–43.
[70] George Wilkins Kendall, *Narrative of the Texan Santa Fe Expedition,* 12–13.
[71] New Orleans *Picayune,* May 18, 1841.

ure-seeking editors, and adventurers of every description, he was confronted with a difficult task at the outset. Lacking a clear knowledge of the route to be traversed and the mobility necessary for safe and efficient travel across the plains, the party journeyed first north and then northwest, ultimately traveling thirteen hundred miles before their arrival in New Mexico. The expected pleasure jaunt was marred by frequent Indian encounters, lack of food, and the uneasy apprehension felt along the way that an unfriendly reception awaited them in New Mexico. The food supply dwindled until the members of the expedition were forced to subsist upon lizards and plants, and the final stroke of bad fortune occurred in the betrayal of their mission by a trusted member of the party.[72]

The President had not attempted to be secretive concerning his pet plan, as his address to the people of Santa Fe will testify. Therefore, upon the publication of Lamar's proclamation and the reception of information from General Manuel Arista, the Mexican commander along the Rio Grande, that an expedition was outfitting for New Mexico, the Governor of New Mexico, General Manuel Armijo, wrote to the Centralist government for the necessary instructions. From Mexico City Santa Anna advised that, although Arista's report indicated the chief purpose of the expedition to be commercial in nature, Armijo was to allow no relations to be established between the Texans and the people of Santa Fe. The governor was also advised that, since the attitude of the inhabitants of the province was somewhat favorable to Texas, McLeod and his force could expect to receive aid from the local populace upon their arrival. Therefore, Armijo was instructed to meet the Texas caravan before it could approach near enough to establish communication with the inhabitants. Santa Anna believed that the people favored the Texas cause because of ignorance and that a timely appeal to their patriotic sentiments might prevent trouble.[73]

Upon their arrival at the outskirts of Santa Fe, the Texans were betrayed by one of their own guides, and the party was forced to surrender. By the terms of the surrender the members of the expedi-

[72] Kendall, *Narrative of the Texan Santa Fe Expedition*, 377. Also see Thomas Falconer, *Letters and Notes on the Texan Santa Fe Expedition, 1841–1842*, 91.
[73] William C. Binkley, "New Mexico and the Texas Santa Fe Expedition," *Southwestern Historical Quarterly*, XXVII (1924), 101.

tion who were citizens of the United States were promised that they would be provisioned with supplies and returned to Texas, and the native Texans were promised that their lives would be spared. In total defiance of this promise most of the members of the party were immediately ordered on a forced march to Mexico City as political prisoners. Many died along the way, and the cruelty of the Mexican officers left in charge of the straggling party was barbaric.

In Texas, though the ultimate fate of the expedition was still unsuspected, there was much criticism of the grandiose scheme fostered by Lamar. Congress was not in session in the summer of 1841, but the opponents of the President promised that as soon as the Legislature reconvened an investigation would be made of the manner in which Lamar had authorized the project without the consent of Congress. David S. Kaufman, representing the county of Nacogdoches in the House, who had been the administration's strongest supporter in eastern Texas, expressed his belief that the Santa Fe expedition was completely unauthorized by Congress,[74] and many attacks of the same nature were forthcoming. The whole foolish plan to subvert the citizens of Santa Fe must go down as the classic blunder of the Lamar administration; however, the conduct of Governor Armijo in his treatment of the prisoners resulted in a renewal of the war spirit in the Republic and tended to obliterate the mistake made by the President in sanctioning the plan in the first place.

In addition to the arbitrary treatment meted out to the members of the expedition, the United States Consul at Santa Fe, Manuel Alvarez, was roughly handled by the Mexican authorities while attempting to secure the release of Kendall as an American citizen and not a full-fledged member of the party. Alvarez had also attempted to intercede for the release of Franklin Combs, the seventeen-year-old son of General Leslie Combs of Lexington, Kentucky, who, it was rumored, was about to receive the appointment as United States minister to Mexico. So pronounced was the popular feeling in Kentucky over the imprisonment of Combs that the Legislature passed a resolution urging the United States to take prompt measures to secure the release of all the prisoners, American citizens

[74] David S. Kaufman to Washington D. Miller, August 15, 1841, Washington D. Miller Papers.

and native Texans alike.[75] Similar action was soon taken in Maryland and Louisiana. In Louisiana the Legislature passed a series of resolutions stating that the United States should intervene not only to effect the release of Kendall and Combs and to have the conditions of surrender fulfilled in so far as they pertained to the citizens of the United States, but also to ensure that the property of the Texans would be returned to them. Public meetings were held in New Orleans and other cities throughout the South condemning Governor Armijo and the authorities in New Mexico.[76]

As might well be expected, Kendall's paper, the New Orleans *Picayune*, led the protest against the treatment accorded members of the party. Concerned with the personal safety of its editor, the New Orleans paper called for a policy of decisive resolution on the part of the United States:[77]

Let us proceed with studied firmness in what we do on this occasion. Our cause is one of high and honorable sentiment. We occupy a position that must draw upon us still closer scrutiny from all the monarchial nations of the old world. Let us be honestly indignant, manly and bold, but descend to nothing intemperate, or to any frothy exhibitions of meaningless declamation. We will tell Mexico that she has enchained American citizens, who were travelling well provided with every necessary protection demanded by the laws of nations.—We will calmly tell the aggressor that *we are wronged*, and our country is too proud of its glorious birthright and the rank it holds within the pale of nations, to submit, at this year of its history, to insult and injustice.

Other similar protests were soon heard. The editor of the New Orleans *Bulletin*, while not above hinting that Kendall's capture may have all been a publicity stunt, did state: "These Mexicans have shown themselves incapable of observing the rules and practices of honorable war between civilized nations."[78] The Texas newspapers joined the chorus, and the government again found itself under pressure.

The Santa Fe expedition represented Lamar's policy at its worst. The administration had been forced to bear the ignominy of surren-

[75] Robert E. McClendon, "Daniel Webster and Mexican Relations," *Southwestern Historical Quarterly*, XXXVI (1933), 296–97.
[76] *Ibid.*, 298.
[77] New Orleans *Picayune*, February 4, 1842.
[78] New Orleans *Bulletin*, n.d., in Houston *Morning Star*, January 13, 1842.

der on the soil of an enemy, and it was also obvious now that no further attempts could be made to secure the friendship of the supposedly disaffected province in New Mexico. The Mexican nation received a decided boost to its military confidence in the failure of the Texas party, and the corresponding injury to the morale of the Texas cause was obvious; the supposed invincibility of Texas troops in any type of military action against Mexican soldiers had not stood the test of practice. The western-frontier sections of the Republic, which had always been the prime support of the government, found nothing in the failure of the mission to justify their hopes of continued emphasis on frontier defense. The British diplomatic representative in Texas, Charles Elliot, informed Lord Aberdeen that the chief result of the expedition was "something little short of the breaking up of the whole Western Country of Texas,"[79] and other reports were in circulation adhering to this view. Finally, the most galling feature of the Santa Fe plan was its complete financial loss. The President had drafted the scheme as a desperate measure to bring some revenue into the empty treasury of the Republic, and, ironically enough, he had been compelled to act in illegal fashion, only to be burdened with a costly failure.

The entire incident acted as the capstone to the President's misfortunes. Coming into office after his predecessor had displayed no great administrative talents, the Georgian had attempted to overturn Houston's policies and thus succeed where the latter had failed. The Lamar party had vigorously waged war against the Indians in direct contrast to the policy followed by Houston. Also, the administration, in contravention of Houston's policies, had acted to strengthen the western-frontier area and had deliberately cultivated that section by causing the seat of government to be removed to Austin. Lamar had hoped to negotiate a peace with Mexico and thus put an end to the frequent skirmishes which had characterized the first Houston administration, but here the President met his first administrative failure. Lamar had taken office fully aware of the mistake made by Houston in allowing the issue of paper money, but in failing to obtain a loan abroad and in authorizing huge and need-

[79] Charles Elliot to Lord Aberdeen, November 2, 1842, in Ephraim D. Adams (ed.), *British Diplomatic Correspondence concerning the Republic of Texas, 1838–1846,* 122.

less governmental expenditures he had only aggravated an already unstable situation. The established currency was virtually without value in the Republic, and the financial condition of the country was at its lowest ebb since the victory at San Jacinto. A Catholic priest attempting to establish a mission at Galveston has left an adequate description of the severity of the times. Writing to a friend in July, 1841, the priest commented:[80]

I arrived last night at this place [Houston] and found the people in pretty low spirits. Everything looks dull. No money in the country, people move back to the States much faster than they came in. . . . I am really out of heart. In the States a log church may be at least put up, but here in Texas there is nothing to be done without money, and money can be had nowhere.

With conditions in this state, and with the feeling pervading the populace that any change would be for the better, the citizens of the Republic turned their attention to the approaching election.

Houston's presidential campaign had begun as early as the spring of 1839. Stopping off at New Orleans on his triumphal tour of the South, the General made a passionate appeal for the cause of temperance. The New Orleans *Picayune* reported that Houston was "very popular and daily becoming more so."[81] The newspaper also informed its readers that the eleventh-hour temperance advocate would most certainly be a candidate for the Presidency in Texas in the election of 1841. The reaction to Houston was the same throughout the South and the General lent credence to the reports of his availability by making a severe attack upon Lamar's policies immediately upon his return to Texas. Houston evidently desired to begin his campaign early, for he began marshaling his forces shortly after his election to the House of Representatives as a member of the Fourth Congress, from the county of San Augustine. As the head of the opposition party in the House, the former President successfully defeated some of the administration's pet measures, such as the ownership of the former Cherokee lands, and introduced certain measures which were calculated to embarrass the government, such as the Franco-Texienne Bill.

[80] J. M. Odin, I.S.C.M. to Monsieur J. Timon, July 16, 1841, in *History of the Diocese of Galveston, 1847–1922*, 66.
[81] New Orleans *Picayune*, March 13, 1839.

As Houston had had presidential experience and was very popular, local officials who wished to sit in Congress and more ambitious politicians who wished to hold cabinet posts in the next administration had no difficulty in deciding upon "Old Sam" as their candidate in 1841. Therefore, because of his recognized chances of success, his selection as the party nominee was a foregone conclusion. In his farewell address made in 1838, Houston did admit that the Presidency had been a "pillar of thorns" to him, but at the same time he indicated that he would run again if the emergency required it.[82] In Houston's own opinion and in the belief of his party followers, the state of the nation was such that Houston should become a candidate. Thus the Houston party had its nominee long before the election of 1841.

If precedent had been followed by electing the vice-president to succeed the Chief Executive, the nomination of the Lamar party should have immediately gone to David G. Burnet. Lamar had received the latter's backing in 1838, and Burnet had consistently favored the policies of the administration, while nursing a lasting hatred for Houston. Burnet, in the words of his contemporary, Ashbel Smith, was "a character that Old John Knox would have hugged with grim delight," and his personal temperament was in opposition to the easygoing, convivial Lamar.[83] The President and his aide worked well together until Lamar was temporarily forced to abandon the Presidency because of illness and Burnet was designated acting President. Apparently flushed with a sense of new-found importance, Burnet proceeded to remove some of Lamar's appointees to the government civil service, though he did attempt to justify his actions in the light of the imperative need to practice the strictest economy. Also, Burnet's inflammatory war message after the failure of Treat's negotiations in Mexico had an adverse effect on Lamar, who still believed that with the help of British mediation peace could be achieved.

The breach between Lamar and Burnet was well known in political circles throughout the Republic. A member of the Lamar party wrote to James Harper Starr informing him of the news:[84]

---

[82] Austin *City Gazette,* February 10, 1841.
[83] Smith, *Reminiscences of the Texas Republic,* 80.
[84] H. J. Jewett to James H. Starr, July 15, 1841, Starr Papers.

Gen. Lamar & Judge Burnet as you know have had a rupture which never will be healed. Burnet treated Lamar ungenerously and by his conduct has completely alienated Gen. Lamar's friends from him. This with Burnet's course while acting President will prevent many from giving him their support. They will I think stay aloof voting neither for Burnet nor old Sam.

In the same vein, Henry Millard, a prominent citizen of Galveston, informed Anson Jones, who stood high in the councils of the Houston party, that "Lamar and Burnet are at outs" and that Lamar would cast his vote for Houston on election day.[85] Finally, James Morgan, in writing to his New York correspondent, Samuel Swartwout, confirmed the news that Lamar and Burnet had severed their political alliance.[86]

With Burnet repudiated by the titular head of the party, the administration faction was forced to find another nominee. Certain elements within the Lamar clique had long favored General Albert Sidney Johnston to succeed the President. James Love, a Galveston merchant who was an influential member of the administration party, reported with pleasure to his chief: "We intend Johnston for our Capt. I am pleased to see that he openly and zealously sustains your course. He did not attend Houston's dinner."[87] Johnston, who had received his first appointment in Texas as commander of the army from Houston, had served with distinction as Lamar's secretary of war. His part in the Cherokee War had estranged him from Houston, and it was felt that because of his own enviable military record Johnston would stand a good chance in a popularity test against Old Sam. However, the potential candidate remained deaf to the pleas of James Love, former Secretary of State James Mayfield, and others of the Lamar party who wanted him to run for the Presidency. Johnston refused to be considered a candidate because of his poor health (he had suffered from malaria while in Texas) and an innate disinclination to assume the cares of office. In May, 1841, Love addressed a letter to Johnston, who was then at Louisville, Kentucky, informing him that "if you desire the presi-

---

[85] Henry Millard to Anson Jones, March 16, 1841, quoted in Gambrell, *Anson Jones*, 207.
[86] James Morgan to Samuel Swartwout, September 1, 1841, Morgan Papers.
[87] James Love to Lamar, April 14, 1841, *Lamar Papers*, III, 371.

dency, your chance is good."[88] But Johnston remained adamant in his refusal to allow his name to be considered, and the Lamar party was forced to conduct a further search for a suitable nominee.

In the election of 1838, Lamar himself had not consented to run until he was assured that Thomas J. Rusk would not also be a candidate for the Presidency. Certain of the fact that he would only face Grayson or Collinsworth in that election, the ever-cautious Lamar had then allowed his name to be used. Lamar's action in 1838 clearly testified to the great popularity enjoyed by Rusk throughout the Republic. The possibility of Rusk's candidacy in 1841 brought the issue to the fore again. James Mayfield wrote to James Harper Starr: "I have written a hasty note to Genl. Rusk of this date. His success is certain if he will at once allow his friends to use his name. Induce him to do this. I shall leave here on Sunday for Houston—thence if possible to Nacogdoches. . . . Write to me and tell me what Rusk will do. It governs much my own actions."[89] With Johnston's refusal an established fact, those members of the Lamar party opposed to Burnet's candidacy determined to press the office upon Rusk.

In the election of 1838 Rusk had refused to be a presidential candidate because of private affairs and inability to meet the thirty-five-year age requirement. He had served as chief justice of the Supreme Court during its first session in the Lamar administration but had retired soon thereafter. His services to the Republic were demonstrated once more in the Cherokee War, when he commanded a detachment of Texas Rangers, but he had again retired to the private practice of law in partnership with James Pinckney Henderson. His law practice had proved to be very lucrative, and, since he had no desire to be President, Rusk once again refused to accept the nomination. It was not the question of age this time, but the honest desire to remain in private life. In addition, Henderson's well-known friendship with the Houston party may have influenced Rusk not to run because of the embarrassment it would cause his law partner.[90]

Confronted by the unconditional refusals of Albert Sidney John-

[88] Love to Albert Sidney Johnston, May ?, 1841, quoted in Johnston, *Life of General Albert Sidney Johnston,* 121.
[89] Mayfield to Starr, March 17, 1841, Starr Papers.
[90] Gambrell, *Anson Jones,* 204.

ston and Rusk, the partisans of the current administration were forced to rally around Burnet as their standard-bearer. Aware that he was decidedly unpopular with certain elements of his own party and that his chances for election were slim at best, the Vice-President still was eager to make the race. Anson Jones characterized Burnet as a man who "lacks tact and judgment, and is always too much under the influences of his prejudices, which are very powerful,"[91] and Burnet's prejudices in this instance were a matter of public record. He had harbored a hatred for Sam Houston beginning with the latter's victory at San Jacinto and increasing in bitterness over the years. Convinced that fate had played him a bad turn in Houston's election as the first president (succeeding Burnet, who was then President of the ad interim government), the disgruntled Burnet hoped for a thorough vindication of his principles in the election of 1841.

The second election in the Republic of Texas marked the nadir of political taste. With neither candidate having any personal respect for the other, the campaign became even more bitter than the typical frontier race. The Burnet forces, realizing that they possessed a weapon in Houston's known penchant for strong drink, exploited this weakness in every possible way. Writing in July, 1840, James Morgan noted that "Genl. H is strongly inclined to be more dissipated than ever,"[92] and the following year Morgan, having some doubt of Houston's ability to survive his great love for ardent spirits, thought that "Gen. Houston, if he lives, will most assuredly be elected Pres."[93] As might be expected, the followers of Burnet gleefully reported every instance of Houston's drinking as evidence of his unfitness for office. From Austin, Edward Fontaine relayed this news to President Lamar: "The people are becoming more and more afraid of trusting the *righting* of the Ship of State into the hands of a hero who can't *stand upright* himself. I found several on the Colorado (Shuff & Browning among the rest) who were his warm friends when I went down, but who have since turned in favor of Burnett."[94] Finally, the Houston *Telegraph and Texas Regis-*

[91] Jones, *Republic of Texas*, 35.
[92] James Morgan to Samuel Swartwout, July 6, 1840, Morgan Papers.
[93] Morgan to Swartwout, April 22, 1841, *ibid.*
[94] Edward Fontaine to Lamar, July 23, 1841, *Lamar Papers*, III, 557.

ter, whose editor, Francis Moore, Jr., bore an intense personal dislike for Houston, informed its readers that "a few days past he *was brought* to this City in such a state of brutal intoxication, that his own friends were filled with shame and disgust... and carried back in the same deplorable condition."[95] Try as they might, the Houston party could not hope to conceal their leader's reputation for drunkenness.

Since Burnet had no personal habits open to ridicule, the backers of Houston claimed that Burnet should stand responsible for the glaring mistakes of the Lamar administration. It was strongly contended that Burnet, as vice-president, acting secretary of state, and acting president, had become the most important figure in the Lamar party and had been looked upon as the natural successor to Lamar long before the election. That these charges had an appreciable amount of effectiveness can be seen by the vehement denial printed by Francis Moore in the column of the *Telegraph and Texas Register:*[96]

Judge Burnet, being merely Vice-President has no control in the Administration, and has so little influence that his opposition to the Santa Fe expedition had no weight, and indeed he does not attempt to interfere in the administration of government. The faults and the merits of the present administration, should rest where they belong, upon the administration itself, and not for base electioneering purposes be thrown upon Judge Burnet.

The Houston forces also held that Burnet had opposed the peace negotiations with Mexico and had foolishly advocated outright war. On the other hand, Burnet's supporters insisted that their candidate should share none of the responsibility for the shortcomings of the Lamar administration and that he had actually opposed some of the government's projects, notably the removal of the seat of government from Houston to Austin. The Burnet men insisted that their nominee was a true independent who was bound to no party at all and was campaigning solely on the basis of his principles.

Houston was also challenged about his position on certain issues. His acknowledged favoritism for eastern Texas rather than the fron-

[95] Houston *Telegraph and Texas Register,* July 28, 1841.
[96] *Ibid.,* August 4, 1841.

tier sections of the Republic was the chief grievance of those who felt they could not accord him their honest backing. The belief was widespread that if Houston was elected he would immediately transfer the seat of government back to the east and that he would not give adequate consideration to the demands of the frontier. Washington D. Miller, later to become Houston's private secretary, but at that point virtually unknown to him, wrote to the candidate about his views on these basic questions:[97]

You are represented by many of your opponents, as being generally inimical to the welfare of the West—as rejoicing in the anticipation of power to dissever from us, in the day of our depression, the strong arm of our defence, protection and prosperity, by a removal of the present seat of government—as viewing us beyond the pale of common justice and equal privileges with the rest of our countrymen—as deeming us unworthy of governmental considerations, or even mercy—as partial to the East because of its strength and hostile to the West because of its weakness.

Houston's candidacy was also criticized because of his advocacy of the Franco-Texienne Bill, which was held to be the result of an understanding between the candidate and the French government whereby the frontiers of the Republic would be turned into a colony of France. Houston's defense of the Cherokee Land Bill and his fair policy in Indian relations were also held up to public opprobrium. The charge was made that if elected Houston would not vindicate the nation's honor in respect to Mexico and would let matters drift rather than settle the issue by the sword or begin again the process of negotiation. Finally, it was contended that Houston could boast of no better financial record in office than Lamar and that upon his election he would recall General Hamilton and thus give up all hope of ever getting the five-million-dollar loan in Europe.[98]

The press of the Republic had a banner day over the election of 1841. The newspapers backed their respective candidates in colorful fashion, and the Houston *Telegraph and Texas Register* set the tone of election editorials as early as March of the election year:[99]

[97] Washington D. Miller to Houston, February 27, 1841, Miller Papers.
[98] Austin *Texas Sentinel*, July 22, 1841.
[99] Houston *Telegraph and Texas Register*, March 31, 1841.

There is one consideration connected with the ensuing presidential election that our citizens should constantly keep in view. The national character is to be sustained, and the private character of the individual elected, should be free from blemish or any degrading vice. . . . Burnet has been tried in adversity and prosperity, and ever found capable and faithful to the best interests of the people. Why then should we hesitate? By electing a drunkard, we cast the high destinies of our beloved republic upon a die, and leave it to blind chance. Whether our bark of state bound on with her sails swelled to the breeze of prosperity, or whether misguided by the *reeling* helmsman, she founders amid rocks of quicksands, to the ruin of the country.

A short while later, the Austin *City Gazette* charged the friends of Burnet with paying for the reissue of the pamphlet *Houston Displayed,* a bitter indictment against the victor of San Jacinto charging him with cowardice at the time of the battle but admitting that the General could not be held accountable for his actions because he was then a slave to the opium habit. The *City Gazette* lamented the fact that the pamphlet had been issued for "electioneering purposes" and noted with satisfaction that this was a "work of which the publisher appears to have been so ashamed, as not to allow his imprint to be printed on it."[100]

Such comments were merely the opening guns in this bitter election. Frontier editors delighted in racy writing under normal, everyday conditions, and an election which was so controversial allowed a wide display of editorial talents. An Austin paper, the *Texas Sentinel,* which supported Burnet for the Presidency, stated as an unqualified truth that Sam Houston would "*blaspheme his God,* by the most horrible oaths, that ever fell from the lips of man."[101] On the other hand, the *Houstonian* of August 18, 1841, published a commentary on Burnet written by Houston, under the pen name "Truth." Referring to Burnet's denunciation of his character, Houston said: "You prate about the faults of other men, *while the blot of foul unmitigated treason rests upon you.* You political brawler and canting hypocrite, whom the waters of Jordan could never cleanse from your political and moral leprosy."[102] Houston followed this by

[100] Austin *City Gazette*, August 11, 1841.
[101] Austin *Texas Sentinel,* July 5, 1841, quoted in Hogan, *The Texas Republic,* 174.
[102] *Houstonian,* August 18, 1841, quoted in *ibid.,* 174.

179

a reference to Burnet as a "hog thief." Confronted with this last assault, the Burnet party was forced to resort to poetry. The following ode was dedicated to Houston:[103]

> A hero was travelling—his labors were o'er
> But sad was the smile his countenance wore,
>   For . . .
> . . . he'd sworn before God 'gainst taking strong drink,
> Now what will I do when my spirits are low,
> Shall I take to friend opium. Ah! it is a worse foe—
> By th' Eternal, I have it. To think more would be idle,
> The Book that I swore on—why, it was not the Bible!
> So give me some whiskey—tis the cheer of Gods! . . .

The Houston faction, confronted with this effort, readily admitted defeat in the realm of poetry. Eschewing the written campaign, both parties then concentrated on winning votes for their respective candidates.

James Pinckney Henderson, supporting Houston because of the rebuff he had received from the Lamar administration while still in Europe, wrote to Anson Jones, instructing him to go on a speaking tour in the east because "you know sufficiently well the effect the presence a candidate has on the sovereigns."[104] In this fashion the Houston party spared no effort in presenting their case to the "sovereigns." Henderson, Jones, Ashbel Smith, and others campaigned arduously, and the ultimate success of their candidate must in part be attributed to their constant efforts. Houston himself went on the stump and brought the full force of his personality to bear on the electorate. Adolphus Sterne, the postmaster at Nacogdoches, noted that Houston was very well received while making an election speech in that town, and the same situation was repeated elsewhere.[105] Burnet, on the other hand, could not be compared to Houston as a stump orator, and there is no extant evidence of any large public assemblies gathered to hear him present his case. In this fashion the two nominees conducted their campaign, with the Houston party putting forth a much more strenuous effort.

[103] Austin *Texas Sentinel*, August 26, 1841, quoted in James, *The Raven*, 319.
[104] Henderson to Jones, June 15, 1841, in Jones, *Republic of Texas*, 164.
[105] Harriet Smither (ed.), "The Diary of Adolphus Sterne," *Southwestern Historical Quarterly*, XXXI (1928), 380.

The general feeling which prevailed in the Republic during the campaign was that Houston would be returned to the Presidency by a substantial margin. This opinion was most clearly reflected in the defeatist tone of correspondence to President Lamar touching upon the election. James Webb, Lamar's closest friend and former agent to Mexico, informed the President that "the almost certain prospect of his election to the Presidency will be the means of returning many Houston men to the next Congress which otherwise could not get there, & such a Congress would do nothing to advance the credit of your administration."[106] In very practical fashion Webb then advised Lamar to replace General Hamilton in England by appointing James Burnley, who was popular with the Houston group, and to replace Barnard E. Bee in Washington with Branch T. Archer, whose great popularity throughout the Republic would preclude his removal by the new administration. James Reily, writing to James Harper Starr, a sworn Houston opponent, predicted that Burnet would not receive one hundred votes in the city of Houston and would be soundly defeated throughout the nation.[107] The most damning commentary on Burnet's chances came from Henry Millard, writing from Austin. The Burnet party realized that they must make a clean sweep of the frontier sections in order to stand a chance in the election. Commenting on this situation, Millard wrote: "Burnet is completely done, he could not now in the western counties be elected fiddler Genl. to the old chief."[108] In truth, the Burnet partisans had seen the handwriting on the wall and virtually conceded defeat before the contest.

In contrast, the Houston party, well aware of the work that had gone into the campaign and certain of the effect of their candidate's personality on the frontier, was very sure of the outcome. After the election but before the returns were counted, James Morgan observed that "in very few Counties no Candidate stood any chance to be elected to Congress unless he first declares himself a *Houston man*. This augurs well for *Old Sam*."[109] Another indication of the prevailing belief in the General's coming victory was the desire of

181

the vice-presidential candidates, Generals Memucan Hunt and Edward Burleson, to identify themselves with the Houston ticket. The Houston party's first choice had undoubtedly been Rusk, but Houston finally gave his blessing to Burleson because that candidate represented the west and thus would give some sectional balance to the ticket as well as offset Houston's acknowledged preference for the east.

Election day dawned quite warm, and the total vote was about what had been expected.[110] Houston was elected, receiving 7,915 votes to Burnet's 3,619. In the race for vice-president, Edward Burleson, the Houston-sanctioned candidate, received 6,141 votes and Memucan Hunt received 4,336.[111] The election results bore out the saltily worded message James Morgan had conveyed to a friend: "Old Sam H. with all his faults appears to be the only man for Texas —He is still unsteady, *intemperate,* but drunk in a ditch is worth a thousand of Lamar and Burnet."[112] In short, Burnet's identification with the disastrous mistakes and extravagances of the Lamar administration and Houston's powerful, compelling personality had returned the Old Hero to the Executive Chair.

[110] Smither (ed.), "The Diary of Adolphus Sterne," *Southwestern Historical Quarterly,* XXXII, 73–74.
[111] Wooten, *A Complete History of Texas,* 274.
[112] James Morgan to Colonel Webb, January 29 ,1841, Morgan Papers.

The Old Hero Once Again

WHATEVER GENERAL HOUSTON has been, it is plain that *He* is the fittest man in this Country for his present station. His education has been imperfect, but he possesses great sagacity and penetration, surprising tact in his management of men trained as men are in these parts, is perfectly pure handed and moved in the main by the inspiring motive of desiring to connect his name with a Nation's rise. Adverting to his general safe and reasonable policy with respect to Mexico, it must certainly be admitted that He sometimes says and writes what appears to be capricious and contradictory. But the truth is that He knows his own people thoroughly, and when He seems to be running with them, He is probably satisfied that opposition would only provoke their precipitate purposes. With hard fare at the point of assembly, skilful delays on the part of the President, and an abundant measure of mutual laudation, the fit passes away innocently enough.[1]

ON ASSUMING OFFICE, that astute politician, Houston, faced the most difficult task which had yet confronted a President of the Republic. The military hero had been returned to office at a time when the fortunes of Texas were at their lowest ebb. Lamar had left his successor the legacy of an impoverished and virtually powerless Republic; his extravagances in office had meant disaster to the country and political disaster to himself. A missionary to Texas at this time noted: "There is no business going on, no money in circulation and provisions are extremely scarce,"[2] and this lamentable observation was on the tongues of many throughout the land. As if the specter of financial ruin were not enough to confront, the Mexican danger still remained, and the President was certain that the forces of the Republic were not adequate to wage war at this time. However, there was the ever-present danger that Mexico, again united under Santa Anna, might well choose this opportune time to attempt a reconquest of her territories. The President also knew that he would have to contend with reckless elements in Congress who would demand a full-scale invasion of Mexico for political purposes, and this fear was to be only too well realized. Finally, the General was faced with the task of defining the relationship of the Republic to the United States and to Great Britain and France; the negotiations for annexation could be renewed again by the new administration, or the Chief Executive could simply allow the matter to be dropped.

In the selection of his cabinet Houston was careful to nominate men of unquestioned loyalty to his principles. The costly mistake Lamar had made in appointing former supporters of Houston to his official family would not be repeated. For secretary of state the President was quick to name Anson Jones. The appointee had previously distinguished himself as minister from Texas to the United States, and he also had actively campaigned for his chief in the recent election. Houston was aware that he harbored a potential rebel

[1] Charles Elliot to William Addington, November 15, 1842, in Adams (ed.), *British Diplomatic Correspondence*, 126.
[2] J. M. Odin, I.S.C.M. to Rev. John Timon, June 20, 1842, in *History of the Diocese of Galveston, 1847–1922*, 74.

in his midst because of Jones's consuming ambition to be President, but the appointment was necessary to preserve harmony, since Jones had the full backing of such influential party stalwarts as Ashbel Smith and James Pinckney Henderson.[3] As secretary of war and marine the President named his personal friend of old Tennessee days, George W. Hockley. The appointee had been at San Jacinto and had always been a devoted follower of Houston's. William H. Daingerfield, a native of Virginia and a fairly recent arrival in Texas, was named secretary of the treasury. He had been an outstanding Houston man in the recent sessions of the Senate and a vigorous opponent of the Santa Fe expedition.[4] For the office of attorney general the President appointed George Terrell, who, curiously enough, had served as Houston's attorney general when Old Sam was governor of Tennessee. Terrell had demonstrated his full loyalty by refusing the position of secretary of state in the Lamar administration, and therefore he was quickly rewarded by the party now in power. The major diplomatic appointments were conferred upon James Reily, named minister to the United States, and Ashbel Smith, in payment for his political support, appointed minister to France and England. To complete the selections, Gail Borden was entrusted with the collectorship of the port at Galveston.[5]

Satisfied with his cabinet appointments, the President devoted a great deal of time and preparation to his inaugural address. Taking the oath of office on December 13, 1841, Houston determined to make the occasion a memorable one by a formidable effort in the delivery of his prepared speech. Josiah Gregg, the famous frontier trader, was a spectator at the ceremonies and has left this description of the gala event:[6]

Today Gen. Sam Houston was inaugurated president of the Republic of Texas. The audience consisted perhaps of about 1000 persons. He appeared on the stage in a linsey-wooley hunting shirt, and pantaloons, and an old wide brimmed white fur hat. I thought in this Gen. Houston

[3] Gambrell, *Anson Jones,* 219.

[4] *Houston Writings,* II, 453.

[5] Wooten, *A Complete History of Texas,* 279. There was no independent cabinet position in the second Houston administration to cover the office of postmaster general. The functions of this appointment were taken over by the department of war and the secretary of state.

[6] Maurice Garland Fulton (ed.), *Diary and Letters of Josiah Gregg: Southwestern Enterprises, 1840–1847,* 109.

demonstrated more vanity than if he had appeared in an ordinary cloth suit. He knew it would be much remarked, and thought it would be popular no doubt, with the body of the people. Gen. Burleson also appeared and was sworn in in his fancy leathered hunting shirt—probably more for the purpose of being in unison with the President than for vanity—though Burleson was a *hunter* of the plainest raising and education.

In his inaugural speech Houston attacked the Lamar administration at all of its weak points. Instead of presenting to the people a series of proposals for the betterment of the Republic, he engaged solely in a bitter condemnation of the recent incumbents. Lamar's Indian policy, his failure to obtain a peace with Mexico, his hasty abandonment of the annexation proceedings, and his admittedly poor showing in the realm of finance were all in their turn castigated and held up to public ridicule. The President characterized the Santa Fe incident as "visionary and unauthorized" and intimated that the funds which had been allocated to increase the size of the navy were also part and parcel of an unconstitutional transaction. The Hero of San Jacinto expressed his thankfulness that the loan was no longer a vital issue and that therefore the Republic would not be lulled into a false sense of security. Finally, Houston strongly condemned Lamar's policy of staffing the government with political "loafers" and served notice on the assemblage that the civil expenses of the government would be reduced from $3,000,000 to the reasonable sum of $300,000.[7]

Houston's address may have been eloquent to his friends in Congress, but to Josiah Gregg it was a distinct disappointment. Concerning the speech, Gregg noted:[8]

He did not demonstrate that extemporaneous eloquence, which I had expected to see and hear: Indeed I could but pronounce the manner of his address rather dry and monotonous. A part of the substance did well enough; but he certainly would have done much better not to have been his own eulogist—I should say he dwelt too much and unbecomingly on the merits of his former services and administration: of which the people generally do not speak near so favorably as he himself. Also he bore much too severely upon the maladministration of his predecessor—this he should have left for others to have censured.

[7] "Inaugural Address," *Houston Writings*, II, 391–94.
[8] Fulton (ed.), *Diary and Letters of Josiah Gregg*, 110.

186

One week later, however, in his first message to Congress, the President formally outlined the policies that would guide his administration. The Chief Executive called for friendship and treaties of peace with the Indian tribes and at the same time for the establishment of a line of garrison-protected trading posts all along the frontier. He then recommended that the customs should be collected in specie, and the direct taxes in a mixed currency of specie and government liabilities. Also, he suggested that the debts and obligations of the Republic should be suspended until their nature and exact amount could be fixed and until there was some certainty of paying them. The President asked for the issuance of not more than $350,000 in exchequer bills to take the place of redbacks, the promissory notes issued during the Lamar administration. These exchequer bills were to be secured by one million acres of the Cherokee lands and by the customs revenues of the government, to be received for duties and taxes only at par, and to be canceled as fast as they were received. Houston expressed his hope that Congress would reduce all expenses, would cut down taxes to one-half their former rates (with payment to be made in coin or par paper only), and would give sanction for a public loan of $300,000. In the realm of foreign affairs, the Executive announced that he would enter into no agreements with the Mexican revolutionists and called for a staunch policy of armed neutrality toward Mexico. He stated that a treaty of commerce with the United States was desirable but made no comment whatever about the thorny problem of annexation.[9]

The Sixth Congress of the Republic, sitting at Austin from November, 1841, to February, 1842, and later at Houston from June to July, 1842, was predominantly an administration-controlled Congress, but there were strong elements of opposition to the President among those legislators who had survived the disastrous defeat of Lamar. As speaker of the House, the Houston forces selected Kenneth L. Anderson, representing the county of San Augustine. In the House, the administration could count on the unqualified support of Nicholas Henry Darnell, also of the county of San Augustine, Jessie Grimes, representing the county of Montgomery, William E. Jones, of Gonzales, Cornelius Van Ness, of Bexar, Isaac Van Zandt,

[9] *Houston Writings*, II, 399–408.

of Harrison, and Robert McAlpin Williamson, of the county of Washington. In the Senate, the Houston sentiment was directed by Senator John A. Greer, of the district of San Augustine, and Senator Kindred H. Muse, representing the combined districts of Nacogdoches and Houston. However, an articulate opposition to the President's leadership existed in both the House and Senate. In the Senate, the antiadministration group was led by William H. Jack, of Brazoria, and the bitterly partisan editor of the Houston *Telegraph and Texas Register,* Francis Moore, sitting for the combined districts of Harris, Liberty, and Galveston. Finally, in the House, opposition strength gathered around William L. Cazneau, of Travis County, Tod Robinson, of Brazoria, and General Sidney Sherman, of Harris County.[10] This was the state of party alignments as the Sixth Congress began its sessions; the Houston forces united under the President, while the opposition had no basis for union other than a common desire to obstruct the government's projected program of legislation.

Irrespective of party loyalty, the legislators were able to agree on the necessity for retrenchment. On January 19, 1842, Congress provided for the issuance of $200,000 in exchequer bills, secured by the customs receipts, and it was further stipulated that these bills should be received only at par for taxes and duties. In rapid fashion the solons then suspended payment of the public debt of the Republic until the nation could meet its obligations. Then, directly repudiating one of Lamar's principal measures, the congressmen repealed the law authorizing the $5,000,000 loan. They also refused to sanction any further loans of any amount, defying the President's wish for a public loan of $300,000. As a further economy measure, Congress decided to lop off the government payroll some political positions which had been created by the previous administration. Accordingly, the offices of commissioner of revenue, translator of the general land office, commissary of subsistence, and quartermaster and paymaster general of the regular army were abolished. Also, the salaries of the President, members of his cabinet, and members of the Supreme Court, as well as the chief clerks in all of the departments, were appreciably reduced. As evidence of their patriotic sin-

[10] Winkler (ed.), *Secret Journals of the Senate,* 204.

cerity, the legislators did not forget to cut down their own pay rate from $5 to $3 per day.[11]

In a letter to his wife, Anson Jones noted: "Every thing goes on here very well so far. The Old Hero keeps perfectly cool and sober. . . . His message has given very general satisfaction."[12] However, this atmosphere of harmony which had resulted in the bipartisan efforts at economy in government was not destined to last long. The President soon displayed his lasting preference for the eastern sections of the Republic by indicating his desire to remove the seat of government from Austin back to Houston. The Executive decided upon this action well aware of the furor it would create, but he allowed his disposition toward the east to sway his judgment. The only satisfactory reason that can be set down to justify the President's action was the constant fear of Indian attack to which the capital city was subject. During Lamar's administration the Comanches had made sporadic raids on the city, and the fear expressed by one citizen that the "Indians are thick as hops about the mountains in this vicinity and occasionally they knock over a poor fellow and take his hair"[13] was a very real one. Houston also felt that the archives of the Republic were not safe at Austin and therefore decided on removal.

The Chief Executive had not wasted any time in demanding the removal of the seat of government. Immediately after his election, but before the inauguration, the administration-sponsored newspaper, the Houston *Morning Star,* referring to Austin, asked its readers to weigh the awful consequences if "the enemy should descend and capture this place, and destroy the public archives and murder or carry into captivity the officers of government, in what a deplorable condition would our Republic be placed? We should become the laughing stock of the world."[14] Once in office the President gathered together his following in Congress, and on January 18, 1842, two bills were introduced in the House of Representatives for the removal. One bill empowered the Executive to remove the archives and such other public property as he might deem desirable

[11] Lubbock, *Six Decades in Texas,* 143–44.
[12] Anson Jones to his wife, December 21, 1841, Anson Jones Papers.
[13] Jack Snively to James H. Starr, n.d., Starr Papers.
[14] Houston *Morning Star,* October 2, 1841.

to a safer place, and the other proposed to fix a new site for the capital by a joint vote of the Senate and House of Representatives. The fight for removal was led by John A. Greer in the Senate and Isaac Van Zandt in the House, and for a while it appeared as if the Houston forces would carry the issue. However, William L. Cazneau, member of the House from Travis County, of which Austin was the principal city, waged a passionate fight against removal, and a deadlock resulted.

Though the President was in favor of removal from Austin, there were elements in his party who doubted the wisdom of this policy. The objection was voiced that if the action could not be secured by legitimate means in Congress then Houston would be forced to resort to an executive order to realize his ends, and it was felt that this would be unwise politically since the President's plan would be met with a storm of disapproval. Washington D. Miller, now private secretary to the President, wrote to his chief in this light: "When the danger is apparent, and the mass of the people see it, then the time has arrived to remove them, and not before. The advice of one of your friends, to *just get scared one time and see if you don't get to Houston with more ease than could be expected won't do*. The emergency must be *real* and the people must see it."[15] This was good political advice, but for once Houston did not play the politician and persisted in his demands that the party followers in Congress push the removal bills through.

The removal of the capital was the most hotly debated issue in Houston's second term of office. To those residing in the western-frontier sections of the Republic who had not voted for the President, it seemed that all their fears about Houston's lack of concern for the welfare of the frontier had come true. At this time Miller informed the Executive:[16]

The people of the West are on this subject sensitive in the highest degree. They are enamored with the idea of the seat of government being located upon the Colorado and I trust I may not be disbelieved when I say that under no circumstances will they consent to its removal so long as it may be practicable for them to prevent it—and under no circumstances will they consent to see the archives of the government removed.

[15] Washington D. Miller to Houston, February 9, 1842, Miller Papers.
[16] Miller to Houston, March 2, 1842, *ibid*.

It is certain that some members of the population around Austin, and in the western counties generally, considered the possibility of armed resistance against any attempts to remove the archives from Austin. Feeling ran high on the matter, and the charges hurled back and forth were of a serious nature. A letter from a settler on the frontier addressed to the President of the Republic gives an indication of the passion aroused at the time:[17]

Sir Old Sam—We did heart that you was goin to move the seat of government and the publick papers and that you swore you would do it, and then when you come to Austin and found out the boys would not let you do it you sed you never was goin to move it. Now Sam you told a dam lie for you did promise the people in Houston that you would move it, and I heard a man say that you told Hockley not to bring all his servants because you would all go back soon. But the truth is that you are afeard you Dam old drunk Cherokee. We dont thank you becase we would shoot you and every dam waggoner that you could start with the papers you cant do it and we ax you no odds. Travis and Bastrop Fayette Gonzales can bring 1000 men out and Ned Burleson and Lewis P. Cook have promised that you shant budge with the papers. I heard them myself and you know Burleson and Cook can make you squat you dam blackguard Indian drunk. Now old fellow if you want to try Ned Burlesons spunk you try to move these papers, and old Ned will serve you just as he did your Cherokee brother when he took the Hat what you give to your Daddy Bowles You shall hear more from me when I am ready.

But the President's luck, which had helped him out of difficult situations before, again came to his rescue. The official account of the unhappy outcome of the Santa Fe expedition reached the Republic soon after Houston took office. Public indignation at the arbitrary manner in which Lamar had authorized the expedition and a general sentiment for offensive war against Mexico acted to force the seat-of-government issue into the background. The congressmen expressed their anger at the fate of the members of the expedition by passing a bill extending the boundaries of Texas to include the Californias, New Mexico, Chihuahua, Sonora, and parts of the Mexican provinces of Sinaloa, Durango, Coahuila, and Tamaulipas —a territory larger than the United States at that time and containing a population of about two thousand Mexicans and Indians.

[17] James Welsh to Houston, n.d., in Gambrell, *Anson Jones*, 247.

POLITICAL HISTORY OF THE TEXAS REPUBLIC

Houston, always a realist in military matters, contemptuously referred to this enactment as a "legislative jest" and lectured Congress that it would "appear curious to nations in amity with us, that a people destitute of means to meet their most pressing wants should assume to govern a country possessing a population of more than thirty to one."[18]

However, in the face of this verbal rebuke, Congress passed the enactment over Houston's veto and thereby succeeded in making a very empty threat against the sovereignty of Mexico. The principle of manifest destiny was truly at work among the legislators, but the fact that the Republic could not financially afford to make good their pretensions should also have been reckoned with. Even so, this state of affairs did not deter Senator Francis Moore, the editor of the Houston *Telegraph and Texas Register*, from waxing eloquent on the glories to be gained through an offensive war against Mexico:[19]

We have been repeatedly assured by many of the most wealthy and influential men of the Mississippi valley, that whenever Texas shall determine to push her standard across the Rio Grande, she will never want for the men and means requisite to plant that standard in triumph on the "walls of the ancient Capital of the Montezumas." We have every reason to believe that these professions are sincere, and we can hardly doubt that the least demonstration on the part of our government to commence or sanction offensive operations against Mexico, would be responded to with joyus acclamations throughout the United States, and especially through the broad and populous valley of the Mississippi. Let the mandate but go forth. "Texas has decided to prosecute an offensive war," and she might in all probability remain almost passive and look on with folded arms to see the great work accomplished.

As if to give the lie to sentiments such as those poured forth by Moore, Mexican troops under the command of General Rafael Vasquez appeared before San Antonio on March 5. Vasquez led some fourteen hundred men, and the hundred or so settlers at Béxar wisely decided to surrender. At about this same time, small parties of Mexican troops entered Goliad and Refugio, but they did no great

[18] "Veto of an Act to Define the Boundaries of the Republic," *Houston Writings,* 464–65.
[19] Houston *Telegraph and Texas Register,* February 2, 1842.

damage and retired in orderly fashion in a few days. This military offensive stemmed from Santa Anna's wish to serve notice that the reconquest of Texas might soon be attempted on a grand scale. With internal troubles now at a minimum, the Mexican government reacted against the Texan's attempt to aid the rebels in Yucatan, the Santa Fe expedition, and many other irritants they had suffered during the Lamar administration. The clear and present danger of a full-scale invasion of Texas soil by Mexican troops was another legacy left to Houston by his predecessor.

The Vasquez raid, while it saved Houston's prestige in the capital fight, still precipitated the first major rebellion within the ranks of his party. The President had been fortunate in escaping this problem throughout his first administration, but the Mexican danger gave Vice-President Burleson an opportunity to consult his own political star. The established way to prominence in the politics of the Republic was through the glories of military conquest, and the Vice-President therefore decided to assume a command in the field. The President's private secretary, Washington D. Miller, informed Houston: "Gen. Burleson and about three companies of horse left here this morning for Bexar. Louis P. Cooke commands one. Burleson has declared unceasing strife until the achievement of a lasting peace; and is warm for the Rio Grande."[20] Realizing that Burleson's actions were to a great extent motivated by political considerations, Houston dispatched Brigadier General Edward Morehouse to inform General Alexander Somervell, commander of the militia at San Antonio, that he was to assume entire command of any military action that might be taken against the retreating Mexicans. When Somervell rode into camp he was told that the volunteers assembled at San Antonio had chosen Burleson as their leader and that they would not serve under the President's appointee. Burleson, shrinking from an open clash with the President, lingered uncertainly for some two weeks and then finally returned to Austin. Somervell, in turn, wisely declined to command those men who did not want him, and the incident was allowed to die. The Mexicans continued their orderly retreat; further preparations were necessary before they would make another attempt at reconquest.

The result of the Mexican raid was unfortunate for the adminis-

[20] Washington D. Miller to Houston, March 13, 1842, Miller Papers.

tration. Houston now had on his hands a restless group of some thirty-five hundred volunteers at San Antonio who were reluctant to return home before attempting an invasion of Mexico. As was to be expected in such cases, the volunteers were proving extremely troublesome. In plaintive fashion, the Houston *Morning Star* informed the men that "Gen. Somervell is an experienced soldier and very amiable in his private deportment, it is to be hoped that the volunteers will rally to his standard, and endeavor to strike an effectual blow against the enemy."[21] Still, the antipathy to the command of the President's appointee continued to display itself, although the sentiment for war remained strong throughout the Republic. Various newspaper editorials caused the Executive great anxiety, for he wished to avoid war and if forced into it wanted the nation to be united under his designated commander. Commenting on the necessity for war, the Austin *City Gazette* said:[22]

Here, then, is to be found the cause of all of our difficulties—the source of a heavy national debt—crippled commerce—neglected if not paralyzed husbandry; and an emigration, less by four-fifths, than it would have been under other circumstances; and it renders cautious and hesitating purchasers of improvements, and operations of every kind, in consequence of this continually threatened invasion. Our Mexican relations must be regarded as the great barrier to our immediate and unrivalled prosperity. . . . Being convinced as to the cause of our present evils, what, then is the remedy? It is an immediate invasion of the northern provinces of Mexico—carry the "war into Africa." The Rio Grande should be the theatre of every battle; and on the enemy should our men subsist, until we have our rights and independence acknowledged.

Because the President would not take effective action and the men themselves would not serve under Somervell, the volunteers quit their campsite on April 2. Houston had suffered in silence throughout the unfortunate affair, but in a letter to Secretary of the Treasury William H. Daingerfield the party leader unburdened himself about Burleson and the insubordination which the Vice-President had displayed:[23]

[21] Houston *Morning Star*, April 14, 1842.
[22] Austin *City Gazette*, March 30, 1842.
[23] Houston to William Henry Daingerfield, April 1, 1842, *Houston Writings*, III, 15.

You would be amused and miserably provoked at some of our "Heroes." It has been reported by rumor (for that has been the only official) that Burleson was at San Antonio with 1500 men & Clark L. Owen with 1000 at Victoria, all burning with revenge to cross the Rio Grande and "damning the President" that he would not let them go on. Oh, they were snorting! Genl Somerville was the only officer that I could by law order to the command Genl of the 1st Brigade and Lieut. Brigadier! Somebody will be taken down a button hole or two.

As the bellicose demands continued and the revolt swelled within his own inner councils, Houston was compelled to make a token bow to the advocates of war. On March 26 the President declared a blockade against all Mexican ports from the coast of Tabasco to Brazos Santiago. The Mexican navy had been seriously damaged in the Pastry War with France, and the blockade could not have been effectively enforced if the Texas Navy had been in the area, but Houston was aware that Commodore Moore was still in Yucatan waters and deliberately delayed ordering the return of the fleet. When Moore returned to the city of Houston and met with the President in May, he was told to proceed with the skeleton navy to New Orleans for repairs. The Executive solemnly assured him that the necessary funds would be forthcoming to cover the cost of repairs, and Moore sailed away. In this fashion, Houston made his gesture to the adherents of war, thus pacifying public opinion. The President then turned his attention to other matters, and the question of the practical enforcement of the blockade was allowed to rest for a time.[24]

The first sessions of the Sixth Congress had been concluded at Austin on February 5, and now Houston determined that the next meetings would be held in his namesake city. The Vasquez raid had strengthened the President's hand in the matter of the removal of the seat of government, for with the Mexican troops able to occupy San Antonio, the capital city of Austin would be in grave danger of attack. In fact, the road to Austin lay open, and had Vasquez wished to make a concerted attempt to capture the city his efforts might well have met with success. Before announcing that the next sessions of Congress would be held in Houston, the Executive made public his desire that the archives be removed from Austin, and the party organ, the Houston *Morning Star*, editorialized on the dangers of allowing the archives to remain at Austin:[25]

> The Archives, therefore, can hardly be considered safe in their present location; and if they are not removed to Houston, we think they should at least be brought *within the settlements* as far as Bastrop. If, by any sudden incursion of the enemy, the Archives of the country should be destroyed, the citizens of Travis county would bitterly regret that any motives of private interest had induced them to retain the Archives at their present hazardous location.

The legislators assembled at Houston on June 27 and sat for less than a month, adjourning on July 23, 1842. The session was one of the most tempestuous that the Republic had ever known. In the face of the disapproval caused by the removal of the capital, Houston at this time made no attempt to have the archives removed from Austin. By this strategy the Executive hoped to convey the impression that the removal was only a temporary measure. And Houston realized that his popularity had always greatly suffered because of his reluctance to sanction an offensive war against Mexico.

Just before the congressmen assembled at Houston, the revolt within the President's party broke into public print. Vice-President Burleson committed the great blunder of defending his recent insubordinate actions in an open letter to the people of the Republic. Stating that the Texans could successfully have crossed the Rio Grande and invaded Mexico if the command had been unified and that it was only the stubbornness of the Executive that had prevented the grand design, Burleson assured the citizenry: "I love my country more than I fear the executive's displeasure. . . . I still believe it of vital importance to the prosperity of Texas, that the campaign should be made upon the valley of the Rio Grande."[26] Houston wisely remained silent and refused to enter into a public controversy with the Vice-President, but in a letter to Daingerfield the President vented his true feelings:[27]

> The exertions which were made by some persons to embarrass the Government and to create *Great* ruin have failed and matters are in

[25] Houston *Morning Star*, March 24, 1842.
[26] Houston *Telegraph and Texas Register*, April 20, 1842.
[27] Houston to Daingerfield, April 27, 1842, *Houston Writings*, III, 38–39.

some degree changed into another channel. They find that they are not so great as they believed, nor will the Government allow them to take the lead. They are now understood and will bear the mark on the forehead.

With this private unburdening of his anger, the President filed away the act of treachery for further reference.

In his message to Congress at Houston, the Chief Executive concerned himself with the question of a definite policy toward Mexico. He told the legislators that he would not assume the responsibility of advising an invasion of Mexico because there was no serious danger of an attempt on the part of that country to subjugate Texas but that Santa Anna would adopt a policy of raiding the frontier and of attempting to make contact with the few tribes of hostile Indians still within the boundaries of the Republic. Houston admitted that some remedy must be found to combat these evils but that at the same time the government must entertain no pretensions of pushing the war beyond the Rio Grande. The President called attention to the fact that many volunteers and militiamen had answered his call for troops and were then on the Nueces and at other points waiting either to be employed in active military operations or to be disbanded. The Executive reminded the legislators that the ultimate decision would rest in their hands and promised to be guided in his actions by the will of Congress.[28]

This decision not to recommend war after the Vasquez raid defied a strong war sentiment within Houston's party. Washington D. Miller had made a trip through certain sections of the Republic in an attempt to discern popular feeling on the matter, and he returned confirmed in the belief that the government must wage war. In a letter to the President, Miller allowed his enthusiasm to run away with him while counseling his chief in this fashion:[29]

It strikes me that we are upon the eve of a great and important crisis in the history of America. Think, General, and think betimes, of the complexity and grandeur of the movements about to be exhibited to the gaze of astonished millions. A great drama is in progress. Two acts have

---

[28] "Annual Message to the Seventh Congress of the Republic," *Houston Writings*, III, 74–83.

[29] Washington D. Miller to Houston, March 5, 1842, Miller Papers.

already passed. The first was the settlement and establishment of the independence of the United States—The second was the settlement and liberation of Texas—The third *will be the conquest of Mexico*. "Westward the *star* of empire makes its way" and like the wise men of old, the Angloamerican will be true to its course. They will follow its light as a beacon of glory. . . . General, I am not raving. I am in earnest.

Upon reading this Houston must have had some good-natured doubts about the reasoning powers of his secretary, but he persevered in his cautious policy, though realizing that he had injured the government's popularity by his refusal to bow to public feeling and declare war.

However, the congressmen, most of whom did not enjoy the Old Hero's personal popularity at the polls, made the necessary obeisance to the public excitement and brought forth a bill which called in strong language for active measures against the Mexican government. Again the President had to contend with a semblance of party revolt, for the leading advocate of the war bill was Isaac Van Zandt, a loyal Houston man, who was serving on the House Military Affairs Committee. In a passionate speech before the House, Van Zandt, who well knew that his policy would incur administrative displeasure, claimed that foreign capitalists, eager for a share of the nation's public domain, would flock to finance the war. Van Zandt implored the Executive to sell or mortgage "millions of acres" without making any "cold and sordid calculation" whether the policy would be "incompatible with the genius of our institutions." Van Zandt argued that if subscription booths were opened throughout the Republic Texans themselves would contribute enough to enable the Executive to begin offensive operations. The congressman concluded his oration by stating that the volunteers were at hand for so popular an enterprise as a march beyond the Rio Grande and that the nation waited only for the President's approval.[30]

As a direct result of the spur provided by Van Zandt, Archibald Wynns, Cooke, and William E. Jones in the House, and John A. Greer in the Senate, the Legislature passed a bill calling for an offensive war. By the provisions of the enactment, the Executive was

[30] Gambrell, *Anson Jones*, 252–53.

designated commander-in-chief in the field and was given virtually dictatorial powers justified only by the existing emergency. Houston was empowered to conscript one-third of that portion of the population able to bear arms and to sell ten million acres of land in order to defray the expenses of the campaign. The resignation of Felix Huston as major general of the militia was accepted, and the President was given the active command in the field. In short, the legislators had concluded that the perilous times justified strong measures and had acted accordingly. If Houston desired to be a military strong man and to pose as the savior of the Republic, the opportunity was now at hand.

A feeling of joy swept through the country when the news of the congressional action was made public. It is certain that a war with Mexico would have been immensely popular with the settlers of Texas. In a letter to Samuel Swartwout, the observant James Morgan reported: "There will be no restraining the volunteers from going ahead. They are almost uncontrollable now, such is their anxiety to get into Mexico." Morgan informed his friend that because of Burleson's disobedience the President was "snarlish as a half starved dog" and stated his belief that Houston would accept the terms of the bill and thereby assume the active command of the nation's armies. Those close to the Executive strongly advised him to sign the bill, both because it was extremely necessary to his political welfare and also because the situation of the nation demanded it.[31]

It was generally assumed that Houston would give his approval to the measure and thus expedite the preparations for war, though a small minority believed the President would veto the bill and refuse to assume the blanket grant of power which some felt to be unconstitutional. This sentiment was expressed by the editor of the Galveston *Civilian* in a comment on what Houston's policy might be:[32]

The war Bill has not yet been acted upon by the Executive, and if I am allowed to prophesy, it will be vetoed, and if so it will elevate Gen. Houston so far above all his enemies that hence forward he will be in-

[31] Morgan to Swartwout, May 17, 1842, Morgan Papers.
[32] Galveston *Civilian*, July 18, 1842.

vulnerable to the shafts so lavishly aimed at him.—His refusal to accept the almost unlimited powers vested in him will display his superior strength of mind in refusing what his enemies have so loudly declared was his only object and desire—the complete control of the purse and sword.

The editor of the *Civilian* proved to be an apt prophet, for after delaying a short time the President returned the bill with his veto. In the message explaining his action, Houston stated that he was opposed to such dictatorial powers being granted to any person in a free government. The Executive believed that a successful invasion of Mexican soil would require at least five thousand men with all the necessary military supplies and equipment and that the Republic could not finance such an army. He noted that the ten million acres of land appropriated would require agents to sell it; no provision had been made for their pay, and the sale itself would bring only a very small revenue, for the Republic had already issued great quantities of land scrip which had no sale except at nominal prices. The Old Hero then gave evidence that all the criticism which had been heaped upon him had reached its mark, for he concluded the veto message with a sarcastic observation that the entire bill was like a "resolution to appropriate ten million acres of blue sky and conferring dictatorial powers on the north wind."[33] Besides his opposition to war, the President's chief objection to this measure was that its provisions were unconstitutional and would prove a serious blow to the civil liberties of the populace.

Houston was also convinced that the economy of the Republic would not allow the waging of an extensive campaign. Writing to his Secretary of State, Anson Jones, the President commented: "Had I sanctioned the war bill, I could not have commanded any means within twelve months, and the ardor of our people while it is restrained, is most impetuous. I would have been in a state of constant vexation, and threats of revolution would have been constant. As things now stand, there can be no censure upon the Executive."[34] In this wistful hope Houston was sustained by a communication from Andrew Jackson. Writing from "The Hermitage," the former

[33] "Message to the House of Representatives, July 22, 1842," *Houston Writings,* III, 116–24.
[34] Houston to Anson Jones, August 2, 1842, in Jones, *Republic of Texas,* 185.

President imparted his reaction to the veto message and at the same time offered some advice to his former protégé:[35]

I hope your Congress had not the design in passing this bill to disgrace you, regardless of the great injury an offensive war would entail upon the republic, if not destroy it by making Texas an easy conquest for St. Anna, after your failure and all your resources consumed. By your veto you have saved your country, and yourself from disgrace. *Stand on the Defensive.*

The special session of Congress which had met at Houston had resulted only in political distress for the party in power. It was now realized that the President had made no effective provisions for defraying the expense of naval repairs and that the phantom Texas fleet would be compelled to lie dormant at New Orleans for want of sufficient funds. The charge was therefore made that the Executive had made false promises to Commodore Moore and that he should be censured for this action. The administration could make no effective answer, and Houston's unfortunate difficulties with Commodore Moore, which took place later in his term, had their origin here.

In addition, Congress had been subjected to party pressure and forced to make a revision of the nation's tariff system. The legislators lowered the 45 per cent ad valorem duties imposed by the final tariff act of the Lamar party to a level averaging 25 per cent, but subjected many more articles to specific duties. Only a very few immigrant goods, Bibles, primary-school books, and livestock could be admitted free of duty, and the weight of the new tariff was placed on the absolute necessities of life, such as breadstuffs, assorted groceries, furniture, dry goods, wearing apparel, and tools. Also, the new act made some unwise changes in the organization of the eastern customs districts. In a vain attempt to combat smuggling activities in the east and to relieve the western sections from the full burden of the tariff, the counties along the Red River—Fannin, Lamar, Red River, and Bowie—were incorporated into a new collectoral district known as Red River, and the boundary for the San Augustine District was moved south of Bowie County.[36] How-

[35] Andrew Jackson to Houston, August 17, 1842, *Houston Writings*, III, 125.
[36] Journal of the House of Representatives, Sixth Congress, Second Session (Houston, 1842), 29.

ever, the change led to no improvement whatever, and since it had been sponsored by the Speaker of the House, Kenneth L. Anderson, a staunch administration man representing eastern Texas, the rumblings of the west grew even louder.

Embittered by such economic pains as these, popular feeling rose higher against the war veto and pacific policy of the President. Indeed, throughout both his administrations Houston was never so vehemently condemned. When news of the veto was made public, the Houston *Morning Star* observed that the "House of Representatives was thrown into some little commotion by the reception of the veto of the President upon the War Bill." The editor, displaying a mastery of understatement, admitted that "popular clamor will be raised against the veto" but implored the citizenry to defer their judgment until "the storm of passion and prejudice has subsided."[37] Despite this plea for tolerance, the storm broke around the President's head, and open threats of assassination were made against him.[38] When a delegation visited the Executive Mansion to implore Houston to accept the position as commander and lead the people to war, the President's advice to "plant corn" only enraged them further. A Catholic priest noted: "The country continues to be in a great state of uneasiness, perplexity and misery."[39] Adolphus Sterne, a backer of Houston's in the presidential election and postmaster at Nacogdoches, reflected the general popular opinion in confiding to his diary:[40]

Oh—dear Texas have I worn chains for thee, to see *such* fellows try to fatten on thy ruin! Confound all demagogues—all Political gamblers, god grant that Texas may belong to the great union of the Land of Washington—if it does not soon I'll give up all hopes of ever seeing this a happy Country!!!

Congress adjourned in late July without taking any further action about the problem of Mexican relations, and the nation was left in a state of fitful anxiety.

Throughout the month of August, rumors circulated within the

[37] Houston *Morning Star*, July 23, 1842.
[38] Corinne Montgomery, *Texas and Her Presidents*, 118–19.
[39] *History of the Diocese of Galveston, 1847–1922*, 75.
[40] Smither (ed.), "The Diary of Adolphus Sterne," *Southwestern Historical Quarterly*, XXXIII (1930), 325.

Republic that Santa Anna would soon attempt a full-scale invasion. San Antonio was considered particularly vulnerable to attack, and the citizens there lived in constant fear. On Monday, September 5, 1842, Judge Anderson Hutchinson, opening the sessions of the district court at San Antonio, noted in his diary that an invasion was not immediately expected; six days later he had been proved wrong. On September 11 the Mexican commander, General Adrian Woll, appeared before San Antonio with fourteen hundred men and captured the city. Samuel Maverick, who was trying a case before the district court at the time Woll and his troops appeared, has left this description of the event:[41]

At day light on the morning of the 11th Sept. we were aroused from our slumbers by the firing of a piece of cannon almost in the edge of town, succeeded immediately by the sound of martial music & the tramp of a body of men—A dense fog obscured them from actual observation until they had advanced into the public square when they were immediately fired upon by our party, who amounted to about fifty in number—the fire was soon returned by the Mexicans—This lasted a few minutes when the fog disappeared discovering to us that we were surrounded on all sides by the bodies of regular troops.

The entire personnel of the district court was captured by the Mexican force, as well as three congressmen who were in San Antonio to try important cases. However, a few Texans managed to escape and quickly spread the news of the raid. In a few days the organized militia, the Texas Rangers, and scattered volunteers banded together under the leadership of the noted Indian fighters Jack C. Hays and Matthew "Old Paint" Caldwell and marched into San Antonio, determined to give battle to Woll and his troops. The Texans numbered some six hundred men, and on September 18 they successfully lured Woll's force into a battle near the Salado River, six miles outside San Antonio. Then, as frequently happened to plague military efforts of the Republic, a dispute took place over the right of command, and before Caldwell was entrusted with the final authority Woll made his escape. A battalion under Hays sniped at the Mexicans as they retreated, but any chance the Texans may

[41] *Memoirs of Mary A. Maverick,* arr. Mary A. Maverick and George Maverick, ed. Rena Maverick Green, 68–69.

have had to win a pitched battle had been thrown away by internal bickering.[42]

In the interim between the adjournment of Congress in July and the Woll raid in September, the enthusiasm for an offensive campaign against Mexico had somewhat subsided, and the President was less harshly censured for his veto. The Houston *Telegraph and Texas Register*, deprecating this pacifist sentiment, complained that "notwithstanding all the ardor manifested by our citizens *in words* to prosecute an offensive war with Mexico, few, very few, are willing to take the field in person. The most trivial excuse is sufficient to silence their scruples and induce them to remain at home."[43] However, after the Woll raid, which constituted an even greater insult to the Republic than the attack by Vasquez in June and seemed to indicate that Mexican troops could raid the Republic with impunity, there was another wave of martial sentiment in Texas. On September 17, only a few days before Caldwell and his men had allowed Woll to slip from their grasp, the Houston *Morning Star* blazoned forth: "To arms! should be shouted throughout the Republic, and every man who can shoulder a rifle should hasten to the aid of our western citizens. One bold and decisive blow at this juncture may completely defeat the contemplated campaign of Santa Anna."[44] The sentiment in the Republic was now overwhelmingly in favor of war, and the populace awaited only the reaction of President Houston.

Thoughtful citizens of the country were aware that Houston sometimes revealed his intentions through the columns of the *Morning Star*. On October 1, 1842, the *Star* published an editorial which seemed to prove beyond a doubt that Houston had at last come to favor forthright action against his old enemy. Commenting on the emergency, the editor wrote:[45]

We have recently received intelligence from Matamoros, that the whole number of troops in the valley of the Rio Grande, including about 2,000 at Matamoros, and the 1,500 under Woll, is less than 5,000

[42] James K. Greer, *Colonel Jack Hays, Texas Frontier Leader and California Builder*, 75–78.
[43] Houston *Telegraph and Texas Register*, August 17, 1842.
[44] Houston *Morning Star*, September 17, 1842.
[45] *Ibid.*, October 1, 1842.

and these are scattered in different detachments, so far apart that it will be difficult, if not impossible, for more than 2,000 to concentrate at any point other than Matamoros. These troops too, are generally ill armed and many of them are unfit for service. An army of a thousand Texians, therefore, could sweep the whole country from Chihuahua to the coast. Intelligent gentlemen who have visited Chihuahua say that it could easily be captured by 500 or 800 Texians, and say that a contribution of $200,000 specie could be levied also, and other towns in proportion. In the valley of the Rio Grande, thousands of horses, cattle, sheep and goats, could be gathered and driven into our settlements. Thus could we extort from Mexico an amount of property greater and more valuable than the whole products of Texas have been for the last five years. Our citizens could not engage in a more lucrative business than in carrying on an offensive war with Mexico.

While the battle at the Salado was in progress, Captain Nicholas Dawson and a regiment of volunteers from Fayette County approached from the east to join Caldwell and Hays. They were cut off by Mexican cavalry, and after a desperate struggle in which half the Texans were killed the other half surrendered upon promise of honorable treatment. However, those who had given themselves up were shot and the "Dawson Massacre" was added to the record of Mexican treachery. The Mexican troops then retreated, and the Texans were forced to disperse. Vice-President Burleson, who had led a detachment of volunteers, made a short speech advising the citizens to prepare for war and defied Houston to vacillate any longer.

The Executive's hand was now forced, and he was ready to take the necessary action. Immediately after the Woll invasion the President had issued an order activating two regiments of the militia, who, along with the volunteers, were to constitute an army for active operations against Mexico, and General Somervell was again given the command. The appointee was still not acceptable to the majority of the troops, who were doubtful about his relish for the fight and who had misgivings that their leader would not carry the war beyond the Rio Grande. However, about seven hundred men assembled at San Antonio in October and November, and a regiment was organized under the command of Colonel James R. Cooke. Chief Justice John Hemphill was commissioned adjutant general of the entire force, and William G. Cooke was named quartermaster general. On November 22, under the leadership of Somervell, they set out for the Rio Grande and after an arduous march, during which the dissatisfaction against Somervell increased, reached Laredo on December 8. The town had been vacated by the Mexican garrison, and Somervell was unable to prevent his men from plundering and looting the civilian populace that had remained.[46] Somervell then marched his troops three miles down the Rio Grande and camped. Because of an absence of adequate supplies and provisions, the discontent against the commander reached alarming proportions, and the men soon made known their desire to cross the Rio Grande and live off the land while campaigning in Mexico. The Texas commander refused to cross the river but instead marched downstream to the mouth of the Salado River, nearly opposite the town of Guerrero. All who wanted to go home had been given the opportunity at Laredo, and about two hundred men had departed, leaving about five hundred men now in the party. They crossed the river on December 15 and camped near Guerrero for two or three days. On December 19 Somervell ordered them to prepare to return to Gonzales or be disbanded. Amid scenes of great confusion and many threats to Somervell's person, about three hundred men refused to obey the order. The malcontents then organized into two companies under the command of Colonel William S. Fisher and prepared to campaign on their own. The volunteers had agreed upon Fisher as their leader primarily because he had previously fought with the Mexican Federalists and was familiar with the local terrain. The other two hundred men, still under the leadership of Somervell, returned to Texas.[47]

Convinced that Houston had deliberately ordered his appointee to turn back once the Rio Grande had been reached and that the whole operation had resulted only from the President's need to make some sort of a concession to war sentiment, the men under Fisher, in deciding to carry on the campaign, in effect committed a calculated act of mutiny. Fisher's party descended the river by makeshift boats and then traveled by land until they reached the

[46] Wooten, A Complete History of Texas, 287–88.
[47] Special Report of the Secretary of War and Marine, Report of Brig. General A. Somervell, Washington, 1843, 71–72.

Mexican town of Mier. On December 23 the men crossed the river and entered the town. After collecting forced contributions from the inhabitants, the Texans took away the local priest and the alcalde as hostages and returned to the Texas side of the river. Two days later they learned that Mexican troops under General Pedro de Ampudia had occupied the town with two thousand troops. Fisher and his men decided to recross the river and give battle.

The ragged band of Texans entered the town of Mier in the cold dawn of Christmas morning and fought throughout the day and a good part of the night. Of the men who took part in the battle, about ten Texans were killed and more than twenty wounded. The engagement soon reduced itself to hand-to-hand combat, and it was rapidly evident that the Texans were sorely outnumbered. On the morning of December 26 the Mexican commander conveyed a message under a white flag stating that he was about to be heavily reinforced and that in order to spare further loss of life on both sides the Texans should capitulate. Actually, at first sight of the white flag, the majority of the Texans felt that the Mexicans wished to surrender. Upon learning that their own leader was considering giving up, the men wanted to continue fighting, but in reality there was no course open to them other than honorable surrender. A written promise was granted that they would be humanely treated and soon exchanged, and upon this guarantee the surrender was accomplished.[48]

Once again the terms of surrender were violated by the Mexican armies. Instead of being returned to Texas, the volunteers were forced to march to Matamoros and then southward to Monterrey and Saltillo. At Salado, a small town between Saltillo and San Luís Potosí, on February 10, 1843, the great majority of the prisoners led by Captain Ewan Cameron attempted to escape. They were able to overpower their guards, and about 193 liberated prisoners started at once for the Rio Grande. For a short while the retreat went well, but fearing the Mexican military forces the Texans turned aside into the barren desert and mountains of northern Mexico. Here in the region sometimes referred to as Tierra de Muerte—"Land of Death" —they were hard pressed to find food and were completely unable to find water. They were forced to kill their mounts for meat and

[48] General Thomas J. Green, *Journal of the Texian Expedition Against Mier*, 165.

drink the blood of their mules. Their guns had been abandoned because of exhaustion, and they were located and easily captured by some Mexican cavalrymen on February 19. Several of the Texans had already perished from hunger and thirst, but those who were captured were returned to Salado. Santa Anna ordered all of them killed at once, but the humanity of some of the Mexican officers modified the order, so that only every tenth man was to be shot. This incident, which has become justly infamous in Texas history, has been described by Thomas J. Green, a member of the expedition to Mier:[49]

The decimation took place by the drawing of black and white beans from a small earthen mug. The white ones signified *exemption,* the black, *death.* One hundred and fifty-nine white beans were placed in the bottom of the mug, and seventeen black beans placed upon the top of them. The beans were not stirred, and had so slight a shake that it was perfectly clear they had not been mixed together. Such was their anxiety to execute Captain Cameron, and perhaps the balance of the officers, that first Cameron, and afterward they, were made to draw a bean each from the mug in this condition.

Though Cameron and the remainder of the leading officers drew white beans, seventeen Texans drew the fatal black beans. Green has described their execution:[50]

Just previous to the firing they were bound together with cords and their eyes being bandaged, they were set upon a log near the wall, with their backs to their executioners. They all begged the officers to shoot them in front, and at a short distance; that 'they were not afraid to look death in the face.' This he refused; and to make his cruelty as refined as possible, fired at several paces, and continued the firing from ten to twelve minutes, lacerating and mangling these heroes in a manner too horrible for description.

Those Texans who had drawn the white beans were marched to Mexico City and made prisoners at the Castle of Perote, a Mexican stronghold on the road from Mexico City to Vera Cruz. Here the prisoners joined their comrades who had previously been captured during the Vasquez and Woll raids on San Antonio. Express orders

[49] *Ibid.,* 169–70.   [50] *Ibid.,* 174.

were given for the execution of Captain Cameron, and the remaining prisoners at Perote despaired for their lives.

It is true that the chief motive impelling the volunteers to undertake the original expedition under General Somervell was the anticipation of great plunder. Times were very hard in the Republic and also in the United States in 1842, and the chance to go adventuring to Mexico City and to raid along the way was too difficult for many a restless youth to resist. James Morgan, at all times an accurate observer of events in the Republic, reported to Samuel Swartwout: "There is no credit handy & but little confidence between man & man in promise to pay! This will account to you for so many leaving Somervell to go & fight on their own hook across the *Rio Grande*. Their object was plunder. They had nothing at home, nor in fact *no homes* & many of them went forward as an alternative, having no fear of Houston."[51]

The President's position in the matter was therefore a very difficult one. His aversion to volunteer armies was well known. His appointment of Somervell was a matter of record, and the insurrection of Fisher and his men was a blow to the dignity of the government. Houston would have been well within his rights had he refused the prisoners the honorable status of Republic soldiers acting with the consent of the government and thus subject to treatment as legitimate prisoners of war. The tense situation was described by the Galveston *Civilian and Gazette*:[52]

. . . this expedition beyond the Rio Grande, whatever may have been the advantages expected from it, or the disasters which have resulted is one with which the Executive has claimed no connection. He did not propose or encourage it—nor did he oppose it. When he found that those engaged were determined to make the movement at all hazards, he very properly recognized them as acting under the sanction of the Government, in order that, in case they were captured, they might stand upon the footing of prisoners of war.

Houston allowed himself only one outburst about the Mier affair, and that was directed to Captain Charles Elliot, the British consul at Galveston. Making a sarcastic reference to the "campaign of the

---

[51] James Morgan to Samuel Swartwout, February 20, 1843, Morgan Papers.
[52] Galveston *Civilian and Gazette*, January 28, 1843.

people" and stating his belief that "now the eyes of the blind are opened," the President argued that the Texans had marched without orders, thereby placing themselves outside the protection of the accepted rules of war.[53] However, because the Mexicans had acted in such arbitrary fashion, Houston requested that Elliot write to the British minister at Mexico City and attempt to intercede for the Texas prisoners. Houston himself, however, was deaf to all entreaties that he personally order the remnants of the Republic's army to proceed to Mexico City to a rescue attempt. The policy which the government intended to follow, though in conflict with popular sentiment, is well summarized in an excerpt from a communication written by Secretary of State Anson Jones to Van Zandt at Washington:[54]

The present policy of the government towards Mexico is to stand on the defensive. This policy has been strictly pursued as far as practicable, and will be continued. Texas has not the means necessary to carry on offensive operations against her enemy. The late Campaign under Gen. Somervell was not projected or recommended by the President. It was merely *sanctioned* to satisfy popular clamor, and as the volunteers under him wished to cross the Rio Grande and were determined to do so right or wrong to clothe the expedition with legal authority that in case it was unfortunate, and our citizens should fall into the power of Mexico they could not be regarded or treated by the authorities of that government otherwise than lawful belligerents acting under sanction of their own government.

A month after the sessions of the Sixth Congress adjourned, the President had issued a proclamation announcing that the next session of Congress would be held at Washington-on-the-Brazos, the site of Texas independence. Houston instructed the congressmen to appear at the new seat of government early in November, 1842. At the same time, the Executive decided that the capital under no considerations would be moved again to Austin, and he therefore ordered that the archives of the government be transferred from Austin to Washington-on-the-Brazos for permanent keeping. Accordingly, Captain Thomas Smith was dispatched to Austin to remove

[53] Houston to Elliot, January 24, 1843, *Houston Writings*, III, 299–300.
[54] Anson Jones to Isaac Van Zandt, February 16, 1843, *Diplomatic Correspondence*, II, 127.

the records. However, the army officer was frustrated in his duty by the interference of a boardinghouse keeper, who discovered what Houston's emissary was about and let fire with a six-pound cannon which had been located on the government grounds at Austin since Lamar's Cherokee War. The shot fired by Mrs. Angelina Eberly was accurate enough to damage the General Land Office Building, which housed the archives. Houston, realizing that another attempt to remove the archives might result in civil war, wisely allowed the matter to die.

Houston's decision to convene Congress at Washington-on-the-Brazos also met with protest. Dr. John Washington Lockhart, one of the leading settlers of the small hamlet, has left this description of the site, the third capital of the Republic within ten months:[55]

Washington in 1840 had a resident population of about 250 souls and a non-resident population of about 50 to 100 more, principally gamblers, horse racers, etc., for this was a great resort for such characters. In almost every other house on the public street you could see games of all sorts being played, both night and day, and, strange to say, nearly all the money of the country was in the hands of this class of people. It was not unusual to see a man one day with his pockets full of money and have the next day not a cent in his possession. Of course, barrooms were plentiful and did a good business. There were a few dry goods stores, which kept only a very inferior quality of goods, a few staple coarse goods, with an enormous price attached to them—so that only a few could afford to purchase from them.

Captain Charles Elliot, the British consul at Galveston and a good personal friend of Houston's, lamented the situation which had forced the President to move the seat of government again. In a letter to a friend back in England, the British observer gave his account of conditions in Texas at this time:[56]

Driven away by some of those springs of local politics, feuds and jealousies, which run into such long streams of talk and knavishness on this side of the Atlantic, and are so insignificant and unintelligible every where else, the President has convened Congress to assemble at Washington on the Brazos, where there are 12 or 13 Wooden shanties, and to

[55] Wallis and Hill, *Sixty Years on the Brazos*, 89–90.
[56] Charles Elliot to William Addington, November 15, 1842, in Adams (ed.), *British Diplomatic Correspondence*, 127.

211

which place there are no means of getting except in an ox train, or on a Bat horse. . . . The President writes to me in a private Note a few days since, that He finds things at Washington rather raw and as He has been accustomed to the elaborate comforts of an Indian wigwam, I presume he must be living in a commodious excavation.

In calling the legislators to meet at Washington-on-the-Brazos, the President had asked Congress to come together three weeks earlier than the law required, and on November 14, 1842, the solons began straggling into town in no good humor. After a week a quorum had still not arrived, and it was not until November 24 that a working majority in the House answered the roll call. As if to indicate the temper of many of the legislators, the first proposal voiced was to adjourn and meet at Austin, and this suggestion was barely voted down. The President did not deliver his message until December 1, and though a quorum had still not been attained in the Senate the members of the upper house who were present graciously consented to hear the speech as individuals. In this address Houston did nothing to assuage the feelings of the congressmen from the western sections. Attacked from all sides, and feeling that many of those present had given their tacit assent to the machinations of Burleson and Fisher at the Rio Grande, the President read the legislators a bitter lecture: "Since the commencement of legislation in Texas . . . we find the proceedings of Congress characterized by selfishness and partiality. . . . Its decline since the year 1838 to its present point of depression, has been regular and more rapid than perhaps that of any country."[57] Houston blamed the frontier difficulties of the nation on niggardly appropriations by Congress at the very time that the delegates were only too willing to sanction every type of grandiose scheme for foreign conquest. He concluded his address by appealing to the patriotism and wisdom of the members of the Seventh Congress, and emphasized that vigorous and unified measures were desperately needed in this time of stress.

The President was facing the most difficult crisis of his political career. His policy of moving the seat of government seemingly at will and his attempt to take the archives from Austin had alienated

[57] "Annual Message to the Texas Congress, December 1, 1842," *Houston Writings*, III, 203–204.

the little backing he may have enjoyed in the western sections at the time of the election. In addition, Houston's indefinite policy toward Mexico and his apparent abandonment of the Mier captives did not suit those who demanded war as a necessary vindication of the Republic's honor. But perhaps the most unfortunate factor politically, was the irreconcilable split between Houston and Burleson. The President had approved Burleson as his running mate in the recent election only because the latter was very popular in the west and would therefore serve as a balance to Houston's recognized strength in the east. Now, because of Burleson's rash disobedience, party unanimity was practically nonexistent, and the Houston forces were well aware that their political fortunes were at a low ebb.

At the same time the differences within the President's party became a matter of official record, the former Lamar supporters, William Cazneau and Hugh McLeod in the House and William H. Jack and James Webb in the Senate, were taking advantage of every opportunity to obstruct the administration's program in Congress. Houston's partisans, who had pushed through the policy of retrenchment at the sessions of the Sixth Congress, were still on hand; but the former Lamar men, voting with the disgruntled delegates from the western districts and those few administration backers who did not condemn Burleson's policy were able in many instances to defeat the Executive's will.

The political situation at Washington-on-the-Brazos has been clearly described by a few interested observers. George Erath, a frontiersman and Indian fighter representing the western county of Milam, recorded in his diary: "At that time I was strong with the West; we were called Western or Eastern according to our bias for or against Houston."[58] Joseph Eve, the representative of the American government in Texas, noted in a letter to a friend that "Genrl. Lamar and his friends, Judge Burnet and his friends, the Vice-President and his friends are all in the opposition."[59] This statement supports the belief that Burleson had completely aligned himself with

[58] Erath, "Memoirs of George Bernard Erath," *Southwestern Historical Quarterly,* XXVII, 140.

[59] Joseph Eve, "A Letter Book of Joseph Eve, United States Chargé D'Affaires to Texas," *Southwestern Historical Quarterly,* XLIII (1940), 487.

the government's most powerful enemies. In commenting upon the geographical differences within the country which had always had political significance, Eve continued: "The whole of the west are most violently hostile to the President, many of them say without reserve that if they are compelled to abandon their homes that his blood shall atone for it. They attribute all their misfortunes to his leaving Austin last winter so soon as Congress adjourned and leaving the whole west exposed to the enemy."[60] Finally, the most concise description of the political difficulties besetting Texas came from the editor of a nonpartisan newspaper, the San Augustine *Red-Lander*:[61]

It is difficult to conjecture what will be the result of the movements of political parties in this country. The political wisdom of the nation now constitutes two distinct and clearly defined parties, who are arrayed against each other for objects and purposes widely different. While one of these adheres to the views and policy of the Executive and evinces a determination to sustain him in his course, the other, with an utter recklessness of purpose displays a marked hostility to every measure proposed by the President.

Houston's scathing lecture to the assembled delegates did nothing to further governmental harmony. The legislators did ratify a treaty negotiated by James Reily, the Texas minister to the United States, which covered routine commercial relations between the two countries, but such violent and partisan remarks were then made concerning Reily's conduct of his office at Washington that the minister felt it his duty to submit his resignation to the President. Houston was then compelled to nominate Isaac Van Zandt for the position, thereby depriving himself of one of his most faithful followers in Congress. Frequent motions were made to move the seat of government back to Austin and to sanction an attack against the Castle of Perote in an attempt to free the Texas prisoners. Relations between the Executive and Congress grew worse as the session drew toward a close. To many observers it seemed that the legislators were not taking their prescribed duties seriously and were interested only in embarrassing the President. The correspondent

[60] *Ibid.*, 490.
[61] San Augustine *Red-Lander*, December 15, 1842.

of the Houston *Morning Star* recorded his disgust at the behavior of the nation's elected representatives:[62]

. . . on Saturday I went to the House of Representatives which is held in the Court House. The Speaker was sitting listlessly in his chair, and before him were a few members, some sitting, some standing, and some leaning against the posts, apparently waiting for a quorum. The Door Keeper was sitting on a log outside the house. Finding little here to interest me, I proceeded to the Senate, which is held in Bailey, Gay and Hoxey's old store, where I found the President looking at the Senators, and the Senators looking at him. The Senate, I learned, was waiting for the House to progress with business, and the House, I suppose, often waits for the Senate, and in the mean time certain members steal away occasionally, and '*consult the book of prophecies*' alias a pack of cards. Thus do our legislators *labor* for their country.

Just as the habits of the congressmen were criticized by a correspondent of the administration's newspaper, the President himself was not free from the censure of his secretary of state. Anson Jones confided to his diary that Houston's tactics found no favor with him: "I have also strenuously opposed his system of petty and vindictive warfare upon individuals, and the 'Honorable Congress' which are gotten up by him to make political capital for himself, but are injurious to the interests and character of the country."[63] It was obvious to all that an impasse had been reached and that no substantial good would result to the nation from this session of Congress.

In the last few days prior to adjournment, however, certain measures were pushed through. A bill for the protection of the frontier was passed over the President's veto. On this bill, which provided for the election of a major general by a joint ballot of both houses and the appropriation of fifty thousand dollars for the defense of the frontier, a few congressmen who had been voting with the Houston bloc turned against the party leader and voted with the west. Thomas J. Rusk was elected major general, and the administration charged that the command had been created only in the hope that Rusk would win military glory in a campaign against Mexico and then allow his name to be put forward as a candidate in the election

[62] Houston *Morning Star*, December 22, 1842.
[63] Jones, *Republic of Texas*, 39.

of 1844. Another act provided for the secret sale of the Texas Navy. Since the President had not received sufficient appropriations to meet the cost of naval repairs, the act was completely in accord with his wishes. The session then adjourned on an unfortunately characteristic note: the legislators failed by only one vote to approve a resolution expressing the official "thanks" of Congress to the residents of Austin who had helped prevent the Executive from removing the archives; and Houston almost succeeded in preventing the Chief Clerk of the House from paying the congressmen for the days they had not been in official attendance at the session.[64]

In the interim between January and December, 1843, when Congress was called into session again, Houston and those who remained loyal to him were under unceasing attack. The Texas Minister at Washington, Isaac Van Zandt, was diligently seeking the United States' intervention in the case of the Texas prisoners in Mexico. Meanwhile, in the Republic the newspapers trumpeted their sentiments about the government's failure to satisfy the national honor. Houston's troubles were magnified when the Houston *Morning Star,* which had consistently supported the party in power throughout all its previous difficulties, refused to support the President's unwillingness to act in behalf of the prisoners. On this question, the paper commented:[65]

It is the duty of the President of the Republic of Texas, also to request foreign powers to interpose their authority, and require Mexico to respect them as Texians, and not as rebels or banditti. We have long been waiting for President Houston to make some effort of this kind. We hoped he would either write to the British, French or American ministers and Mexico and inform them that these troops were entitled to all the rights and privileges of Texians, and consequently entitled to be treated as prisoners of war, or if he were unwilling to communicate with those ministers, that he would at least make some public notice that they were entitled to the rights of Texian soldiers. But we have waited in vain. . . . Let the President, therefore, even at this late period, atone in some degree for past neglect, and accord justice to his oppressed and suffering fellow-citizens.

[64] Journal of the House of Representatives, Seventh Congress, Second Session (Houston, 1843), 121–25.
[65] Houston *Morning Star,* June 3, 1843.

In the midst of these charges and others of the same nature, the administration was suddenly confronted with a vital decision to make about the Mexican difficulties. Shortly after Congress adjourned in January, 1843, James Robinson, who had been captured in Woll's raid on San Antonio and was a prisoner at Perote, came forth with a plan. He addressed a letter to Santa Anna in which he stated that if a personal interivew was granted he would furnish the Mexican ruler with an important body of information about how a lasting peace between Texas and Mexico might be accomplished. The Texas captive pictured his fellow countrymen as eager for peace and a reunion of the two countries, provided that certain conditions could be agreed upon. The most important of these were amnesty for all past actions and a separate government for Texas under Mexican sovereignty. Santa Anna indicated his interest and Robinson was granted a hearing. As a result of the meeting, an agreement was reached which proposed that Robinson proceed to Texas and offer a settlement on the following terms: (1) Texas to acknowledge the absolute sovereignty of Mexico; (2) a general act of amnesty to be passed for former acts of the Texas government; (3) Texas to form an independent department of Mexico; (4) Texas to be represented in the general Mexican Congress; (5) Texas to institute or originate all local laws, rules, and regulations; (6) no Mexican troops under any pretext whatever to be stationed in Texas. This agreement was signed by Santa Anna on February 18, 1843, and given to Robinson, who promised to transmit it to President Houston along with his strong recommendation that it be adopted.[66]

Robinson made his bid for peace in the hope that his participation in the affair would secure his own personal freedom. His fellow prisoners were well aware of this and condemned the self-appointed emissary in no uncertain fashion. One of the captives at Perote expressed his feelings in a letter to a friend at home:[67]

I see in a late *Pickayune* the *proposition* of *Santa Anna* through Roberson the worst man that Texas ever had within her *borders*—say to him

---

[66] Schmitz, *Texan Statecraft: 1836–1845*, 195–96.

[67] A. Barkley to H. G. Woods, May 8, 1843, quoted in L. U. Spellman (ed.), "Letters of the Dawson Men from Perote Prison," *Southwestern Historical Quarterly*, XXXIX (1935), 252.

for me that his blood shall atone for his conduct towards us His conduct is the sole cause of our lengthy confinement here in this hell I might call it.

If I am fortunate enough to have oppertunity will give them the sentiments of 9/10 of the men confined in this *Prison*—it is as folowes—Should Texas listen to any propositions Santa Anna could make that they will leave the Country as soon as God will let them and constant prair is should she listen to anything short of her Independence that like Sodum & Gomora will be burned by a fire from *Heaven*.

Robinson arrived in Texas at the end of March and proceeded to the seat of government, where he presented the document to the President. Congress was not then in session, and the envoy was aware that neither Congress nor the President would ever agree to any terms which did not guarantee the complete independence of Texas. Houston did listen to Robinson's proposals, however, and for this harmless action he was again taken to task by the Texas press. The editor of the now unfavorable Houston *Morning Star* expressed astonishment that the President had listened to Robinson's proposals, which were made only to put Texas off her guard and which the editor felt were an insult to the nation.[68] In a private letter to Joseph Eve, Houston stated that the entire episode was ridiculous and that its only value was to "file away as a curiosity for after times."[69] However, the Executive did see in Robinson's mission a desire for peace on the part of Mexico, and he therefore requested the British consul, Charles Elliot, to ask the British minister at Mexico City, Richard Pakenham, to take the necessary steps toward armistice negotiations.[70]

There were other problems that the government had to contend with in the spring of 1843. The President had sanctioned his own type of Santa Fe expedition in the equally unfortunate Snively affair. Because the treaty negotiated by James Reily at Washington had not been ratified by the United States Senate, the Republic of Texas still claimed the vast territory lying west of the hundredth meridian between the Arkansas River and the Rio Grande. Therefore, if the claim was valid then the commerce between Missouri

---

[68] Houston *Morning Star*, May 4, 1843.
[69] Houston to Joseph Eve, April 22, 1843, *Houston Writings*, IV, 183.
[70] Houston to Charles Elliot, May 13, 1843, *ibid.*, III, 388–89.

and Santa Fe had to be regarded as contraband and the operations of the Santa Fe trade as an infringement upon the sovereignty of Texas. The President, to test these conclusions, gave his approval to an expedition under Colonel Jacob Snively which set out in April to capture a wagon train of Mexican traders on the way from Missouri to Santa Fe. By the terms of Snively's commission, half the spoils would become the property of the government and the other half would be rightfully claimed by Snively and his men, who should not number more than three hundred. Unfortunately, the Mexican caravan escaped attack when the Texans were arrested by officers of the United States Army, on the charge that the Texans were on American soil with intent to do harm. The members of the party were eventually returned to Texas, but the administration had involved itself in a dispute with the United States at the exact time the support of that nation was being sought for the captives in Mexico. Because of his faulty strategy, the Executive suffered once again.[71]

Another problem confronting the administration was the acute possibility of civil war within the Republic. Once again disturbances broke out in the "neutral ground" section, recalling the escapades of Haden Edwards at the time of the Fredonian Rebellion, prior to the winning of independence. Disputes over the forging of land titles and the like were still common, but the disturbances in Shelby County in the spring of 1843 arose mainly from personal differences. In the congressional elections of 1842 Charles Jackson, a fugitive from Louisiana, ran for Congress in Shelby County. He was defeated and blamed his setback on certain persons involved in land frauds, which he declared he would expose to the General Land Office. When Joseph Goodbread, a leader of the faction that had defeated Jackson, threatened to run him out of the county, Jackson shot and killed him at Shelbyville. Before Jackson could be brought to trial he organized a force which he called the Regulators, while his opponents organized themselves as the Moderators, and civil war in east Texas resulted. In the development of the issue, more than fifty men were killed, and both camps were preparing for a fight to the finish when Houston finally called out the militia to

[71] Rex Wallace Strickland, "Anglo-American Activities in Northeastern Texas, 1803–1845." (Ph.D. dissertation, University of Texas, 1937), 376.

quell the disturbance. Once more the government was censured for apparently neglecting to take forceful action.[72]

As a further irritant, Houston, by virtue of his dominating personality, was continually involving himself in violent disputes with those around him. His controversy with Vice-President Burleson serves as an example of that unhappy trait. However, it was the dispute with Commodore Moore that must rank as the most bitter feud in which the Executive participated. It will be remembered that a secret act of the Seventh Congress had provided for the sale of the Texas Navy, and that this act had met with the decided approval of the President. In accordance with the terms of the act, Houston commissioned James Morgan and William Bryan to proceed to New Orleans and inform Commodore Moore that his ships were to be sold and that he and his men were to return to Galveston. Moore, however, had entered into an agreement with certain capitalists in New Orleans who were willing to finance a freebooting expedition to Yucatan, with the ultimate profits to be divided between the backers of the cruise and the treasury of Texas. To this final expedition, which was unauthorized and a direct act of disobedience, Morgan foolishly gave his approval. William Bryan returned to Texas, and the President, furious at Moore's insubordination, promised to declare Moore a pirate if he did not return to Galveston immediately.[73] Morgan's account of what followed, preserved in a letter to a friend, affords the best description of the affair:[74]

You know it was my intention when I left, to proceed direct to Galveston with the vessels, and should have done so but at the Balize, we met with two vessels just arrived that brought such news of the situation of the Mexn. Navy—and the lonely situation of the Montezuma at *Telshac*, that I felt justified in taking the Coast of Yucatan on our way. The fact was, I found our vessels in such apple pie order—the officers so anxious to proceed on the Cruise—such bully crews: and knowing if the vessels did go into Galveston harbor they would never come out again as *Texas* vessels—if not at all—considering still farther that many of the officers never recd one cent of pay for the last two years—and if the navy was laid up or sold they probably never would—That now an opportu-

---

[72] John W. Middleton, *History of the Regulators and Moderators and the Shelby County War in 1841 and 1842 in the Republic of Texas*, 15.

[73] Hill, *The Texas Navy*, 175.

[74] James Morgan to Joseph Reed, May 11, 1843, Morgan Papers.

nity offered to do something for themselves & their adopted Country—a full stop was to be put to the expedition & close it at Galveston—For these & other *still more cogent reasons,* I concluded to stretch my authority as Commissioner, a little, and authorize Com. Moore to go ahead: believing we could visit the Coast of Yucatan & accomplish every object we had in view, in 20 or 30 days at fartherest. . . . I expect to learn that 'Old Sam' will *hang me* for I have travelled out of the course his instructions dictated. But as we have played h——ll with the enemy's arrangements and calculations in this quarter, He may be afraid to overlook the matter.

The President was particularly angered by Moore's action because of the government's hope for an armistice with Mexico. Moore's insubordination took place soon after Elliot had written to Pakenham in the hope of effecting an armistice, and Houston had given the British consul his word that no attack would be made against Mexico while the negotiations were still in progress. But the President used his Indian cunning in the conduct of diplomacy, and his plans were not common knowledge, so his proclamation declaring Moore a pirate was vehemently attacked in the press. The editor of the Houston *Morning Star* strongly condemned the Executive's action:[75]

If Commodore Moore has violated the laws of his country, he merits censure, and when convicted of guilt, will be justly condemned by every friend of good order. But this proclamation does not merely involve him in guilt, it virtually declares that all his subordinate officers and innocent crews are pirates, and if by the fortunes of war they are captured by the enemy, (which heaven forbid) they will not be regarded as prisoners of war; but may under the sanction of this proclamation be all *shot or hung as pirates!* Com. Moore cannot be arrested or punished unless in accordance with the laws of the Republic, and if these are insufficient for the purpose, the President only subjects the government and the country to disgrace by issuing proclamations, which like the bulls of the Pope, are only evidences of the impotence and imbecility of their author.

Houston issued the proclamation, and Moore, after a short and insignificant cruise, returned to Galveston. As was his habit, the President declined the usual challenge to a duel, and the Commodore was forced to stand trial for piracy. The ultimate disposition of

[75] Houston *Morning Star,* May 11, 1843.

the matter was left to the Anson Jones administration, but the incident did indicate the abject state of the President's popularity.

As a result of all these misfortunes, Houston's political stock in the summer of 1843 was at its lowest point. The administration planned to marshal support for its armistice negotiations by electing followers of Houston to the Eighth Congress, which would convene in December. However, at the same time, a movement sprang up for the impeachment of Houston, with the understanding that Vice-President Burleson would succeed to the Executive office. This plan gained some currency among the former Lamar men, led by Cazneau and Webb, though many of Houston's opponents felt that impeachment would only make a martyr out of the President. It was also thought that the administration party could be defeated at the polls in the next election and that it was better policy to ensure that event than to resort to impeachment. The correspondent of the New Orleans *Picayune*, whose paper had always been anti-Houston, stated the case for impeachment:[76]

We frankly acknowledge that we are among those who have always thought Sam Houston honest, and our charity still clings to this hope, although his actions would indicate anything but purity of purpose; but if honest he is demented, and the people over whom he presides should no longer suffer themselves to be disgraced by the mad acts of an imbecile or a lunatic. Violent measures we cannot recommend; but an inspired people can certainly devise some constitutional means to rid themselves of an incubus so destructive of their various interests. In a case like the present, why cannot the Vice President, who is certainly an honest man, call Congress together? He may not have full authority so to do, but in an emergency so pressing he might assume a point, convene the Congress, and have Houston impeached at once, either as a traitor or an imbecile—one or the other of these charges can certainly be sustained. Should the Vice President, Gen. Burleson, pursue this course, he would be justified by nine-tenths, aye, a greater proportion of the people, and would rid Texas of the only impediment which now stands in the way of a successful prosecution of the war against Mexico, and the attainment, at no distant period, of a full and unconditional independence.

In the face of constant criticism, Houston went ahead with his

[76] New Orleans *Picayune*, May 20, 1843.

plans to achieve an armistice through the intervention of the British minister at Mexico City. As a result of his interview, Robinson advised Santa Anna that Houston was willing to agree to an armistice period of several months in order to give the populace adequate time to think over any propositions which might be made for permanent peace. Robinson had also been told that the Republic did not want to commit itself in irrevocable fashion but would agree to a cessation of hostilities on a temporary basis. When Santa Anna received this information from Robinson he readily agreed to an armistice and informed Pakenham of his decision. This news was relayed to Houston by Captain Elliot, and on June 15, 1843, the Executive issued a proclamation of armistice declaring hostilities suspended, pending negotiations for peace. It was stipulated that the armistice was to continue until due notice of resuming hostilities was officially announced through the British legation. Santa Anna then took similar action.[77]

By the terms of the armistice agreement, each government appointed commissioners to meet at the town of Sabinas, a point near the Rio Grande. The Texas commissioners were Samuel Williams, an influential citizen and financier in Galveston, and George W. Hockley, who had served in the Houston cabinet as secretary of war and marine. The agents were instructed to arrange the terms of a general armistice and to agree upon the appointment of a commission, to meet at some future date in Mexico City and try to arrive at terms for a permanent peace. It was also stipulated that whatever agreements the two agents made about a final peace would be subject to the President's ratification.

The armistice agreement was signed in the summer of 1843 and caused a varied reaction throughout the Republic. The correspondent of the New Orleans *Picayune* noted that many were "lauding Sam the First to the skies," but the journalist himself believed that peace could be obtained with "priest-ridden Mexico only by battering down some of her towns, and thus bringing her to a right sense of things."[78] From London, the Texas minister to England and France, Ashbel Smith, reported that the armistice had done "a world of good" and that the cause of Texas had profited in Europe

[77] Schmitz, *Texan Statecraft: 1836–1845*, 198–99.
[78] New Orleans *Picayune*, September 7, 1843.

by the agreement. The attacks against Houston's policy were mostly directed at England's intervention in the affairs of Texas and the necessary influence the British would now exert in the Republic. The editor of the *Brazos Planter* lamented the fact that the Republic had seen fit to acquire a "monarchial nurse."[79] The President, who by now was hardened to this type of abuse, continued in his usual, determined fashion.

Houston's agreement to an armistice stemmed either from his conviction that the arrangement would not hamper negotiations for annexation by the United States or from his desire that Texas remain independent with the implied backing of England. Throughout the summer of 1843 the Executive and other cabinet officials went on speaking tours in an attempt to gain the election of a favorable Eighth Congress, which would meet at Washington-on-the-Brazos. The Houston group was well aware that annexation would be the chief topic of discussion at the sessions of Congress, and though the President had kept his exact feelings on the matter from most of his intimates the word had been passed on that every effort would be made to elect legislators favorable to the administration.

In addition to his constant speechmaking throughout the summer months, the Executive negotiated treaties with the Comanches and other Indian tribes. These colorful spectacles, which took place at the capital, also afforded a chance for political oratory. Finally, in a speech delivered at Huntsville, Houston made an attempt to quiet the fears that had been circulating throughout the country concerning the influence of England in Texas affairs. The President phrased his words in this fashion:[80]

I question very much, my friends, whether England would have us, if she could get us. To my mind it is clear that England does not *care* about the abolition of slavery. . . . She knows very well that a slave population will develop the resources of a new country in one-eighth of the time it would take free labor. England don't want you in my opinion, gentlemen! She has a great many mischievous and unruly subjects to govern already.

This speech concluded the campaign waged by the administration

[79] *Brazos Planter*, in Houston *Morning Star*, November 23, 1843.
[80] *Houston Writings*, III, 448.

in the interests of party solidarity; the elections were now in the hands of the people.

When the congressmen again straggled into the dusty town of Washington-on-the-Brazos in December, 1843, it was apparent that Houston, while on circuit, had lost none of his appeal as a politician. Although William H. Jack and James Webb had retained their seats as opposition members of the Senate, their strength had been offset by the election of David Kaufman and Robert McAlpin Williamson, both staunch supporters of the government's policies. To the House of Representatives came Thomas Jefferson Green, a prominent member of the ill-fated Mier expedition who had succeeded in escaping from the Castle of Perote, and his presence was a constant reminder of the Executive's unpopularity on that score. William Cazneau had also retained his seat in the House on the basis of his western support, but the opposition could point to no sizable gains in strength in the House. The majority of the Houston men had been returned, and in addition the President could count on the backing of two new members, Richardson A. Scurry, of San Augustine County, and Harvey W. Kendrick, representing Matagorda County.[81] Thus assured that the opposition could not override his program at will, the Executive looked with anticipation to the sessions of the Eighth Congress.

In his message of welcome to the congressmen, the President dwelt upon the improvements that had taken place during his administration. By practicing the strictest economy, and particularly by refusing to authorize increased expenditures for the navy, the nation's treasury had now achieved a precarious balance. Because of the armistice the President had negotiated, the country was free from the continual threat of Mexican invasion, and the peace treaties which had been signed removed the fear of Indian attack. The Executive observed that the trade of the nation was flourishing, that the French government was considering the establishment of direct steamship trade with Texas, and that William Daingerfield had been appointed minister to the Hanse towns, Belgium, and Holland in order to cultivate trade relations with those powers. Houston noted that England had acted as mediator in the armistice talks, and he strongly advised that the friendship of that nation be pre-

[81] Lindley (comp.), *Biographical Directory*, 37–38.

served. On the other hand, Texas had received nothing but harsh treatment from the United States. That country had refused to ratify the commercial treaty drawn up in 1842 and, as a further indignity, had sanctioned the arrest of Texas soldiers on territory rightfully claimed by the Republic. This last was a reference to the Snively expedition, which had become a sore point to the Texans in their relations with the United States government.[82]

The sessions of the Eighth Congress are important because the delegates concerned themselves primarily with the question of annexation. The troublesome issues in the political history of the Republic—the financial problems, Indian relations, the location of the seat of government, and peace with Mexico—had all been settled by the party in office. And although their decisions were under constant attack the settlement of these issues allowed Congress to concentrate on the question of annexation. Houston had favored a speedy union with the United States in 1836 and a referendum had indicated the overwhelming support of the people at that time. However, because of Jackson's reluctance to embarrass his handpicked successor, Van Buren, by introducing a question that was certain to stir sectional animosity, the possibility of annexation had disappeared. Houston had only been successful in obtaining recognition by the United States by the time his first term expired. Lamar, rather than negotiate for annexation, had preferred to fish in the troubled waters of peace talks with Mexico, a policy which had merely led to one humiliation after another.

James Reily, the Texas minister in Washington, had been unable to discover any notable sentiment for annexation in the United States, and upon his retirement from office in the winter of 1842 he informed his successor, Isaac Van Zandt, not to be too hopeful for a union of the two nations. Therefore, Van Zandt made no effort to reopen the troublesome question for discussion, and he received no instructions from the Texas government to do so. However, in London Ashbel Smith was continually stressing in his reports the concern that the British government indicated for the diplomatic recognition of Texas' independence, an attitude that had been illustrated by the willingness with which Britain had offered its services

[82] "Annual Message to the Texan Congress, December 12, 1843," Houston Writings, III, 459–74.

as mediator between Texas and Mexico. Smith also reported that the commercial elements in England were willing to go to virtually any lengths to bring an end to slavery in the Republic. This group was responsible for the meeting of the World's Convention of Abolitionists in London in June, 1843. Prominent American abolitionists, such as Lewis Tappan and Stephen F. Andrews, attended, and various resolutions were drawn up for effecting the abolition of slavery in Texas.[83] A committee of antislavery men called upon Lord Aberdeen to secure his assistance in their proposals, but other than displaying his friendly interest the British foreign minister took no direct action.

When the news of the abolitionists' activities reached the United States, an unfounded rumor circulated that Aberdeen was ready to act with the group and guarantee a Texas loan if the Republic would abolish slavery. This report reached the White House, and Abel Upshur, the secretary of state, sent letters of inquiry to the ministers of the United States in Texas and England. From both these sources the Secretary was informed that there was no real danger from the British on the question of abolition and that their only concern was of a commercial nature. However, even after Upshur received these assurances, he continued to believe that, though England would not take the slavery approach in her relations with the United States, still the British government was concerned enough with Texas to make some move to block any agreements between the United States and the Republic.[84] Therefore, Upshur began to exert pressure on President Tyler to negotiate for annexation, and, on October 16, 1843, the Secretary of State addressed a note to Van Zandt indicating that he would be willing to reopen deliberations whenever the Texas Minister was furnished with the proper powers. Upshur was truthful enough to add that he could not guarantee acceptance of any treaty in the Senate, but he did pledge that the administration would back the negotiations in the strongest fashion.[85] Van Zandt promised to write to his government for instructions and to confer with Upshur at a later date.

[83] Adams, *British Interests and Activities in Texas, 1838–1846*, 170–71.
[84] Schmitz, *Texan Statecraft: 1836–1845*, 202–203.
[85] Randolph G. Adams, "Abel Parker Upshur," in Bemis (ed.), *The American Secretaries of State and Their Diplomacy*, V (1928), 95–96.

These new developments took place at the very time that sentiment for annexation was again taking shape in Texas. The hard times besetting the Republic, combined with a common heritage and tradition, made a union with the United States continually desirable to the people of Texas. In this light, the Houston *Morning Star* reported: "So far as our own observation extends, we consider that there is at this time as great a proportion of the people in favor of annexation, as there was at the time of the adoption of the Constitution."[86] Houston, with his recognized facility for discerning the public will, was aware of the popular demand but wanted to make absolutely sure that the United States was sincere in its desire for annexation. Accordingly, he informed Van Zandt that the administration must decline to enter into the deliberations until some assurance was given that the United States Senate would approve the prospective treaty. In his letter to Van Zandt informing him of the Executive's decision, Secretary of State Jones called attention to the following arguments, which Van Zandt was to set before Upshur:

1. Should treaty negotiations begin, Mexico might be induced to terminate the armistice, and England and France would discontinue their efforts to arrange a lasting peace between Texas and Mexico.

2. If annexation did result, it would not matter; but if the treaty should fail to be ratified in the Senate, the hostility of Mexico would again be aroused, and the position of Texas would be worse than if the original proposition for annexation had not been made.

3. Finally, Van Zandt was to imply that Houston would in all probability bring the matter before the Texas Congress and attempt to learn the will of that body.[87]

The Executive's entire policy in the annexation proceedings was based on the idea of prompting the United States to accept annexation by making the most of English friendship. However, Houston's hope that the Republic could maintain an unconcerned pose toward the policy of the United States was destroyed when virtually nine-tenths of Congress signed a round robin circular indicating the desire of the legislators for a speedy union. Faced with this situation,

[86] Houston *Morning Star,* October 5, 1843.
[87] Anson Jones to Isaac Van Zandt, December 13, 1843, *Diplomatic Correspondence,* II, 232–33.

Houston appeared before both houses of Congress on January 20 and pointed out that since the annexation issue would soon be debated in Washington it would be well for the Republic to have a special representative on the scene. The President then asked for an appropriation to defray the expenses of sending a special minister, and this was duly granted. James Pinckney Henderson, the accomplished minister to England and France during the Lamar term of office, was nominated for the task, and his appointment was immediately confirmed by the Texas Senate. The Senate Foreign Relations Committee then recommended that annexation be consummated by treaty and suggested that if Texas should be refused once again the project should be abandoned for good and the Republic should maintain its independent state.[88]

Houston, who had grave doubts about the ultimate success of the proceedings, expressed his feelings in a letter to his old political tutor, Andrew Jackson. Writing to the former President, Houston said:[89]

Now, my venerated friend, you will perceive that Texas is presented to the United States as a bride adorned for her espousal. But if now so confident of the union, she should be rejected, her mortification would be indescribable. She has been sought by the United States and this is the third time she has consented. Were she now to be spurned, it would forever terminate expectation on her part and it would then not only be left for the United States to expect that she would seek some other friend, but all Christendom would justify her in a course dictated by necessity and sanctioned by wisdom.

Before Henderson could arrive in Washington, Van Zandt had taken another important step. He secured from Upshur the promise that the Secretary would ask President Tyler whether the United States would, if necessary, undertake to extend military and naval protection to Texas, thus preventing or combating Mexican invasion while a treaty was under consideration in the Senate. With Upshur's belief that this guarantee could be given, Van Zandt was confident enough to enter unofficially into preliminary discussions con-

[88] Smith, *The Annexation of Texas*, 165–66.
[89] Houston to Andrew Jackson, February 16, 1844, quoted in William Cary Crane, *Life and Select Literary Remains of Sam Houston*, 373.

cerning the provisions of the treaty.[90] Van Zandt then wrote that he had the main points of the treaty settled, but it was just at this point that the explosion occurred on board the *Princeton* in which Upshur lost his life. This stroke of bad luck, which happened almost concurrently with Henderson's arrival, placed the Texas representative in an extremely bad humor that was not eased by nagging letters from his wife. After one such epistle, Van Zandt burst out:[91]

Now let me ask you My dear if you know what is the extent of my mission, what business I have to do, Whether it will take one Month, two Months, one year or any particular time. Now do you think it is like a crop of potatoes or cabbage which if you cant make in a particular season you cant make at all, Or that I must be governed by the movements of Congress, now I have no more to do directly here with the Congress than I have with the Congress of Mexico. . . . I am certainly not here on a trip of pleasure.

Upshur's death brought John C. Calhoun into office as secretary of state. Calhoun's wish for the annexation of Texas as a boon to the slaveholding states was well known, and friends of the measure rightly felt that the South Carolinian would spare no efforts to draw up a treaty and place it before the Senate. The annexation question now became a truly national issue, and the press of the United States violently debated the wisdom of the proposed action. The New Orleans *Picayune*, long the advocate of expansion and a spokesman for the militant South, commented:[92]

There is apparently little difference of opinion, among nearly every class of people in this section of the country, as to the justice, policy, and absolute necessity of adding Texas to the Union. To recover back for the United States a magnificent territory, which John Q. Adams, in his able letters to Senor de Onis in 1818, proved incontestably to belong to us; to do away with the necessity of protecting a long line of frontier from smugglers; to defeat the insidious policy of England, for it is believed that she is aiming to attack us in our slave property by erecting another Canada upon our borders; in fine, to prevent Texas, now that many of her first men find it impossible to support a government with so small a population, from either throwing herself into the arms or falling

[90] Schmitz, *Texan Statecraft: 1836–1845*, 203–204.
[91] Isaac Van Zandt to his wife, February 6, 1844, Van Zandt Papers.
[92] New Orleans *Picayune*, March 26, 1844.

into the clutches of Great Britain—on these and other grounds the South will almost to a man sustain the policy of the President in bringing about annexation.

Calhoun signed the treaty of annexation with Henderson and Van Zandt on April 12, and ten days later it was sent to the United States Senate with a message urging ratification. The treaty could not have been presented to the Senate at a more unfavorable time, for the presidential campaign in the United States was just beginning and the annexation issue soon became tied up in national politics. It was certain that the major candidates would have to approach the Texas question with caution, and the Washington correspondent of the New Orleans *Picayune* likened its political effects to the "grain of mustard which in a season shoots up into a large tree."[93] As matters developed, Henry Clay, the nominee of the Whig party, attempted to side-step the ticklish question by stating that without the hazard of war with Mexico, and under conditions that would satisfy both the North and the South, annexation might be accomplished. This evasion proved disastrous to the oft-defeated Clay. In a preconvention statement the expected Democratic nominee, former President Van Buren spoke against annexation; this so enraged the powerful group of Southern Democrats that they successfully blocked his nomination at the convention and placed the name of James Polk before the nation. Polk was elected to the Presidency on a frank platform of expansion—"the reoccupation of Oregon and the reannexation of Texas."[94]

After the political conventions, but before the election which resulted in Polk's victory, the annexation treaty came before the Senate. Powerful efforts had been made to keep the treaty buried in committee, but the friends of the measure successfully brought the question to a vote on June 8. The treaty was defeated in the Senate by a vote of 35 to 16. The Whigs voted solidly against it, and of the Northern states only Pennsylvania supported it by the vote of the entire delegation. The New Hampshire and Indiana votes were split, and the other support the treaty received came from the Southern states. The group in favor of the treaty consisted of fifteen

[93] *Ibid.*, May 14, 1844.
[94] Oscar D. Lambert, *Presidential Politics in the United States, 1841–1844*, 71–75.

Democrats and one Whig, Henderson of Mississippi. Those opposed included twenty-eight Whigs and seven Democrats. Woodbury of New Hampshire was the only New Englander who voted for ratification.[95]

The vote on annexation had been conducted solely on a sectional basis, and the abolition sentiment in Congress had been successful in picturing the treaty as one more step in the expansion of slavery. Added to this, many of the Southern newspapers had been intemperate in their advocacy of the Texas cause and in their veiled threats to secede in the event they were defeated. John Quincy Adams, the leading abolitionist in Congress, sincerely believed in the justice of his convictions, yet the account in his diary of the failure of the treaty indicates the heights of feelings which were aroused:[96]

The vote in the United States Senate on the question of advising and consenting to the Texas Treaty was, yeas, 16; nays, 35. I record this vote as a deliverance, I trust by the special interposition of Almighty God, of my country and of human liberty from a conspiracy comparable to that of Lucius Sergius Catalina. May it prove not a mere temporary deliverance, like that, only preliminary to the equally fatal conspiracy of Julius Ceaser! The annexation of Texas to this Union is the first step to the conquest of all Mexico, of the West India islands, of a maratime, colonizing, slave-tinted monarchy, and of extinguished freedom.

The rejection of the treaty allowed Houston once again to display his talents as an accomplished diplomat. Throughout the Republic the reaction to the news of rejection was a determination to avoid such an embarrassing situation in the future. The Houston *Morning Star* reported that the whole affair had resulted in a "useless expenditure of public money, mortification and disgrace"[97] and recommended to the President that he cultivate the good offices of England and France to guarantee the independence of Texas. Houston, although he had given his approval to the treaty after Van Zandt's assurance that it would be ratified, had not cut off all ways of retreat. The President had always been friendly with Cap-

[95] Smith, *The Annexation of Texas*, 273.
[96] Nevins (ed.), *The Diary of John Quincy Adams, 1794–1845*, 570–71.
[97] Houston *Morning Star*, July 6, 1844.

tain Elliot, the British representative, and because of his support of De Saligny at the time of the latter's difficulties with the Lamar administration Houston also enjoyed the friendship of the French minister. Therefore, the party leader was willing to strike for the independence of Texas or at least for a favorable treaty with Mexico.

It will be remembered that the President had sent commissioners to Mexico in the hope that a permanent peace might be achieved. However, the Executive recalled his agents when the negotiations for annexation began, on the promise of American military protection while the annexation talks were in progress. In recalling the commissioners, the President refused to officially recognize the few stipulations they had agreed to. The Mexican government then declared that hostilities would be resumed. At about the same time, Secretary of State Calhoun made public his correspondence with the British minister at Washington about the slavery question. The American secretary called attention to the fact that Great Britain had long been the advocate of abolition, and Calhoun contended that if annexation was not consummated at once British interests would be extended to Texas and from that point would menace slavery in the United States.[98] Unfortunately, however, Calhoun's action had an effect exactly opposite to the one he had hoped for. His outburst only served to antagonize the British government and caused Lord Aberdeen to be willing to go to extreme lengths to prevent annexation.

Soon after the annexation treaty was lost in the United States Senate, the Foreign Office at London proposed that a "Diplomatic Act" be passed to enforce peace between Mexico and Texas and that the independence of the Republic be recognized. Lord Aberdeen informed Ashbel Smith that if Mexico refused to acknowledge the independence of Texas she would forfeit the friendship of England and France. Smith was enthusiastic about the plan and forwarded to Houston his recommendation that it be adopted. Pakenham, now British minister to the United States, was less vigorous in support of the proposal, advising Aberdeen that any interference on the part of the British government would only result in addi-

[98] Adams, *British Interests and Activities in Texas, 1838–1846*, 161–63.

tional strength for those in favor of annexation and that the entire issue would be decided once and for all at the polls.[99] Aberdeen realized the logic of Pakenham's words and gradually lost interest in the plan. Houston, however, was eager to give the proposal a chance and advised Anson Jones that Smith might be instructed to join in the "Diplomatic Act" by giving the necessary pledges. However, by this time Jones was President-elect, and in the belief that any further decisions on this question were rightfully his to make he quietly ignored the order. The reasons set down by the Texas Secretary of State to justify his inaction ended the concern of the Houston administration with the problem. Try as he might, Houston had been unable either to secure annexation or to make certain the independence of the Republic. On Houston's order, Jones commented:[100]

The within order cannot be obeyed, for it would either defeat Annexation altogether, or lead to a war between Europe and America. Besides, it would directly complicate our relations and entangle us with France and England, produce disturbances and revolutions at home, and probably render it very difficult, if not impossible, for me to administer the government of Texas successfully. Gen. H. has furnished no explanation of his motives for the course of policy. If they be to defeat Annexation, produce a war, or break down my administration, (about to commence) I cannot favor any of these objects, and can conceive of no other.

The annexation issue was carried over into the next Texas administration, and, accordingly, the presidential race of 1844 was very significant in the political fortunes of the Republic. A visitor to Texas in that year, commenting on the political habits of the citizenry, observed: "The election is the prevailing topic of conversation; indeed, it seems to me, that both in the United States and Texas, this sort of excitement is so popular, that no sooner is a President elected, then there commences all the excitement of canvassing for, and choosing his successor."[101] The speculation about Houston's successor began soon after the Old Hero assumed office for the second time. The candidates in 1844 were also aware that

[99] *Ibid.*, 166.

[100] Anson Jones to ?, September 28, 1844, quoted in Schmitz, *Texan Statecraft: 1836–1845*, 210.

[101] Matilda Charlotte Houstoun, *Texas and the Gulf of Mexico; or, Yachting in the New World*, 170.

they would base their campaigns either on the merits of the Houston administration or on the mistakes of the party in power. Because politics were always of a personal nature in the Republic, the backing of Houston was to be eagerly cultivated, and no one understood this more than the President himself.

The campaign bore some similarity to previous election races in Texas. For one thing, Thomas J. Rusk was again sought for the candidacy in the political councils of the nation, and again Rusk declined the nomination. Also, this campaign was conducted very much as the election of 1841 had been—on a low level and with frequent resort to personal abuse. However, one basic difference was present in 1844: the lack of concrete political issues. The difficulties with Mexico had dominated the Houston party's second term, and the refusal of annexation had been a disappointment to both parties in the Republic. It was true that Houston had earned the hatred of the west by the removal of the seat of government from Austin, but that and the President's refusal to sanction an offensive war against Mexico were virtually the only grounds upon which the administration was open to attack. The President and his party had succeeded in maintaining the sovereignty of Texas against Mexican invasion and had brought a nominal amount of economic prosperity to the land.

In July, 1843, James Pinckney Henderson, always an important figure in the politics of Texas, informed Anson Jones that General Rusk had again declined the nomination for the Presidency and had advocated that Henderson and his followers shift their support to Jones. Henderson informed Jones that as secretary of state he would receive the blessing of the President and that he should allow his name to be considered. Henderson believed that because of Houston's break with Vice-President Burleson there were many potential candidates who might receive Houston's approval. Accordingly, it would be wise for the Secretary of State to declare his intentions so that the President might have adequate time to reflect upon his important decision.[102] M. P. Norton, a prominent lawyer of central Texas, wrote to Jones at a later date informing him that Henderson was considering becoming a candidate and that the chief justice of the Supreme Court, John Hemphill, could easily be in-

[102] Henderson to Jones, July 23, 1843, in Jones, *The Republic of Texas*, 231–32.

duced to make the race.[103] Norton, who assumed the role of Jones's political adviser, urged the Secretary not to delay but to indicate whether or not he would run. Upon receiving this letter, and fully believing that he would ultimately receive the President's backing, Jones informed Norton that his name might be used.

It was no secret in the Republic that Burleson intended to be a candidate. The Vice-President was eager for a public vindication of his insubordination in the affair of the Vasquez attack on San Antonio, and he expected to command the favor of the Lamar-Burnet men. It was at one time expected that Lamar would consent to run again, and Jones originally expected to make the contest against Lamar rather than Burleson. James Webb, Albert Sidney Johnston, Barnard E. Bee, and others who had been notably associated with the Lamar party attempted to induce the former President to run, but after some consideration Lamar refused to give his consent.[104] Therefore, the supporters of Lamar rallied around Burleson and sponsored him as the antiadministration candidate. In addition to the backing of Webb, Johnston, and Bee, such Lamar stalwarts as William Cazneau, Thomas J. Green, Hugh McLeod (who had been in command of the Santa Fe expedition), and Branch T. Archer (who had separated from his former friend because of Houston's refusal to declare war upon Mexico) all gave their support to the Burleson candidacy.[105] Finally, Lamar himself made a personal appearance at the meeting which was called to nominate Burleson in January, 1844, and gave his endorsement to the Vice-President.

Before the campaign became the dominant issue in the Republic, there were mild attempts to nominate Abner Lipscomb and Kenneth L. Anderson. Lipscomb had served for a short time as Lamar's secretary of state, and he could point to some support from former adherents of Lamar. Anderson had served as speaker of the House of Representatives during the sessions of the Seventh Congress and was the favorite of a certain element in the Houston party which felt that Jones had no independent policies of his own and thus could not be elected. However, these short-lived attempts failed,

[103] M. P. Norton to Jones, March 29, 1844, in *ibid.*, 332–33.
[104] James Reily to James H. Starr, August 5, 1844, Starr Papers.
[105] Lubbock, *Six Decades in Texas*, 152–53.

and the election of 1844 became a race between Jones and Burleson.

Lamar's personal appearance in favor of Burleson had displayed to the electorate the sentiment of that faction. It remained only for Houston to officially sanction the administration's candidate. This the President did in an open letter to "Messrs. Black, Ruthven, Hadley and Others" written just a month prior to the election but in time to place the favor of the government squarely behind the Secretary of State. Referring to the fact that he and Burleson had followed different paths during the recent term, the President commented that he had had little personal intercourse with his subordinate: "During the last session of Congress I had the pleasure of meeting him but twice & then in the streets. He did not visit me." Then, after stressing the fact that Jones had served him well both as minister to the United States in 1838 and as secretary of state, Houston officially damned Burleson's candidacy: "On almost every question affecting the policy of the present administration, which required the casting vote of the vice President, he gave it *against* the Executive."[106] The election slate was now complete; Jones had become the administration candidate.

The election of 1844 was not marked by basic differences on political issues. Burleson promised if elected to move the seat of government back to Austin, but Jones also indicated that he would not oppose such a move if Congress gave its approval. Both candidates adopted a wait-and-see attitude on the question of annexation, and if union with the United States was not forthcoming both favored maintaining independence. Burleson had indicated his distrust of British meddling in the internal affairs of Texas, and Jones suffered because of Houston's obvious willingness to pay court to the British.[107] Therefore, with election issues at a minimum, the campaign quickly took on many of the features of the election of 1841. In place of Burnet the Jones group was able to link Burleson with the mistakes of the Lamar administration. That Burleson so eagerly accepted the backing of the discredited followers of Lamar does not

[106] Houston to Messrs. Black, Ruthven, Hadley and Others, August 5, 1844, *Houston Writings*, IV, 354–57.
[107] Gambrell, *Anson Jones*, 348.

speak well of his political sagacity, and he was saddled with the burden at the time of the election. As a case in point, the Jones men ridiculed the treaty made by General Hamilton, Lamar's diplomatic representative at London, for the mutual suppression of the slave trade. The editor of the Houston *Morning Star* commented on the way in which the Jones group had construed Hamilton's action to their own advantage:[108]

> The disparagement of Gen. Burleson is not very obvious to ordinary perceptions, but is clearly effected in this way; by proving Gen. Hamilton an ignoramus or a traitor to our country, they of course implicate Gen. Lamar in his treason and ignorance; and although Gen. Burleson was totally unconcerned with Gen. Lamar's administration, and knew nothing of those treaties, until they were submitted to the Senate for their approval; yet, as they have attached him to the Lamar party, they have nothing to do but to condemn every thing done by Lamar or his ministers, and consequently Gen. Burleson is at once politically annihilated. This is manifestly one of the great advantages gained by the introduction of this new theory in diplomatic science. On the one hand Dr. Jones is to be forced upon the people by the merits of Gen. Houston; and on the other hand, Gen. Burleson is to be sacrified by the demerits of Gen. Lamar.

Francis Moore, Jr., the vitriolic editor of the Houston *Telegraph and Texas Register* and still the implacable opponent of all that Houston stood for, joined those protesting the linking of Burleson with the excesses of the Lamar term in office. Condemning this policy, Moore editorialized:[109]

> In the first place by what authority, by what presumption, by what shadow of reasoning, do they identify Gen. Burleson with Gen. Lamar's administration? Did he ever belong to the cabinet? No. Did he ever assist, either in advising or carrying out any of his obnoxious measures? No. Is he either directly or indirectly involved in the unfortunate and therefore unpopular Santa Fe expedition—No, he censured . . . only the fight against the Cherokees, and that because he held a military command under the Administration.

Having successfully identified Burleson with the Lamar group, Jones's followers next concentrated on personalities. Burleson's

---

[108] Houston *Morning Star*, July 13, 1844.
[109] Houston *Telegraph and Texas Register*, July 10, 1844.

origin had been humble, and he had been a hunter and frontiersman all his life. It was true that he could not read with any profi-
ciency, and he was particularly clumsy as an orator, given to classical allusions which had been ghostwritten for him and which he
was at loss to understand.[110] The editorial support in his favor could
not hide the impression that the Vice-President was of rude attain-
ments in his reading habits, but an attempt was made to combat
the slurs on Burleson's chosen way of life. In an effort to add luster
to the candidate's agricultural pursuits, one newspaper drew a favorable comparison with a former President of the United States:[111]

General Burleson is the antipodes of the office hunters of the day.
Silent and unobstrusive in his deportment—fond of retirement and devoted to the pursuits of agriculture, he has always been either a farmer
or soldier—never an office hunter or a speech maker. It is a remarkable
fact, that the very objections that are now urged against Gen. Burleson,
are those which were urged against Gen. Harrison previous to his
election.

The attacks continued apace on the abilities and personal char-
acteristics of Burleson, but Anson Jones found himself no less a tar-
get for the barbed shafts of his enemies. Of course, the principal
charge against Jones was that he had been directly selected by
Houston and that if he was elected to the Presidency he would do
the Old Hero's bidding on all matters. Jones was pictured as having
no will of his own and as being subject to every whim of Houston's.
A friend, nettled by this type of criticism, wrote to Jones:[112]

Are you a candidate for the Presidency? If so, do you run on the
strength of Houston's popularity, or upon your own merits? In other
words, are you the Administration candidate? My personal predilictions
in your favor have been too unequivocally expressed to permit any
doubts in your mind, in regard to my friendship. But I could not consent
to vote for anyone who depended on the popularity of Sam Houston and
the fame of San Jacinto. . . . I do not think it would be necessary for you
to denounce the administration, or even to attempt to conceal your warm
friendship for Gen. Houston; but I do not think you should permit your

[110] Gambrell, *Anson Jones,* 350–51.
[111] Houston *Morning Star,* June 8, 1844.
[112] James Burke to Anson Jones, October 31, 1843, in Jones, *The Republic of
Texas,* 264.

name to be run as the *nominee and special* favorite and candidate of the administration, as Van Buren was of Jackson. I do not think that popularity is transferable in Texas as in the United States.

The editor of the La Grange *Intelligencer* took a leaf from Burleson's notebook and presented a classical reference to point up the folly of Jones's chosen course:[113]

Caligula, the depraved and worst of all the tyrants that ever ruled Rome, after having trodden the spirit of his people into the most abject slavery, showed his contempt for them by making his *horse* a Consul. Gen. Houston, thinking the people of Texas in a like condition, evinces a much greater contempt for them, by wishing to impose Dr. Anson Jones upon the Republic as President—*a less noble animal.*

Because of his close association with the administration, Jones was labeled pro-British in his sentiments. Also, because the candidate's first official task as minister to the United States in 1838 had been to withdraw the Texas petition of annexation, there were many who believed that Jones was personally hostile to a union with the United States. This was the most telling charge against Jones, and the Burleson forces made the most of their weapon. The Clarksville *Northern Standard,* in expressing its opinion of the position of Jones toward England, commented:[114]

Dr. Jones' organ has long been speaking in disparaging terms of the Government of the United States. . . . HE HAS ALL ALONG BEEN OPPOSED TO ANNEXATION. . . . he does not consider that an allegiance with the United States can be as much to our advantage as one with England. Does Anson Jones believe the people of this country so base and mean spirited as to feel a pride in helping to swell the wealth and overgrown power of England? Yet this is the ambition and this is the policy of Anson Jones. . . . While our friends in the United States are making the most active exertions, Anson Jones is at the same time prosecuting negotiations with England which will give her a monopoly of our commerce and will forever exclude us from the Union.

As the election day approached, political feeling ran high throughout the Republic. Francis Moore noted that "the party spirit

---

[113] La Grange *Intelligencer*, June 13, 1844.
[114] Clarksville *Northern Standard*, August 19, 1844, quoted in Gambrell, *Anson Jones,* 351.

in the United States is tame and mild compared to the bitter, malignant, demoniac zeal which is displayed in many instances by the partisans of our candidates."[115] However, this was an overstatement, for the election was in no way different from the two that had preceded it. Prior to election day the editor of the Houston *Morning Star* had complained that "we know of no party in this country based upon measures,"[116] and this observation was basically true. As was generally predicted, Burleson carried the sparsely settled western areas, and Jones the thickly populated eastern sections. Jones, as the secretary of state in office, had the official duty of counting the votes recorded in the election. This proved a pleasant task, for the Secretary polled nearly ten thousand votes and was thus assured of a decisive victory.

William Kennedy, a member of the British legation at Galveston, sent this version of the election to Lord Aberdeen: "Mr. Jones owes his election to Houston's influence, and to the impression which he has himself countenanced, that he will follow in his footsteps."[117] It remained only for James Morgan to record his sentiments in his habitually breezy style:[118]

Dr. *Anson Jones* is certainly elected to the Presidency—there is no doubt of it—though all the returns are not in yet—He had no popularity of his own—rode in on Old Sam's Shadow! His opponent Burleson is a very illeterate man & would have disgraced the Republic in that office— (if it can be disgraced)—Genl. Hamilton—Col. Bee—Genl. Johnston & a host of others will be sadly disappointed in the election as all expected to ride if Burleson was elected, which was generally looked for as Jones had no popularity of his own. But Old Sam can beat the D——l himself when he trys and make anyone president.

[115] Houston *Telegraph and Texas Register*, June 4, 1844.
[116] Houston *Morning Star*, June 25, 1844.
[117] William Kennedy to Lord Aberdeen, September 23, 1844, in Adams (ed.), *British Diplomatic Correspondence*, 366.
[118] James Morgan to Samuel Swartwout, September 28, 1844, Morgan Papers.

The End of an Era

YET, ANSON, WITHOUT TALENTS, without political honesty, or popularity, has had greatness thrust upon him. His elevation shows to the world *King Log* in his native colors, and shows a little mind swelled to fancied greatness. Truly does he remind one of the fabled frog trying to swell up to the size of the ox: and now Anson tries to strut a patriot, statesman, and hero. "Shame where is thy blush!" . . . Sir, take your old post in the rear, and leave this question for the Texas people to decide, for you cannot induce any one to believe that your opposition to annexation arises from any native sentiments.[1]

THE SHORT ADMINISTRATION of Anson Jones was almost wholly occupied with the final disposition of the annexation ques-

[1] La Grange *Intelligencer*, March 31, 1845.

tion. Realizing that his term in office might be short and that his administration would therefore formulate no new or distinct policies, Jones retained the majority of the Houston appointees as members of his own cabinet. Ebenezer Allen, who had replaced George Terrell as attorney general, stayed on, as did George W. Hill, who had replaced George Hockley as secretary of war and marine. William T. Ochiltree was given the treasury portfolio, and, through the suggestion of Houston, Ashbel Smith was recalled from Europe to be secretary of state. In regard to the major diplomatic appointments, Houston had the pleasure of seeing Reily return to Washington, and George Terrell was sent to England and France as a replacement for Smith. Finally, William Daingerfield was allowed to remain minister to Belgium, Holland, and the Hanse towns.[2] The selection of the official family complete, the new President then confronted the problem of union with the United States.

The final impetus for annexation came not from Texas but from the United States. President Tyler, who had always been a strong advocate of the measure, had rightly interpreted the election of Polk as a mandate from the American people.[3] Polk had stressed as one of his election promises the "reannexation of Texas," and because of his own decisive election victory Tyler decided to act. In his annual message to Congress, delivered on December 4, 1844, President Tyler forcefully stated why he favored annexation. Reviewing the passage of events in Texas since the beginning of the Revolution, Tyler placed emphasis upon the continual warfare between Texas and Mexico. Recalling the massacre at Goliad and the siege of the Alamo, Tyler reasoned that Texas must become an integral part of the Union or be forced to fight a war to the death with Mexico. Then, mentioning the possibility of British influence if Texas remained independent, the President stated that Polk's victory was to him a popular mandate that Texas be annexed. Finally, Tyler contended that, since both governments had already agreed on the terms of annexation as written into the recent treaty that had failed in the Senate, the matter might be accomplished in direct fashion by a joint resolution.[4]

[2] Gambrell, *Anson Jones*, 360.
[3] Oliver P. Chitwood, *John Tyler: Champion of the Old South*, 362–63.
[4] James D. Richardson (ed.), *Messages and Papers of the Presidents*, IV, 341–

Also, Tyler had done more than speak for annexation. Two days after the treaty negotiated by Calhoun and the Texas agents had failed in the Senate, the President sent the documents to the House of Representatives with the plea that the Texas question be favorably settled in some form compatible with the Constitution. The session of Congress was too near its close for any important action to be taken, but the President did receive the promise of House leaders that the issue would be given a full hearing at the next session of Congress. Accordingly, after Congress assembled again in December the House set to work drafting a bill which embodied the President's wishes. The bill, as ultimately adopted by the House of Representatives, was a complete departure from the treaty which had failed at the previous session. It provided that Texas be admitted into the Union with a republican form of government which was to be adopted before July 1, 1846, upon the following basic conditions:

1. All boundary questions were to be adjusted by the United States.

2. The state of Texas was to retain its own public lands and apply the income from those to the debts of the Republic.

3. With the consent of Texas, new states, not to exceed the number of four, might be forced out of the territory, provided that slavery was prohibited in such new states as would fall north of the extended Missouri Compromise line.

In this fashion, the resolution passed the House on January 25, 1845.[5]

In the Senate, debate occupying most of January and February focused upon the constitutionality of the joint resolution. The debate was generally on party lines; the Democrats were in favor of the proposal, and all but two of the Whig Senators were opposed. An agreement was made possible only when an amendment was added which empowered the President, if he chose to do so, to negotiate with the Republic of Texas on such new terms as might be agreed upon by the two governments. In effect, President Tyler

46. The idea for a joint resolution which succeeded where the regular treaty had failed originated with James Pinckney Henderson.

[5] Smith, *The Annexation of Texas*, 332–33.

was authorized to determine the specific manner in which Texas was to enter the Union. Tyler, therefore, could do but two things: act on the plan as proposed by the House, or work for annexation on terms to be agreed upon at a later date. The Senate gave its approval to the amended resolution on February 26, 1845, and the House speedily approved the amendment which the Senate had made to the original House bill. The proposal received the formal approval of the Executive on March 1, 1845. Tyler then received an affirmative vote from his cabinet, and on March 3, 1845, only hours before his administration came to an end, Tyler dispatched the resolution to Texas, urging the Texas Congress to act immediately and without amendment.[6]

In this manner the government of the United States finally extended the offer of annexation to the Republic of Texas. When the policy of the United States had been made public, the Mexican Minister at Washington, Juan Almonte, instantly demanded his passports and left the country. Polk was then faced with the difficult problem of trying to anticipate the official policy of Mexico. Santa Anna had again been driven out of power, and General Herrera had been appointed interim President by the Mexican Council of State. Luis Gonzaga Cuevas was designated minister of foreign affairs, and upon him and Herrera rested the decisions which would have to be made. If Mexico once and for all recognized the independence of Texas, then the Republic would forever maintain its independence. However, Mexico feared that an independent Texas would become the natural ally of the United States and thus support the expansionist pretensions of that government.[7] The annexation of Texas would mean the extension of the American boundary to the frontiers of Mexico. It was at this point in the dilemma that England made its final attempt to decide the issue.

After the election of Polk had indicated that the United States would look with favor upon annexation, Lord Aberdeen received intelligence from different sources that the problem must not be considered settled. Richard Pakenham, writing from Washington, Charles Bankhead from Mexico City, and Elliot from Texas all in-

[6] Chitwood, *John Tyler*, 371.
[7] George L. Rives, *The United States and Mexico, 1821–1848*, I, 698–700.

dicated that if England acted quickly and in a decisive manner annexation might still be prevented.[8] George Terrell, the Texas minister commissioned to England and France by President Jones, also gave Aberdeen the same impression in private conversations. Therefore, stimulated by these observations that a forthright policy might still induce Texas to remain independent, Aberdeen approached the French Foreign Minister, Guizot, and proposed that both countries instruct their agents in Mexico to work for Texas independence.

President Polk, determined to carry through the annexation proceedings initiated by Tyler, had commissioned President Jackson's former private secretary, Andrew Jackson Donelson, as his envoy to the Republic. The fact that his three most recent predecessors had died while performing their duties in Texas did not deter Donelson, and he set out on his mission with high hopes. In a letter to Jackson, he expressed his beliefs about his task:[9]

The main point is to get Texas on the same footing we did Louisiana in 1803. Once in the Union there will be of course no fear of foreign influence, and the issues to be presented on the questions of slavery and number of states can be settled calmly and peaceably. Texas would not come into the Union on Mr. Benton's terms. She would want all the rights and privileges that Louisiana had, and would spurn the idea of receiving them by permission of Mexico. She has no fear of Mexico. On the contrary, Houston could march into the Territory and compel her to give independence to his country. He is only restrained by the wish to spare the further effusion of blood, and to maintain a position favorable to the measure of reannexation.

Donelson arrived at Galveston on April 29 and thereafter was employed in convincing the Texas Congress to accept the terms of annexation.[10]

In truth, President Jones and the majority of his advisers were anything but ardent advocates of annexation to the United States. Reminiscing at a later date, Ashbel Smith, the secretary of state, recalled that he and Attorney General Allen were decidedly hostile

[8] Adams (ed.), *British Interests and Activities in Texas, 1838–1846*, 167–68.
[9] Andrew J. Donelson to Jackson, December 28, 1844, *Jackson Correspondence*, VI, 349.
[10] Annie Middleton, "Donelson's Mission to Texas in Behalf of Annexation," *Southwestern Historical Quarterly*, XXIV (1921), 255.

to the American offer and that Secretary of the Treasury William Ochiltree was the only cabinet member who actually favored the proposal.[11] Also, the major diplomatic appointments made by Jones were calculated to place in positions of importance men who were on record against the proposal. As minister to the United States, Jones had entrusted the delicate negotiations yet to come to James Reily. In a letter to Houston's private secretary, Washington D. Miller, Reily unfolded his sentiments on the crucial issue:[12]

... hence I would warn those who in their executive & representative characters are to control the destinies of Texas, not to hang with desperate grasp to annexation, whilst every year of her miserable uncertainty is sapping her energies. War with Mexico there will not be. Invasion of her territory is not probable. She is free to all purposes. And it is with deepest sincerity I utter the wish that annexation had never been proposed, or since proposed that the measure was ended one way or the other & that right speedily. We must either have annexation or peace before we can prosper and Peace we could with independent action have at once.

In the same manner, the appointee to Britain and France, George Terrell, explained to Jones:[13]

... But this great *friendship for Texas!* The friendship of the lion for the lamb. Look at all the arguments of the statesmen and letter writers on the subject—from the venerable sage of the Hermitage, (God save his soul) down to Felix Huston—is there one single argument in favor of Texas to be found in all of them? According to these gentlemen, Texas is to stand as an outpost to the great Union; she is to form an 'iron hoop' to support the United States. Again, 'it is necessary to the safety of the United States that they should have Texas,' and if they once get their eagle talons fastened upon the country, they are prepared to adjust with Mexico all questions growing out of annexation, *including boundary,* upon the most *liberal* terms, viz: to surrender the territory from the Rio Grande to the Nueces.

Against this favorable setting the ministers of England and France, Elliot and De Saligny, set to work to prevent annexation.

[11] Smith, *Reminiscences of the Texas Republic,* 81.
[12] James Reily to Washington D. Miller, December 24, 1844, Miller Papers.
[13] George W. Terrell to Anson Jones, February 13, 1845, in Jones, *Republic of Texas,* 429.

Proceeding to Washington-on-the-Brazos, where the first Congress under the new administration was in session, the diplomats presented their case before the President and his Secretary of State, Ashbel Smith, in a series of interviews. In these sessions Jones stressed the point that the people of the Republic were eager for annexation and that all efforts to avert it would be useless. However, Elliot still firmly believed that something could be done, particularly since it was understood that the President did not greatly favor the American offer. Elliot therefore suggested that the Texas government accept the good offices of England and France for mediation purposes, to be based on the Mexican acknowledgment of Texas independence.

In his book *The Republic of Texas*, Anson Jones set down his own attitude toward the prevailing topic: "I was acting in good faith simply, to all the powers interested, and was not engaged in *exclusive* efforts for annexation. I was certainly laboring for annexation and independence both at the same time."[14] Because the President retained an open mind on the matter, he was tempted by Elliot's offer. There was every reason to feel that the British minister was acting in sincere fashion and that the support of the government at London would be rapidly forthcoming. However, Jones also realized that the populace in Texas would be eager for annexation as soon as the success of the joint resolution in the United States Congress became a matter of public knowledge. Therefore, if the administration hoped to negotiate with Mexico in the face of the action taken by the United States, it would be absolutely necessary to offer something more than glib assurance. Jones wanted concrete proof that Mexico would be willing to recognize the independence of Texas at once.

Upon the basis of this understanding, it was agreed to draw up certain preliminary conditions to be submitted to the Mexican government. If these conditions were accepted, a proclamation announcing the preliminaries of peace and recognition would be issued. The terms agreed upon by the British and French ministers after conferences with Jones and Ashbel Smith were: (1) Mexico must agree to acknowledge the independence of Texas; (2) Texas must agree to stipulate in the treaty not to annex herself or become

---

[14] Jones, *Republic of Texas*, 430.

subject to any country whatever; (3) limits and other conditions to be matters of arrangement in the final treaty; (4) Texas must be willing to remit disputed points respecting territory and other matters to the arbitration of umpires.[15] Thus Jones in effect gave sanction to the final attempts of Britain and France to forestall action by the United States.

By the terms of the agreement, ninety days was established as time enough in which to receive an answer on the propositions from Mexico. It was also agreed that Elliot was to go directly to Mexico City to present the document stating the conditions of recognition and that he was to use his personal influence to achieve governmental approval. Jones also consented to send Ashbel Smith to Europe so that an accredited agent would be on hand at the European courts, pending the decision of the Mexican government. Finally, it was stipulated that the agreement in the protocol was not to be binding in any way and that if the people of Texas preferred to accept annexation instead the government would be at liberty to act accordingly. Jones did promise, however, to wait the ninety days before submitting the propositions of the United States for popular approval. The protocol was officially signed in late March, 1845, and Smith prepared to depart for Europe.[16]

As Elliot and De Saligny were leaving Washington-on-the-Brazos after signing the protocol, they encountered the representative of the United States, Donelson, who brought news of the successful passage of the joint resolution at Washington. Donelson attempted to communicate with Ashbel Smith but was informed that the Secretary of State had been granted a leave of absence and that Ebenezer Allen was now in charge of the conduct of foreign relations. During a private interview President Jones indicated to Donelson that he had intended to call a special session of Congress to discuss the basic question before the Republic, but in view of the existing situation Jones now felt that it would be best to place the issue squarely before the people in a convention.

Jones, in his desire to call a popular convention, was motivated by political considerations. As the news of the American offer spread, the popular demand for a convention grew increasingly

[15] Schmitz, *Texan Statecraft: 1836–1845*, 230.
[16] Smith, *The Annexation of Texas*, 437.

stronger. Commenting on this development, the Houston *Telegraph and Texas Register* noted:[17]

Now that a law has been passed by the Government of the United States, authorizing the people of Texas to establish a State Government under the Constitution of that country; much anxiety is manifested to ascertain what course will be adopted by our Government to consummate the measure. The main object must be to ascertain whether the terms offered by the United States will be acceptable to a majority of the people of Texas. This can be ascertained only by the direct vote of the people. It is important that the vote should be taken at as early a period as practicable; but, the question arises, how is the question to be submitted to the people? Shall it be done by the proclamation of the President? by an act of Congress? or shall the people acting in their sovereign capacity, call meetings in each county, and decide the question as they decided the question of a separation from Mexico?—the latter course would be a revolution, but the question of itself involves a revolution.

In addition to the desire for annexation, the latent hatred felt by most Texans toward the pretensions of Great Britain began to make itself felt. Many of the fathers of those who were concerned with the annexation question had fought in the War of 1812, and anti-British prejudice was still keenly felt in 1845. As early as December, 1844, the New Orleans *Picayune* had called attention to the dangers presented by the activities of Lord Aberdeen. Commenting on the British disposition to meddle, the newspaper asked its readers to ponder the following questions:[18]

Does the United States or Texas attempt to interrupt the British Government in her conquests. Have they remonstrated against the extension of her empire in India, the subjugation of Afghanistan, the seizure of the Sandwich Islands, the occupation of the Cape of Good Hope, the colonization of Australia, the dismemberment of the Chinese possessions, or the lodgments she has made in every sea and upon every continent? What would England or the civilized world say if the United States were to protest against the annexation of Pondichery to the British Crown, if both England and the colony desired it? Would not such interference be considered impertinent?

[17] Houston *Telegraph and Texas Register*, March 26, 1845.
[18] New Orleans *Picayune*, December 27, 1844.

As events developed in the Republic, within two weeks after Donelson's arrival virtually every county had held a mass demonstration in favor of accepting the offer of the United States. The meeting held at Houston on the ninth anniversary of the Battle of San Jacinto serves as an example of what was happening throughout Texas. The citizens at Houston declared their "full confidence in the honor and justice of the American people" and their belief that the people of the United States would in time extend to them "every privilege that freeman can grant without dishonor, and freemen accept without disgrace."[19] Donelson, believing that former President Houston favored his cause and understanding that Houston's opinion would be very influential, secured a statement from the Old Hero. Houston announced himself in favor of annexation but expressed the opinion that union on the basis of a treaty which would secure Senate approval would give the Republic a better chance to bargain for terms. Donelson then had another interview with Jones on April 12, 1845, and received from the President the promise that he would interpose no further obstacles in the path of annexation. Jones then said that he would call Congress at an early date and shortly announced that it would convene on June 16, thereby giving himself two more months to await word of Elliot's efforts at Mexico City.[20]

The extremists in favor of annexation were not satisfied with the call for a session of Congress and asked that a popular convention be quickly set up. This demand was bolstered by the argument that a convention would be necessary to form the new state constitution, for two of the conditions of the joint resolution were that the constitution must be formed in convention and that it must be adopted with the consent of the existing government. However, there was great diversity of opinion on the apportionment of the representatives for this convention. The west, although depopulated by the running war with Mexico, was still accorded representation and voting strength on a prewar census. As a result, President Jones was provided with a convenient pretext for delaying.[21]

---

[19] Houston *Telegraph and Texas Register*, April 23, 1845.
[20] Middleton, "Donelson's Mission to Texas in Behalf of Annexation," *Southwestern Historical Quarterly*, XXIV 276.
[21] Schmitz, *Texan Statecraft: 1836–1845*, 232.

POLITICAL HISTORY OF THE TEXAS REPUBLIC

Still, the demand for direct action was so concerted that by the first of May many counties had taken it upon themselves to instruct their senators and representatives to meet at Washington-on-the-Brazos on the third Monday in May, assume the conventional powers, and take whatever legal steps were deemed necessary to carry out the will of the people. This precipitance forced the President's hand, and he then issued a proclamation announcing the election of delegates and calling the convention to assemble on July 4, 1845. This satisfied Donelson, who was now confident that his labors for annexation would be successful.

Meanwhile, Captain Elliot had been laboring at Mexico City. After more than a month of constant entreaty, Cuevas, the foreign secretary, agreed to the terms which had been drawn up by Jones and Elliot recognizing the independence of Texas on the condition that the Republic would not annex herself to the United States. Elliot delivered the treaty to Jones on June 3, and the following day the President made public the news that the peace treaty had been accepted by Mexico. Jones therefore proclaimed a cessation of hostilities by land and sea and promised that he would submit the entire question of the Mexican propositions at the next session of Congress.[22]

Congress convened at Washington-on-the-Brazos on June 16 and sat only until June 28, 1845. In his message to the special session the President submitted the offers of both the United States and Mexico and included the correspondence relating to the treaties. Jones presented the case in a fair spirit and left the ultimate decision to the people. However, there was no doubt at all about the prevailing sentiment of the general populace. Mexico was still not to be trusted, and the legislators were extremely wary of any agreements with that country. A short while before the meeting of Congress, the Houston *Telegraph and Texas Register* commented on the talks in progress with Mexico:[23]

The object of the Mexican government is to lie and deceive us, and thus to delay measures until the opponents of Annexation can gain strength to defeat the measure. They may dupe some of our statesmen; but they will not dupe the people of Texas. Their march is onward.

[22] *Ibid.*, 234.
[23] Houston *Telegraph and Texas Register*, April 23, 1845.

Their attention is fixed upon one object, and they are determined to consummate it in spite of every obstacle.

Ashbel Smith also noted that the people were frantic in their opposition to dealing with Mexico, and it is certain that the popular will was for annexation.[24]

The offer of the United States was unanimously accepted by Congress, and approval was also given to the proclamation previously issued by the President, which provided for the election of deputies to a convention to draw up a state constitution. The efforts of Elliot and De Saligny had failed, and Ashbel Smith, only recently arrived in Europe, confined his labors to closing the Texas legations at London and Paris.

The convention met at Austin on July 4, 1845, and passed an ordinance accepting annexation with but one dissenting vote. By the terms of the joint resolution, Texas was to enter the Union as a state without going through the usual territorial stage. New states, not exceeding four in number, could, with Texas' consent, be created out of the new territory, and any of these states north of the 36°30′ line were to be nonslaveholding. Texas was also to pay her own public debt but would retain her public lands. These terms were cheerfully accepted by the convention, and with this formality completed the delegates set to work to draw up a state constitution. The convention was thus occupied for some two months, and on October 13 the state constitution and the annexation propositions were submitted to the people for ratification, which was unanimous. Upon certifying to Congress that the Constitution of Texas met the requirements of a "republican form of government," Polk signed the bill admitting Texas on December 29, 1845. On February 16, 1846, the Lone Star was replaced by the flag of the United States, and James Pinckney Henderson was sworn in as the first governor of Texas.

The annexation of Texas was therefore effected by the people of the Republic and not by their elected officials, most of whom were hostile to the proposal. The correspondence of Terrell, Reily, and Jones serves to indicate the disfavor with which the government regarded the measure. John S. Ford, a member of Congress at this

[24] Smith, *Reminiscences of the Texas Republic*, 72.

time, has stated that the opposition of Jones and his cabinet advisers to annexation was a matter of common knowledge.[25] Finally, this question, like many which had preceded it in the nine-year history of Texas independence, had led to strong controversy. A particular segment of opinion felt that the Republic had achieved something unique in American political history, that the nation had already triumphed over its most difficult trials, and that union with the United States destroyed any potentialities the Republic might have had as a powerful, independent country. James Morgan, whose primary aim in coming to Texas was land speculation, settled permanently and came to love the land. In a somewhat bitter vein he described his reaction to annexation:[26]

It seems that 'the long agony is over' and Texas is to be tacked on to the fag end of the U States, a little behind *Arkansas,* or any repudiating state thereof, *Nolens Volens!*—Worse than all, we shall be annexed with the Curses of fully one-half of the people of the U.S., who have been deriding us and abusing us for Cutthroats, villains, and bestowing upon us every vile epithet and during the whole time of the canvass between Mr. Clay and Gov. Polk, and at it yet! Just, too, as our Independence was about being acknowledged by Mexico! . . . Well, all my projects, I fear, are knocked in the head—and I shall die for want of excitement of some kind.

However, in contrast to these perverse feelings, a fitting epitaph to the history of the Republic was recorded in her diary by Mary Maverick: "July, 1845. Thank God, we are now annexed to the United States, and can hope for home and quiet."[27]

The act of annexation brought to a conclusion a story which had begun with the arrival of the first settlers in Texas. In a twenty-five year span Texas was an outlying province of the Spanish Empire, part of a state within the Mexican Confederation, an independent nation, and ultimately a state in the American Union. Continuous change and transition from one political allegiance to another was the dominant feature of early Texas history.

[25] Memoirs of John S. Ford, 364–65.
[26] James Morgan to Anson Jones, March 28, 1845, Morgan Papers.
[27] Maverick, *Memoirs of Mary A. Maverick,* 89.

The American colonists who migrated to Texas following the lure of a new frontier soon found themselves at odds with their Mexican rulers, and the inevitable Texas desire for independence was culminated on the battlefield at San Jacinto. Thus by force of arms was the struggle for political rights and privileges accomplished. The Republic of Texas survived many tribulations, and it was due to the statesmanship of Presidents Houston, Lamar, and Jones that the nation maintained its right to independent status. At times the problems of finance, military defense, foreign relations, and the haughty bearing of the United States toward annexation appeared to be overwhelming, but in each instance the obstacles were surmounted. At the time of annexation the Republic had experienced its most difficult days, and the future was viewed in an optimistic light.

In the period immediately following statehood the history of Texas continued to be fast-paced. Within a year Texas took an active part in the Mexican War; and in 1861, over the bitter but futile opposition of General Houston, the state pledged its support to Jefferson Davis and the Confederacy. That the period of the Republic has had a lasting impression upon the subsequent history of the state of Texas cannot be denied. The era that produced such patriots as Austin, Houston, Lamar, and the rest and witnessed the birth of modern Texas history will continue to profoundly influence the state in every area in which history, culture, and politics play a vital role.

Bibliography

Bibliography

PRIMARY SOURCES
Manuscript
Bee, Barnard E. Papers. Archives Collection, University of Texas Library.
Briscoe, Andrew. Papers. San Jacinto Museum of History.
Bryan, Moses Austin. Papers. Archives Collection, University of Texas Library.
Douglass, Kelsey H. Papers. Archives Collection, University of Texas Library.
Ford, John Salmon. Memoirs. Typescript, Archives Collection, University of Texas Library.
Jones, Anson. Papers. Archives Collection, University of Texas Library.
Lewis, Ira R. Papers. Archives Collection, University of Texas Library.
Miller, Washington D. Papers. Archives, Texas State Library.
Morgan, James. Papers. Archives, Rosenberg Library, Galveston, Texas.
Reily, James. Papers. Archives Collection, University of Texas Library.
Rusk, Thomas Jefferson. Papers. Archives Collection, University of Texas Library.
Smith, Ashbel. Papers. Archives Collection, University of Texas Library.
Starr, James Harper. Papers. Archives Collection, University of Texas Library.
Van Zandt, Isaac. Papers. Archives Collection, University of Texas Library.

Printed

Adams, Ephraim Douglass. *British Diplomatic Correspondence concerning the Republic of Texas, 1838–1846.* Austin, Texas State Historical Association, 1917.

Barker, Eugene C. (ed.). *The Austin Papers,* III. Austin, University of Texas Press, 1927.

—— (ed.). *The Correspondence of Stephen F. Austin, American Historical Association Annual Report, 1919.* Washington, Government Printing Office, 1924. 2 vols.

Bassett, John Spencer (ed.). *Correspondence of Andrew Jackson.* Washington, Carnegie Institution, 1926–35. 7 vols.

Binkley, William C. (ed.). *Official Correspondence of the Texan Revolution, 1835–1836.* New York, D. Appleton and Company, Inc., 1936. 2 vols.

Fulton, Maurice Garland (ed.). *Diary and Letters of Josiah Gregg.* Norman, University of Oklahoma Press, 1941–44. 2 vols.

Garrison, George P. (ed.). *Diplomatic Correspondence of the Republic of Texas, American Historical Association Annual Report, 1907.* Washington, Government Printing Office, 1908–11. 3 vols.

Gray, William Fairfax. *From Virginia to Texas, 1835: Diary of Col. Wm. F. Gray Giving Details of His Journey to Texas and Return in 1835–1836 and Second Journey to Texas in 1837.* Houston, Gray, Dillaye and Company, 1909.

Gulick, Charles A., Jr., and others (eds.). *The Papers of Mirabeau Buonaparte Lamar.* Austin, VonBoeckmann-Jones, 1921–27. 6 vols.

Lubbock, Francis R. *Six Decades in Texas; or, Memoirs of Francis Richard Lubbock, Governor of Texas in War Time, 1861–63: A Personal Experience in Business, War, and Politics.* Ed. C. W. Raines. Austin, Ben C. Jones and Company, 1900.

Memoirs of Mary A. Maverick. Arr. Mary A. Maverick and George Maverick. Ed. Rena Maverick Green. San Antonio, Alamo Printing Company, 1921.

McCaleb, Walter F. (ed.). *The Memoirs of John H. Reagan.* New York, Neale Publishing Company, 1906.

Nevins, Allan (ed.). *The Diary of John Quincy Adams, 1794–1845.* New York, Longmans, Green & Company, Inc., 1928.

Williams, Amelia W., and Eugene C. Barker (eds.). *The Writings of Sam Houston, 1813–1863.* Austin, University of Texas Press, 1938–43. 8 vols.

Public Documents

Unless otherwise noted, the following records are all situated in the archives of the Texas State Library, Austin. The records are also included in the microfilm collection of the *Library of Congress, State Records Series,* at the Fondren Library, Rice Institute, Houston, with the exception of the Richardson and Winkler volumes.

Debates of the Annexation Convention, July 4–August 28, 1845.
Department of State—Letterbooks, Home Letters, Foreign Letters, Foreign Legation Letters and Journals, 1836–1845.

Executive Department Journals, 1836–1845.

Journal of the Consultation, October 16, 1835–November 14, 1835. Archives Collection, University of Texas Library.

Journal of the General Council, November 14, 1835–March 11, 1836. Archives Collection, University of Texas Library.

Journals of the Senate of the Republic of Texas, 1836–1845.

Laws Passed by the Legislature of Coahuila and Texas. San Jacinto Museum of History.

Messages of the Presidents of the Republic of Texas, 1836–1845.

Ordinances and Decrees of the Consultation. Washington, Library of Congress.

Proceedings of the House of Representatives of the Republic of Texas, 1836–1845.

Richardson, James D. (ed.). *A Compilation of the Messages and Papers of the Presidents, 1789–1897.* Washington, Government Printing Office, 1896–99. 20 vols.

Session Laws of the Congresses of the Republic of Texas, 1836–1845.

Supreme Court Records, 1841–1845.

Winkler, Ernest W. (ed.). *Secret Journals of the Senate, Republic of Texas, 1836–1845.* Austin, Austin Printing Company, 1912.

SECONDARY SOURCES

Manuscript

Chambless, Beauford. "The Ad-Interim Government of the Republic of Texas." M.A. thesis, Rice Institute, 1949.

Covington, Nina. "The Presidential Campaigns of the Republic of Texas of 1836 and 1838." M.A. thesis, University of Texas, 1929.

Crane, Robert E. L., Jr. "The History of the Revenue Service and the Commerce of the Republic of Texas." Ph.D. dissertation, University of Texas, 1950.

Cravens, John Nathan. "The Life and Activities of James Harper Starr, 1809–1890." Ph.D. dissertation, University of Texas, 1948.

Strickland, Rex Wallace. "Anglo-American Activities in Northeastern Texas, 1803–1845." Ph.D. dissertation, University of Texas, 1937.

Printed—Books

Acheson, Sam. *35,000 Days in Texas: A History of the Dallas News and Its Forbears.* New York. The Macmillan Company, 1938.

Adams, Ephraim Douglass. *British Interests and Activities in Texas, 1838–1846.* Baltimore, Johns Hopkins Press, 1910.

Bailey, Thomas A. *A Diplomatic History of the American People*. New York, Appleton-Century-Crofts, Inc., 1946.

Bancroft, Hubert Howe. *History of the North Mexican States and Texas*. San Francisco, A. L. Bancroft and Company, 1884. 2 vols.

Barker, Eugene C. *The Life of Stephen F. Austin, Founder of Texas, 1793–1836: A Chapter in the Westward Movement of the Anglo-American People*. Austin, Texas State Historical Association, 1949.

———. *Mexico and Texas, 1821–1835*. Dallas, P. L. Turner Company, 1928.

———. *Public Opinion in Texas Preceding the Revolution, American Historical Association Annual Report, 1911*. Washington, Government Printing Office, 1913. 2 vols.

———. (ed.). *Readings in Texas History*. Dallas, Southwest Press, 1929.

Bemis, Samuel Flagg. (ed.). *The American Secretaries of State and Their Diplomacy*. New York, Alfred A. Knopf, Inc., 1927–29. 10 vols.

Binkley, William C. *The Texas Revolution*. Baton Rouge, Louisiana State University Press, 1952.

Braunfels, Prince Carl Solms. *Texas 1844–1845*. Houston, Anson Jones Press, 1936.

Brown, John Henry. *Life and Times of Henry Smith, the First American Governor of Texas*. Dallas, A. D. Aldridge and Company, 1887.

Bruce, Henry. *Life of General Houston, 1793–1863*. New York, Dodd, Mead, & Company, 1891.

Burleson, Georgia J. (comp.). *The Life and Writings of Rufus C. Burleson, D.D., LL.D., Containing a Biography of Dr. Burleson by Harry Haynes*. [Waco?], privately printed, 1901.

Callcott, Willfrid Hardy. *Santa Anna; the Story of an Enigma Who Once Was Mexico*. Norman, University of Oklahoma Press, 1936.

Castañeda, Carlos M. *The Mexican Side of the Texan Revolution*. Dallas, P. L. Turner Company, 1928.

Chitwood, Oliver P. *John Tyler: Champion of the Old South*. New York, D. Appleton-Century Company, Inc., 1939.

Coit, Margaret L. *John C. Calhoun: American Portrait*. Boston, Houghton Mifflin Company, 1950.

Coleman, R. M. *Houston Displayed; or, Who Won the Battle of San Jacinto*. Velasco, Texas, privately printed, 1837.

Crane, William Cary. *Life and Select Literary Remains of Sam Houston of Texas*. Dallas, W. G. Scarff and Company, 1884.

De Shields, James T. *They Sat in High Places: The Presidents and Governors of Texas*. San Antonio, The Naylor Company, 1940.

Dewees, William B. *Letters from an Early Settler of Texas*. Louisville, printed by the *New Albany Tribune*, 1858.

Dixon, Sam H. and Louis W. Kemp. *The Heroes of San Jacinto*. Houston, Anson Jones Press, 1932.

Dobie, J. Frank. *The Flavor of Texas*. Dallas, Dealey and Lowe, 1936.

Duval, J. C. *Early Times in Texas*. Dallas, Tardy Publishing Company, 1936.

Edward, David B. *The History of Texas: or the Emigrant's, Farmer's, and Politician's Guide to the Character, Climate, Soil, and Productions of That Country*. Cincinnati, J. A. James and Company, 1836.

Falconer, Thomas. *Letters and Notes on the Santa Fe Expedition, 1841–1842.* New York, Dauber and Pine, 1930.

Field, Joseph E. *Three Years in Texas.* Austin, The Steck Company, 1935. Reprint of the original edition published at Greenfield, Mass., in 1836.

Foote, Henry S. *Texas and the Texans.* Philadelphia, Thomas Cowperthwait and Company, 1841. 2 vols.

Foreman, Grant. *Pioneer Days in the Early Southwest.* Cleveland, Arthur H. Clark Company, 1926.

Frantz, Joe B. *Gail Borden, Dairyman to a Nation.* Norman, University of Oklahoma Press, 1951.

Friend, Llerena. *Sam Houston: The Great Designer.* Austin, University of Texas Press, 1954.

Gambrell, Herbert. *Anson Jones, the Last President of Texas.* Garden City, Doubleday & Company, 1948.

Gouge, William M. *The Fiscal History of Texas; Embracing an Account of Its Revenues, Debts, and Currency, from the Commencement of the Revolution in 1834 to 1851–52.* Philadelphia, Lippincott, Grambo, and Company, 1852.

Graham, Philip. *The Life and Poems of Mirabeau B. Lamar.* Chapel Hill, University of North Carolina Press, 1938.

Green, General Thomas J. *Journal of the Texian Expedition against Mier.* New York, Harper & Brothers, 1845.

Greer, James K. *Colonel Jack Hays, Texas Frontier Leader and California Builder.* New York, E. P. Dutton & Co., Inc., 1952.

Hatcher, Mattie Austin (ed.). *Letters of an Early American Traveller: Mary Austin Holley, Her Life and Her Works, 1784–1846.* Dallas, Southwest Press, 1933.

Hawkins, Walace. *The Case of John C. Watrous, United States Judge for Texas; a Political Story of High Crimes and Misdemeanors.* Dallas, Southern Methodist University Press, 1950.

Hill, Jim Dan. *The Texas Navy, in Forgotten Battles and Shirtsleeve Diplomacy.* Chicago, University of Chicago Press, 1937.

History of the Diocese of Galveston, 1847–1922. Galveston, privately printed, 1922.

Hogan, William R. *The Texas Republic: A Social and Economic History.* Norman, University of Oklahoma Press, 1946.

Horgan, Paul. *Great River: The Rio Grande in North American History.* New York, Rinehart & Company, 1954. 2 vols.

Houston, Andrew J. *Texas Independence.* Houston, Anson Jones Press, 1938.

Houstoun, Matilda Charlotte.*Texas and the Gulf of Mexico; or, Yachting in the New World.* London, J. Murray and Company, 1844.

James, Marquis. *The Raven: A Biography of Sam Houston.* Indianapolis, The Bobbs-Merrill Co., Inc., 1938.

Johnston, William P. *The Life of General Albert Sidney Johnston.* New York, D. Appleton & Company, 1879.

Jones, Anson. *Memoranda and Official Correspondence Relating to the Republic of Texas, Its History and Annexation—Including a Brief Autobiography of the Author.* New York, D. Appleton & Company, 1859.

Kendall, George Wilkins. *Narrative of the Texan Santa Fe Expedition*. Chicago, R. R. Donnelley & Sons Company, 1929. 2 vols.

Kennedy, William. *Texas: The Rise, Progress, and Prospects of the Republic of Texas*. London, R. Hastings, 1841.

Lamar, Mirabeau B. *Lamar's Prosecution of Santa Anna*. Ed. Sinclair Moreland. Austin, The Texas Historical Press, 1935. Reprint of Lamar's original pamphlet.

Lambert, Oscar D. *Presidential Politics in the United States, 1841–1844*. Durham, Duke University Press, 1936.

Lathrop, Barnes F. *Migration into East Texas, 1835–1860*. Austin, Texas State Historical Association, 1949.

Lawrence, Reverend A. B. *Texas in 1840: The Emigrant's Guide to the New Republic*. New York, W. W. Allen, 1840.

Leclerc, Frederic. *Texas and Its Revolution*. Houston, Anson Jones Press, 1950.

Lindley, E. K. (comp.). *Biographical Directory of the Texan Conventions and Congresses, 1832–1845*. Huntsville, printed by order of the House of Representatives, 1941.

Linn, John J. *Reminiscences of Fifty Years in Texas*. New York, D. & J. Sadlier and Company, 1883.

Looscan, Adele B. *Harris County, 1822–1845*. Austin, State Historical Association, 1915.

Lowrie, Samuel H. *Culture Conflicts in Texas, 1821–1835*. New York, Columbia University Press, 1932.

Lundy, Benjamin. *The War in Texas: A Review of Facts and Circumstances Showing That This Contest Is a Crusade against Mexico, Set on Foot and Supported by Slaveholders, Land-Speculators, &c., in Order to Re-Establish, Extend, and Perpetuate the System of Slavery and the Slave Trade*. Philadelphia, Merrihew and Gunn, 1837.

Maillard, N. Doran. *The History of the Republic of Texas*. London, Smith, Elder, and Company, 1842.

Malone, Dumas. (ed.). *Dictionary of American Biography*. New York, Charles Scribner's Sons, 1928–1944. 21 vols.

Marshall, Thomas Maitland. *A History of the Western Boundary of the Louisiana Purchase, 1819–1841*. Berkeley, University of California Press, 1914.

Maverick, Samuel A. *Notes on the Storming of Bexar, in the Close of 1835*. San Antonio, privately printed, 1942.

Middleton, John W. *History of the Regulators and Moderators and the Shelby County War in 1841 and 1842, in the Republic of Texas*. Fort Worth, Loving Publishing Company, 1883.

Miller, Edmund T. *A Financial History of Texas*. University of Texas Bulletin No. 37. Austin, A. C. Baldwin and Sons, 1916.

Montgomery, Corinne. *Texas and Her Presidents*. New York, Winchester, 1845.

Morton, Ohland. *Terán and Texas, A Chapter in Texas-Mexican Relations*. Austin, Texas State Historical Association, 1948.

Newell, Reverend Chester. *History of the Revolution in Texas, Particularly of the War of 1835 & '36; together with the Latest Geographical, Topographi-

cal, and Statistical Accounts of the Country. New York, Wiley and Putnam, 1838.

Parkes, Henry Bamford. *A History of Mexico.* Boston, Houghton Mifflin Company, 1938.

Reeves, Jesse S. *American Diplomacy under Tyler and Polk.* Baltimore, Johns Hopkins Press, 1907.

Richardson, Thomas C. *East Texas, Its History and Its Makers.* New York, Lewis Historical Publishing Company, 1940. 4 vols.

Rippy, J. Fred. *The United States and Mexico.* New York, Alfred A. Knopf, 1926.

Rives, George Lockhart. *The United States and Mexico, 1821–1848.* New York, Charles Scribner's Sons, 1913. 2 vols.

Robinson, Duncan W. *Judge Robert McAlpin Williamson, Texas' Three-Legged Willie.* Austin, Texas State Historical Association, 1948.

Schmitz, Joseph W. *Texan Statecraft: 1836–1845.* San Antonio, Naylor Company, 1941.

———. *Thus They Lived; Social Life in the Republic of Texas.* San Antonio, Naylor Company, 1935.

Shearer, Ernest C. *Robert Potter, Remarkable North Carolinian and Texan.* Houston, University of Houston Press, 1951.

Silver, James W. *Edmund Pendelton Gaines, Frontier General.* Baton Rouge, Louisiana State University Press, 1949.

Smith, Ashbel. *Reminiscences of the Texas Republic,* Galveston, Historical Society of Galveston, 1876.

Smith, Justin H. *The Annexation of Texas.* New York, Barnes and Noble, Inc., 1941.

Smithwick, Noah. *The Evolution of a State; or, Recollections of Old Texas Days.* Austin, Gammel Book Company, 1900.

Stephenson, Nathaniel W. *Texas and the Mexican War: A Chronicle of the Winning of the Southwest.* New Haven, Yale University Press, 1921.

Stiff, Edward. *A New History of Texas.* Cincinnati, G. Conclin Printers, 1847.

Tyler, George W. *The History of Bell County, Texas.* San Antonio, Naylor Company, 1936.

Van Deusen, Glyndon. *The Life of Henry Clay.* Boston, Little, Brown & Company, 1937.

Wallis, Jonnie Lockhart, and Laurance L. Hill. *Sixty Years on the Brazos: The Life and Letters of Dr. John Washington Lockhart, 1824–1900.* Los Angeles, privately printed, 1930.

Wharton, Clarence. *History of Fort Bend County.* San Antonio, Naylor Company, 1939.

Williams, Alfred M. *Sam Houston and the War of Independence in Texas.* New York, Houghton Mifflin Company, 1893.

Williams, Elgin. *The Animating Pursuits of Speculation: Land Traffic in the Annexation of Texas.* New York, Columbia University Press, 1949.

Wiltse, Charles M. *John C. Calhoun: Sectionalist, 1840–1850.* Indianapolis, The Bobbs-Merrill Co., Inc., 1951.

Winkler, Ernest W. *Platforms of Political Parties in Texas.* University of Texas Bulletin No. 53, Austin, 1916.

265

Wooten, Dudley G. *A Complete History of Texas*. Dallas, The Texas History Company, 1899.

Yoakum, Henderson. *History of Texas, from Its First Settlement in 1685 to Its Annexation to the United States in 1846*. New York, J. S. Redfield, 1855. 2 vols.

Printed—Articles

Barker, Eugene C. "The Influence of Slavery in the Colonization of Texas," *Southwestern Historical Quarterly*, XXVIII (1924).

———. "Land Speculation as a Cause of the Texas Revolution," *Quarterly of the Texas State Historical Association*, X (1906).

———. "Notes on Early Texas Newspapers, 1819–1836," *Southwestern Historical Review*, XXI (1917).

———. "Notes on the Colonization of Texas," *Mississippi Valley Historical Review*, X (1923).

———. "President Jackson and the Texas Revolution," *American Historical Review*, XII (1907).

———. "The Texas Declaration of Causes for Taking Up Arms against Mexico," *Quarterly of the Texas State Historical Association*, XV (1912).

———. "The Texas Revolutionary Army," *Quarterly of the Texas State Historical Association*, IX (1906).

———. "The United States and Mexico, 1835–1837," *Mississippi Valley Historical Review*, I (1914).

Binkley, William C. "The Activities of the Texan Revolutionary Army After San Jacinto," *Journal of Southern History*, VI (1940).

———. "New Mexico and the Texas Santa Fe Expedition," *Southwestern Historical Quarterly*, XXVII (1924).

Boucher, Chauncey S. "In Re That Aggressive Slaveocracy," *Mississippi Valley Historical Review*, VIII (1921).

Bugbee, Lester G. "Slavery in Early Texas," *Political Science Quarterly*, XIII (1898).

Castañeda, Carlos. (trans.). "Statistical Report on Texas, 1835," *Southwestern Historical Quarterly*, XXVIII (1925).

Christian, Asa K. "Mirabeau Buonaparte Lamar," *Southwestern Historical Quarterly*, XXIII–XXIV (1920).

Clopper, Nicholas. "The Clopper Correspondence, 1834–1838," *Quarterly of the Texas State Historical Association*, XIII (1909).

Dealey, James Q. "The Spanish Sources of the Mexican Constitution of 1824," *Quarterly of the Texas State Historical Association*, III (1900).

Denton, Bernice B. "Count Saligny and the Franco-Texienne Bill," *Southwestern Historical Quarterly*, XLV (1941).

Dienst, Alexander. "The Navy of the Republic of Texas," *Quarterly of the Texas State Historical Association*, XIII (1909).

Drummond, Lorena. "Five Texas Capitals: An Account of the Seats of Government in Texas since the Adoption of the Declaration of Independence," *Texas Monthly Magazine*, V (1930).

Edwards, Herbert R. "Diplomatic Relations between France and the Republic of Texas, 1836–1845," *Southwestern Historical Quarterly*, XX (1917).

Erath, Lucy A. "Memoirs of George Bernard Erath," *Southwestern Historical Quarterly*, XXVII (1923).

Eve, Joseph. "A Letter Book of Joseph Eve, United States Chargé D'Affaires to Texas," *Southwestern Historical Quarterly*, XLIII (1940).

Graham, Philip (ed.). "Mirabeau B. Lamar's First Trip to Texas," *Southwest Review*, XXI (1936).

Howren, Alleine. "Causes and Origin of the Decree of April 6, 1830," *Quarterly of the Texas State Historical Association*, XVI (1913).

Hynds, Alexander. "General Sam Houston," *Century Magazine*, XXVIII (1884).

Jordan, H. Donaldson. "A Politician of Expansion: Robert J. Walker," *Mississippi Valley Historical Review*, XIX (1932).

Lang, Aldon S. "Financial Aspects of the Public Lands in Texas," *Southwestern Political and Social Science Quarterly*, XIII (1932).

McClendon, Robert E. "Daniel Webster and Mexican Relations," *Southwestern Historical Quarterly*, XXXVI (1933).

Middleton, Annie. "Donelson's Mission to Texas in Behalf of Annexation," *Southwestern Historical Quarterly*, XXIV (1921).

Muckleroy, Anna. "The Indian Policy of the Republic of Texas," *Southwestern Historical Quarterly*, XXVI (1923).

Muir, Andrew F. "Diary of a Young Man in Houston, 1838," *Southwestern Historical Quarterly*, LIII (1950).

———. "The Free Negro in Harris County, Texas," *Southwestern Historical Quarterly*, XLVI (1943).

———. "The Mystery of San Jacinto," *Southwest Review*, XXXVI (1951).

———. "Railroad Enterprise in Texas, 1836–1841," *Southwestern Historical Quarterly*, XLVII (1944).

Rather, Ethel Zively. "Recognition of the Republic of Texas by the United States," *Quarterly of the Texas State Historical Association*, XIII (1910).

Schoen, Harold. "The Free Negro in the Republic of Texas," *Southwestern Historical Quarterly*, XLI (1937).

Smith, W. Roy. "The Quarrel between Governor Smith and the Provisional Government of the Republic," *Quarterly of the Texas State Historical Association*, V (1902).

Smither, Harriet (ed.). "Diary of Adolphus Sterne," *Southwestern Historical Quarterly*, XXX–XXXVIII (1926–35).

Spellman, L. U. (ed.). "Letters of the Dawson Men from Perote Prison," *Southwestern Historical Quarterly*, XXXIX (1935).

Steen, Ralph W. "Analysis of the Work of the General Council of Texas, 1835–1836," *Southwestern Historical Quarterly*, XLI (1938).

Stenberg, Richard R. "Some Letters of the Texas Revolution," *Southwestern Political and Social Science Quarterly*, XXI (1941)

———. "The Texas Schemes of Jackson and Houston, 1829–1836," *Southwestern Political and Social Science Quarterly*, XV (1934).

Wharton, Clarence. "Early Judicial History of Texas," *Texas Law Review*, XII (1934).

Winkler, Ernest W. "The Seat of Government in Texas," *Quarterly of the Texas State Historical Association*, X (1906).
Worley, J. L. "The Diplomatic Relations of England and the Republic of Texas," *Quarterly of the Texas State Historical Association*, IX (1905).

Printed—Newspapers

Austin *City Gazette*, 1840–42.
Austin *Daily Bulletin*, 1841.
Austin *Texas Sentinel*, 1841.
Galveston *Civilian*, 1842.
Galveston *Civilian & Gazette*, 1843.
Houston *Morning Star*, 1839–44.
Houston *Telegraph and Texas Register*, 1836–37, 1839–42, 1844–45.
La Grange *Intelligencer*, 1844–45.
Matagorda *Bulletin*, 1838.
New Orleans *Picayune*, 1837–39, 1841–44.
Niles' Weekly Register, 1836–37.
Richmond *Telescope & Register*, 1839.
San Augustine *Journal and Advertiser*, 1840–42.
San Augustine *Red-Lander*, 1842.

Index

Index

Aberdeen, Lord: 163, 171, 227, 233, 241, 245–46, 250; rejects loan request, 164; proposes "Diplomatic Act," 233

Abolitionists, opposition of, to annexation: 76

Adams, John Quincy: 230; diary of, quoted, 74, 232

Ad interim government: 32, 35, 54, 62, 99, 102; election to offices in, 33–34; unpopularity of, 42

Advocate of the People's Rights (Brazoria, Texas): 19

Alamo: 5, 30, 34, 40–41, 59, 243

Allen, Augustus C.: 58

Allen, Ebenezer: 243, 246, 249

Allen, John K.: 58

Allen, William Y.: 104

Almonte, Juan: 60, 126, 245; surveys Texas, 21 (n. 58)

Alvarez, Manuel: 169

Ampudia, Pedro de: 207

Anahuac, Texas: 12, 21

Anaya, Pedro: 129

Anderson, Kenneth L.: 187, 202, 236

Andrews, Stephen F.: 227

Annexation: 44, 72, 74, 76, 84, 121, 184, 224, 228; Texans' desire for, 47, 53, 56, 85–86, 228, 248, 251; Austin's attitude toward, 47; Houston's attitude toward, 61, 226, 228, 251; British opposition to, 74 (n. 107), 87, 226, 248; issue of, in U.S. politics, 76, 231; refused by U.S., 87,

271

Burton, Isaac W.: 93 (n. 156), 110, 143

Burton, James W.: 108

Bustamante, Anastasio: 126, 131–32; president of Mexico, 73, 122

Butler, Anthony: 15

Caddo Indians: 39, 82

Caldwell, Matthew: 203–204

Calhoun, John C.: 230, 244; fears British influence, 233

Cambreling, Churchill C.: 77

Cameron, Ewan: 207–209

Cameron, John: 67

Campbell, Isaac: 110

Canales, Antonio: 129, 133

Cañedo, Juan: 131–32, 135

Capital of Texas: dispute over location of, 81, 190; *see also* Austin, Texas; Houston, Texas

Carson, Samuel: 33

Cass, Lewis: 88

Castle of Perote: 208–209, 214, 217

Cayuga Indians: 166

Cazneau, William: 188, 213, 225, 236; opposes removal of capital from Austin, 190; favors Houston's impeachment, 222

Chalmers, John C.: 166

Cherokee Indians: 10, 39, 107, 143–44; commissioners treat with, 28; Houston lives with, 49; land titles in Texas, 67; Lamar denies claims of, 104; expulsion of, 108–109

Cherokee Land Bill: 143, 178

Cherokee War: 143, 167, 174, 211; political effects of, 109; *see also* Bowl, John

Cheves, Langdon: 5

Chickasaw Indians: 39

Childress, Robert: 43

Chriesman, Horatio: 81 (n. 127)

Clay, Henry: 254; on U.S. recognition, 44; on annexation, 231

Coahuila: 13, 17

Coles, John P.: 15

Collinsworth, James: 45–46, 48, 63, 65, 72, 99, 175; commissioner to U.S.,

43; chief justice of Texas Supreme Court, 56; candidate for president of Texas, 98; death of, 98

Colorado River: 34, 106–107, 110–11

Columbia, Texas: 22, 51, 57

Comanche Indians: 50, 83, 166, 224; raid Austin, 189

Combs, Franklin: 169–70

Combs, Leslie: 169

Convention of 1835: *see* General Consultation

Cooke, James R.: 205

Cooke, Louis P.: 191, 193, 198

Cooke, William G.: 206

Copano, Texas: 23, 30

Córdova, Vicente: 83, 107

Corzine, Shelby: 56

Cós, Martín Perfecto de: 19, 21–23, 27

Cox, Nathaniel: 8

Crawford, Alan: 87

Creek War: 49

Crockett, David: 30

Crockett, Texas: 96

Cuevas, Louis G.: 245, 252

Daingerfield, William H.: 194, 196, 225, 243; secretary of treasury of Texas, 185

Darnell, Nicholas H.: 187

Davis, Samuel P.: 142

Dawson, Nicholas: 205

Deffaudis, Baron: 89

Delaware Indians: 39, 82

De Saligny, Alphonse: 118, 233, 247, 249; inspection trip of, to Texas, 89, 115; recommends French recognition of Texas, 116; on French loan, 119; minister to Texas, 157; defends Franco-Texienne Bill, 158; and "pig incident," 160–61; breaks diplomatic relations, 161–62

Dewees, W. B.: 145

"Diplomatic Act": 233–34

Donelson, Andrew Jackson: 249, 251; on annexation, 246

Douglass, Kelsey H.: 68, 71, 108

Dryden, William G.: 165

Dunlap, Richard G.: 141, 147; secretary of treasury of Texas, 103; minister to U.S., 122

Dunn, John: 93 (n. 156)

Eberly, Angelina: 211

Edwards, Haden: 10, 219

Elliot, Charles: 209, 233, 247, 252; on Santa Fe expedition, 171; on Houston's policy, 183–84; Houston requests aid of, 210, 218; on Texas politics, 211–12; efforts of, for armistice, 218, 221; on annexation, 245

Ellis, Powhatan: 122, 128

Ellis, Richard: 32

England: 73, 84–85, 91, 119, 129, 148, 163, 184, 232, 240; refuses Texas recognition, 85–88; fails to make loan, 115; signs treaties with Texas, 150; helps secure armistice, 224; Texas' prejudice against, 250; see also Annexation

Erath, George: 213

Eve, Joseph: 213, 218

Everitt, Stephen H.: 56, 59, 140; endorses Lamar, 93

Falcón, J. Miguel: 16

Fannin, James W.: 27, 34, 37, 55; and Goliad campaign, 28–30; friendship of, for Lamar, 102

Farías, Gómez: 17, 21

Financial problems: see Republic of Texas

Fisher, S. Rhoads: 79; endorses Austin, 47; secretary of navy, 55

Fisher, William: 66, 206, 209, 212

Flood, George: 161

Flores, Manuel: 107

Fontaine, Edward: 176

Forbes, John: 67

Ford, John S.: 94, 254

Forsyth, John: 72, 78, 85–86, 122; U.S. secretary of state, 60; negotiates boundary treaty, 91

Fox, Henry S.: 115 (n. 30)

France: 73, 85, 91, 141, 148, 184, 232; Mexican difficulties with, 89; treaty of, with Texas, 118–19; recognizes

Texas, 119; refuses loan, 163; see also Annexation

Franco-Texienne Bill: 158—59, 172, 178

Franklin, Benjamin C.: 56

Fredonian Rebellion: 11, 219; see also Edwards, Haden

Gaines, Edmund P.: 35

Galveston, Texas: 39, 95–96, 127, 134, 167, 174, 221, 246

Gant, William: 71

García, Carlos: 16

General Consultation (Convention of 1835): 24, 42, 45, 143; sanctions Cherokee claims, 67

Goliad, Texas: 18, 27, 37, 59; captured by Mexicans, 30

Gonzales, Texas: 23, 81, 206; Texans occupy, 27

Goodbread, Joseph: 219

Gorostiza, Manuel: 125

Grant, Dr. James: 30

Gray, William Fairfax, diary quoted: 26, 33–34, 78

Grayson, Peter W.: 20, 45–46, 48, 72, 175; commissioner to U.S., 43; on annexation, 90; candidate for president of Texas, 95–96; death of, 96

Great Britain: see England

Great Saline River: 108

Green, Thomas J.: 48, 55, 64, 139; in Texas Army, 41–42; on election of 1838, 96; and Mier expedition, 208; opposes Houston, 225

Greer, John A.: 81 (n. 127), 107, 188, 190, 198

Gregg, Josiah: 185–86

Grimes, Jessie: 187

Guadalupe River: 30

Guerrero, Mexico: 206

Guerrero, Vicente: 11

Gulf of Mexico: 86, 133

Hainai Indians: 83

Hall, Edward: 97

Hamilton, George: 43

Hamilton: James: 121, 123, 127, 141,

Indians—*Continued*
Hainai; Kickapoo; Lipan Apache;
Shawnee; Waco
Ingram, Ira: 56
Inquisition Prison: 17
Invincible (ship): 41
Irion, Robert: 87–88, 90

Jack, Patrick C.: 12–14
Jack, Spencer H.: 20
Jack, William H.: 45, 52, 188, 213,
225; defends Lamar, 142
Jackson, Andrew: 35, 72, 75, 77, 83,
240, 246; on U.S. recognition,
43–45, 73–74; mediation by, requested, 46; Houston serves under,
49; friendship of, for Houston, 51;
policy of, toward Santa Anna, 59,
68; applauds Houston's policy, 201
Jackson, Charles: 219
Johnson, Benjamin H.: 129
Johnson, Francis W.: 27–28, 30
Johnston, Albert Sidney: 109, 236;
commands Texas Army, 66; duel
with Felix Huston, 66; secretary of
war of Texas, 103; in Cherokee War,
108; declines Texas presidential candidacy in 1841, 174
Jones, Anson: 92, 104, 116, 180, 200,
235; annexation policy of, 91, 228,
240, 248; minister to U.S., 91; endorses Rusk, 95; in Texas Congress,
141–42; on Houston, 147, 215; secretary of state of Texas, 184; Mexican policy of, 210; opposes "Diplomatic Act," 234; candidate for president of Texas, 236; charges against,
in 1844 campaign, 239; calls annexation convention, 252; *see also* Republic of Texas
Jones, Oliver: 18
Jones, William E.: 103, 165, 187

Karnes, Henry W.: 83
Kaufman, David S.: 105, 169, 225
Kendall, George W., and the Santa Fe
expedition: 167, 169–70
Kendrick, Harvey W.: 225
Kennedy, William: 241

Kickapoo Indians: 84
King, Amon B.: 30

La Bahía, Texas: 39
La Branche, Alcée: 77–78, 91
Lacey, Martin: 107
Lafitte and Company: 162
La Grange, Texas: 81
Land law of 1837: 70–72, 82, 97
Land Office: established, 62; Houston
refuses to open, 70, 72
Land speculation: 5, 11; *see also* Mon-
clova land speculations
Lamar, Lucius Q. C.: 101–102
Lamar, Mirabeau B.: 93, 115, 127, 131,
213, 238; policy of, toward Santa
Anna, 40–41; secretary of war of
Texas, 40; appointed to command of
Texas Army, 42; vice-president of
Texas, 55; candidate for president of
Texas, 94; charges against, in 1838
campaign, 97; platform of, 97;
Anson Jones characterizes, 100; biographical sketch of, 101–103; criticism of, 103; Indian policy of, 104–
106; financial policy of, 104–105,
119–20; relations of, with Mexican
Federalists, 105, 129, 133, 155; annexation policy of, 105; favors loan,
113; urges Mexican peace, 121–22,
128, 134, 156; poor congressional
relations of, 138; party leader, 139,
171–72; demands war with Mexico,
147; ill health of, 147–48; authorizes
Santa Fe expedition, 164–66; breach
of, with Burnet, 173–74; endorses
Burleson, 236; declines candidacy in
1844, 236; *see also* Cherokee War;
Republic of Texas
Lamar, Tabatha Jordan: 101
Laredo, Texas: 27, 206
Law of April 6, 1830: 18; immigration
features of, 12; Austin's objections
to, 15
Lester, James S.: 93 (n. 156), 142
Lewis, Ira: 29
Liberty, Texas: 96
Lipan Apache Indians: 39
Lipscomb, Abner: 134, 236
Lizardi and Company: 123, 125